Investigating Computer-Related Crime

Investigating Computer-Related Crime

Peter Stephenson

CRC Press
Boca Raton   London   New York   Washington, D.C.

Library of Congress Cataloging-in-Publication Data

Stephenson, Peter.
     Investigating computer-related crime : handbook for corporate
investigators / Peter Stephenson.
          p.   cm.
     Includes bibliographical references and index.
     ISBN 0-8493-2218-9 (alk. paper)
     1. Computer crimes—United States—Investigation.   I. Title.
HV6773.2.S74   1999
363.25'968—dc21   99-34206
                                                                                   CIP

No claim to original U.S. Government works
International Standard Book Number 0-8493-2218-9
Library of Congress Card Number 99-34206
Printed in the United States of America   2 3 4 5 6 7 8 9 0
Printed on acid-free paper

Preface

The introduction of the IBM Personal Computer in 1982 fostered a technology revolution that has changed the way the world does business. Prior to that historic milestone, several personal computers existed, e.g., Apple, TRS 80, but they were primarily used by individuals, schools, and small businesses. When computer mainframe giant, International Business Machines (IBM) entered the personal computer market in 1982, the event quickly captured the attention of corporations and government agencies worldwide.

Personal computers were no longer thought of as toys and almost overnight they were accepted as reliable business computers. Since their introduction, IBM PCs and compatible computers have evolved into powerful corporate network servers, desktop computers, and notebook computers. They have also migrated into millions of households, and their popularity exploded during the 1990s when the world discovered the Internet.

The worldwide popularity of both personal computers and the Internet has been a mixed blessing. The immediate popularity of the IBM PC was not anticipated. The DOS operating system installed on the original personal computers back in 1982 was never intended for commercial use and therefore was not designed to be secure. In the interest of maintaining compatibility with the early versions of DOS, upgrades to the operating system could not adequately address security issues. As a result, most corporate desktop PCs and notebook computers lack adequate security.

Millions of personal computers are used as tools to conduct financial transactions and to store trade secrets, sensitive personal medical data, and employment information. Many of these computers and more are also connected to the Internet to send and receive e-mail and to browse the wealth of information on the World Wide Web. The designers of the Internet never envisioned that it would become the hub of international commerce. As a result, security was not built into the original design of the Internet. The wide acceptance of the personal computer and the Internet has created some concerns for security that are just now being realized. The dramatic increase in computing speeds has added to the dilemma because such speeds aid hackers in breaking into systems.

The inherent security problems associated with personal computers, tied to their popularity in the workplace, have fostered new corporate problems. Now internal audits involve the examination of computer records. Criminal investigations and civil investigations routinely involve computer evidence and such inquiries require new methods and tools for investigators and internal auditors alike. That is what this book is all about, and its coming has been long overdue. It deals with practical methods and techniques that have proven to be effective in law enforcement and military circles for years. Only recently has this type of information and tools been available to corporate auditors and investigators.

Michael R. Anderson

Mr. Anderson retired after 25 years of federal law enforcement service and is currently the president of New Technologies, Inc., a corporation that provides training and develops specialized forensic tools for use in computer evidence processing. While employed by the federal government, he developed some of the original computer evidence training courses for the federal government and is currently a member of the faculty of the University of New Haven, Connecticut. He is also a co-founder of the International Association of Computer Investigative Specialists and is a training advisor to the National White Collar Crime Center. He can be reached via e-mail at mrande@teleport.com regarding computer evidence- and security review-related questions.

About the Author

Peter Stephenson has been a network consultant and lecturer for 18 years, specializing in information protection for large enterprises. His seminars on information security have been presented around the world.

Mr. Stephenson founded Intrusion Management and Forensics Group with approximately 20 associates and independent contractors, to test networks for security problems and devise solutions. After 15 years of consulting, he joined Enterprise Networking Systems, Inc., Redwood City, CA, as Director of Technology for the Global Security Practice.

Acknowledgments

My thanks to Nan Poulios, my business partner of more than ten years, who contributed to this in ways not immediately obvious, like writing reports I should have been writing while I wrote this.

I am grateful to Michael Anderson and the folks at NTI for their support as I wrote this. I recommend their products and training.

Also, although we have never spoken directly, I, and all computer incident investigators, owe a debt of thanks to Ken Rosenblatt for his contributions to our art. I can think of no other book* than his that I would want as a companion to this one on my bookshelf.

I have also benefited from the expertise of Chuck Guzis — for some of the finest evidence-processing tools an investigator could want. Don't stop now, Chuck!

To Rich O'Hanley at Auerbach Publications for his encouragement and help to find this book a home after wandering in the publishing wilderness for nearly a year. And, finally, my thanks to Becky McEldowney, my editor at CRC Press LLC, for not nagging me when the manuscript was late and for providing encouragement and support as I made changes to keep up with technologies that never seem to slow down.

Oh, and to Andrea Demby, CRC Press Production, who left this book substantially as I wrote it, a rare circumstance, indeed. Thanks, Andrea — let's do this again sometime.

---

* Rosenblatt, K.S., *High Technology Crime — Investigating Cases Involving Computers,* KSK Publications, San Jose, CA, 1995.

Dedication

For Debbie, who thought this book would never get written.

Contents

Section 1

The Nature of Cyber Crime

1 Cyber Crime as We Enter the Twenty-First Century

We begin our excursion into cyber crime with both a definition and a discussion of the issues surrounding various forms of computer crime. Throughout this section of the book we will be concerned about what cyber crime is, what its potential impacts are, and the types of attacks that are common.

Computer crime takes several forms. For the purposes of this work, we have coined the term "cyber crime." Strictly speaking things "cyber" tend to deal with networked issues, especially including global networks such as the Internet. Here, we will use the term generically, even though we might be discussing crimes targeted at a single, stand-alone computer.

The exception to this rule will occur in Chapter 6 — "Analyzing the Remnants of a Computer Security Incident." Here we will be very specific about the differences between cyberforensic analysis (networks), computer forensic analysis (stand-alone computers), and software forensic analysis (program code).

Now that we've set the ground rules, so to speak, let's move ahead and begin with a discussion of cyber crime in today's environment.

WHAT IS CYBER CRIME?

The easy definition of cyber crime is "crimes directed at a computer or a computer system." The nature of cyber crime, however, is far more complex. As we will see later, cyber crime can take the form of simple snooping into a computer system for which we have no authorization. It can be the freeing of a computer virus into the wild. It may be malicious vandalism by a disgruntled employee. Or it may be theft of data, money, or sensitive information using a computer system.

Cyber crime can come from many sources. The cyberpunk who explores a computer system without authorization is, by most current definitions, performing a criminal act. We might find ourselves faced with theft of sensitive marketing data by one of our competitors. A virus may bring down our system or one of its components. There is no single, easy profile of cyber crime or the cyber criminal.

If these are elements of cyber crime, what constitutes computer security? Let's consider the above examples for a moment. They all have a single element in common, no matter what their individual natures might be. They are all concerned with compromise or destruction of computer data. Thus, our security objective must be *information protection*. What we call computer security is simply the means to that end.

There are many excellent books available which discuss elements of computer security. Therefore, in general terms at least, we won't go into great detail here. It is sufficient to say at this point that we are concerned with protecting information and, should our protection efforts fail us, with determining the nature, extent, and source of the compromise.

We can see from this that it is the data and not the computer system *per se* that is the target of cyber crime. Theft of a computer printout may be construed as cyber crime. The planting of a computer virus causes destruction of data, not the computer itself. It becomes clear, from this perspective, that the computer system is the means, not the end. A wag once said that computer crime has always been with us. It's just in recent years that we've added the computer.

However, investigating crimes against data means we must investigate the crime scene: the computer system itself. Here is where we will collect clues as to the nature, source, and extent of the crime against the data. And it is here that we will meet our biggest obstacle to success.

If we are going to investigate a murder, we can expect to have a corpse as a starting point. If a burglary is our target, there will be signs of breaking and entering. However, with cyber crime we may find that there are few, if any, good clues to start with. In fact, we may only suspect that a crime has taken place at all. There may be no obvious signs.

Another aspect of cyber crime is that, for some reason, nobody wants to admit that it ever occurred. Supervisors have been known to cover up for obviously guilty employees. Corporations refuse to employ the assistance of law enforcement. Companies refuse to prosecute guilty individuals.

While most of us would detest the rapist, murderer, or thief, we tend to act as if computer crime simply doesn't exist. We glamorize hackers like Kevin Mitnick. We act that way until it affects us personally. Then, occasionally, we change our minds. Statistically, though, the computer criminal has less than a 1% chance of being caught, prosecuted, and convicted of his or her deeds.

So where, as computer security and audit professionals, does that leave us in our efforts to curb cyber crimes against our organizations? It means we have a thankless job, often lacking in support from senior executives, frequently under-staffed and under-funded.

That, though, doesn't mean that we can't fight the good fight and do it effectively. It certainly does mean that we have to work smarter *and* harder. It also means that we will have to deal with all sorts of political issues. Finally, there are techniques to learn — technical, investigative, and information gathering techniques. It is a combination of these learned techniques, the personal nature that seeks answers, and the honesty that goes with effective investigations that will help us become good cyber cops — investigators of crimes against information on the information super-highway, or on its back roads.

HOW DOES TODAY'S CYBER CRIME DIFFER FROM THE HACKER EXPLOITS OF YESTERDAY?

"A young boy, with greasy blonde hair, sitting in a dark room. The room is illumi-nated only by the luminescence of the C64's 40-character screen. Taking another long drag from his Benson and Hedges cigarette, the weary system cracker telnets to the next faceless '.mil' site on his hit list. 'Guest — guest,' 'root — root,' and 'system — manager' all fail. No matter. He has all night ... he pencils the host off of his list, and tiredly types in the next potential victim ...

This seems to be the popular image of a system cracker. Young, inexperienced, and possessing vast quantities of time to waste, to get into just one more system. However, there is a far more dangerous type of system cracker out there. One who knows the ins and outs of the latest security auditing and cracking tools, who can modify them for specific attacks, and who can write his/her own programs. One who not only reads about the latest security holes, but also personally discovers bugs and vulnerabilities. A deadly creature that can both strike poisonously and hide its tracks without a whisper or hint of a trail. The übercracker is here."[1]

This is how Dan Farmer and Wietse Venema characterized two types of hackers when they wrote the white paper, "Improving the Security of Your Site by Breaking Into It" a few years back. Certainly the cyberpunk, "... young, inexperienced, and possessing vast quantities of time to waste ...," is the glamorous view of hackers. That hacker still exists. I learned how to mutate viruses in 1992 from a fourteen-year-old boy I had not and still have not met. I have no doubt that he is still writing virus code and hacking into systems like the bank intrusion that got him his first day in court at the age of fifteen.

However, even the überhacker ("super hacker"), characterized by Farmer and Venema, is a changed person from the days they penned their white paper. There is a new element to this beast that is cause for grave concern among computer security professionals: today's überhacker is as likely as not to be a professional also. In the strictest terms, a professional is one who gets paid for his or her work. More and more we are seeing that such is the case with computer criminals.

Rochell Garner, in the July 1995 *Open Computing* cover story says, "The outside threats to your corporate network are coming from paid intruders — and their actions have gotten downright frightening. So why are corporate security experts keeping silent — and doing so little?"[2]

In 1996, Ernst & Young LLP, in their annual computer security survey, reported attacks by competitors represented 39% of attacks by outsiders followed by customers (19%), public interest groups (19%), suppliers (9%), and foreign governments (7%). The Computer Security Institute, San Francisco, reported that security incidents rose 73% from 1992 to 1993.

Scott Charney, chief of the computer crime division of the Department of Justice, was quoted in the Garner story as saying, "Our caseload involving the curious browser who intends no harm has stabilized and even diminished. Now we're seeing a shift to people using the Net for malicious destruction or profit."[2]

Today's computer criminal is motivated by any of several things. He or she (an increasing number of hackers are women) is in the hacking game for financial gain, revenge, or political motivation. There are other aspects of the modern hacker that are disturbing. Most proficient hackers are accomplished code writers. They not only understand the systems they attack, most write their own tools. While it is true that many hacking tools are readily available on the Internet, the really effective ones are in the private tool kits of professional intruders, just as lock-picking kits are the work tools of the professional burglar.

In the late 1980s and early 1990s, the personal computer revolution brought us the virus writer. Early viruses were, by accounts of the period, a vicious breed of bug. As virus writing became a popular underground pastime, virus construction kits appeared. Now anyone with a compiler and a PC could write a virus. The problem, of course, was that these kits were, essentially, cut-and-paste affairs. No really new viruses appeared — just different versions of the same ones. The anti-virus community caught up, breathed a sigh of relief, and waited for the next wave. They didn't have long to wait.

Shortly after the virus construction laboratory was created by a young virus writer named Nowhere Man, another virus writer, who called himself Dark Avenger, gave us the mutation engine. There is controversy about where the mutation engine actually came from (other writers, such as Dark Angel, claimed to have created it), but the undisputed fact was that it added a new dimension to virus writing. The mutation engine allowed a virus writer to encrypt the virus, making it difficult for a virus scanner to capture the virus's signature and identify it. The race between virus writer and anti-virus developer was on again.

Today, although at this writing there are over 7,000 strains of viruses identified, the anti-virus community seems to have the situation under control. Organizations no longer view virus attacks with fear and trembling — and, perhaps, they should — because there are adequate protections available at reasonable prices. The underground still churns out viruses, of course, but they are far less intimidating than in years past.

The hacking community has followed a somewhat different line of development, although in the early days it seemed as if they would parallel the virus community's growth. Both virus writers and early hackers claimed to "be in it" for growth of knowledge. Historically, there is some evidence this certainly was the case. However, somewhere along the way, evolution took one of its unexplained crazy hops and the virus community stopped developing while the hacker community evolved into a group of professional intruders, mercenary hackers for hire, political activists, and a few deranged malcontents who, for revenge, learned how to destroy computer systems at a distance.

Today, profilers have a much more difficult time sorting out the antisocial hacker from the cold-blooded professional on a salary from his current employer's competitor. Today, the intrusion into the marketing files of a major corporation may be accomplished so smoothly and with such skill that a computer crime investigator has a difficult time establishing that an intrusion has even occurred, much less establishing its source and nature.

However, in most organizations, one thing has not changed much. The computers are still vulnerable. The logging is still inadequate. The policies, standards, and practices are still outdated. So the environment is still fertile ground for attack. Even though today's cyber crook has a specific goal in mind — to steal or destroy your data — he or she still has an inviting playing field.

Yesterday's intruder came searching for knowledge — the understanding of as many computer systems as possible. Today's intruder already has that understanding.

He or she wants your data. Today's cyber crook will either make money off you or get revenge against you. He or she will not simply learn about your system. That difference — the fact that you will lose money — is the biggest change in the evolution of the computer cracker.

Much has been made in the computer community about the evolution of the term "hacker." Hacker, in the early days of computing, was a proud label. It meant that its owner was an accomplished and elegant programmer. It meant that the hacker's solutions to difficult problems were effective, compact, efficient, and creative.

The popular press has, the "real" hackers say, twisted the connotation of the term into something evil. "Call the bad guys 'crackers,'" they say. "You insult the true computer hacker by equating him or her with criminal acts." If we look at the professional "cracker" of today, however, we find that he or she is a "hacker" in the purest traditions of the term. However, like Darth Vader, or the gun in the hands of a murderer ("guns don't kill, people do") these hackers have found the "dark side" of computing. Let's call them what they are — hackers — and never forget not to underestimate our adversary.

THE REALITY OF INFORMATION WARFARE
IN THE CORPORATE ENVIRONMENT

Northrup Grumman, in an advertisement for its services, defines information warfare as "The ability to exploit, deceive, and disrupt adversary information systems while simultaneously protecting our own." Martin Libicki, in his essay, "What Is Information Warfare?"[3] tells us:

> Seven forms of information warfare vie for the position of central metaphor: command-and-control (C2W), intelligence-based warfare (IBW), electronic warfare (EW), psychological warfare (PSYW), hacker warfare, economic information warfare (EIW), and cyberwarfare.

His essay, written for the Institute for National Strategic Studies, begins by quoting Thomas Rona, an early proponent of information warfare:

> The strategic, operation, and tactical level competitions across the spectrum of peace, crisis, crisis escalation, conflict, war, war termination, and reconstitution/restoration, waged between competitors, adversaries or enemies using information means to achieve their objectives.

"Too broad," says Libicki. If we take this definition, we can apply it to just about anything we do or say.

Additionally, popular proponents of information warfare have used the concept to further their own careers at the expense of a confused and concerned audience. Even these proponents, however, have a bit to add to the legitimate infowar stew. Their concept of classes of information warfare, like Libicki's seven forms, adds to our understanding of what, certainly, is a new metaphor for competition, industrial espionage, and disinformation.

The idea of three classes of information warfare allows us to focus on the important aspects: those that affect business relationships. Class 1 infowar, according to the champions of classes of information warfare, involves infowar against individuals. Class 3 is information warfare against nations and governments. And the class we're concerned with here, Class 2, is infowar against corporations. A simplistic approach, to be sure, but at least this set of definitions lacks the jargon and gobbledygook of some other, more lofty, descriptions.

If we examine all of these attempts at pigeonholing information warfare, we can probably get the best feeling for what we are dealing with from the Grumann ad. Infowar is, simply, an effort to access, change, steal, destroy, or misrepresent our competitor's critical information while protecting our own. If this sounds like traditional industrial espionage dressed up in the *Coat of Many Colors* of the cyber age, you're not far off.

That, unfortunately, does not change the facts one iota. Your competition is out to get your secrets. Disgruntled employees are out to destroy your data for revenge. And thieves, in business for their own personal gain, are out to steal whatever they can from you. As the wag said: we only have added the computer. There is nothing new under the sun.

Adding the computer, however, changes the equation somewhat. Fighting cyber crime solely with traditional methods is a bit like trying to bring down a B-52 with a BB gun. It simply won't work. We need to bring new techniques into our tool kit. There is, of course, one very important point we need to make here: adding new tools to the kit doesn't mean that we throw away the old ones. There is much benefit to be gained, you will soon see, in the tried-and-true techniques of research, developing clues, interviewing witnesses and suspects, examining the crime scene, and developing a hypothesis of how the deed was done. So don't toss out the old tools yet.

The techniques we will discuss in this book will allow you to take your experience and apply it to the brave new world of information warfare. If your tool kit is empty because investigating crime of any type is new to you, you'll get a bright, shiny new set of tools to help you on your way. Remember, though, cyber crime and information warfare is real. The old question of "why would anyone do that?" usually can be answered easily in cases of cyber crime. Motivation for these acts is, most often, money, revenge, or political activism. All three pose real challenges to the investigator.

INDUSTRIAL ESPIONAGE — HACKERS FOR HIRE

Consider the following scenario. A very large public utility with several nuclear power plants experiences a minor glitch with no real consequences. The requisite reports are filed with the Nuclear Regulatory Commission and the matter is forgotten — officially. Internal memos circulate, as is common in these situations, discussing the incident and "lessons learned."

One evening, a hacker in the employ of an anti-nuclear activist group, using information provided by a disgruntled employee, gains access to the utility's network, searches file servers until he finds one at the nuclear plant, and, after compromising it, locates copies of several of the lessons-learned memos. The hacker delivers the memos to his employers who doctor them up a bit and deliver them with a strongly worded press release to a local reporter who has made a life-long career out of bashing the nuclear industry. Imagine the potential public relations consequences.

Or, how about this: a large corporation with only one major competitor hires an accomplished hacker. The hacker's job is to apply at the competitor for a job in the computer center. Once hired, the hacker routinely collects confidential information and, over the Internet, passes it to his real employer. Such a situation was alleged in 1995 when a Chinese student, working in the United States for a software company, started stealing information and source code and funneling it to his real employer, a state-owned company in China.

There are many instances of such espionage. Unfortunately, most of them don't get reported. Why? The loss of confidence in a company that has been breached is one reason. Another is the threat of shareholder lawsuits if negligence can be proved. Estimates of the success of prosecuting computer crime vary, but the most common ones tell us that there is less than a 1% probability that a computer criminal will be reported, caught, tried, and prosecuted successfully. With those odds, it's no wonder that the professional criminal is turning to the computer instead of the gun as a way to steal money.

Rob Kelly, writing in *Information Week* back in 1992 ("Do You Know Where Your Laptop Is?"), tells of a wife who worked for the direct competitor to her husband's employer. While her husband was sleeping, she logged onto his company's mainframe using his laptop and downloaded confidential data which she then turned over to her employer.[4]

A favorite scam in airports is to use the backups at security checkpoints to steal laptops. Two thieves work together. One goes into the security scanner just ahead of the laptop owner, who has placed his or her laptop on the belt into the X-ray machine. This person carries metal objects that cause the scanner to alarm. He or she then engages in an argument with the security personnel operating the scanner. In the meantime, the victim's laptop passes through the X-ray scanner. While the victim waits in line for the argument ahead to be settled, the confederate steals the laptop from the X-ray belt and disappears.

You can bet that the few dollars the thieves will get for the laptop itself are only part of the reward they expect. Rumors in the underground suggest that as much as $10,000 is available as a bounty on laptops stolen from top executives of Fortune 500 companies. To paraphrase a popular political campaign slogan, "It's the data, stupid!" Information in today's competitive business world is more precious than gold. Today's thieves of information are well-paid professionals with skills and tools and little in the way of ethics.

These examples show some of the ways industrial espionage has moved into the computer age. There is another way, this one more deadly, potentially, than the other two. It is called "denial of service" and is the province of computer vandals. These vandals may be competitors, activists intent on slowing or stopping progress of a targeted company, or disgruntled employees getting even for perceived wrongs.

Denial of service attacks are attacks against networks or computers that prevent proper data handling. They could be designed to flood a firewall with packets so that it cannot transfer data. It could be an attack intended to bring a mainframe process down and stop processing. Or, it could be an attack against a database with the intent of destroying it. While the data could be restored from backups, it is likely that some time will pass while the application is brought down, the data restored, and the application restarted.

One question that I hear a lot at seminars is, "How can we prevent this type of activity?" The answer is complex. As you will see in the emerging glut of computer security books, planning by implementing policies, standards and practices, implementation of correct security architectures and countermeasures, and a good level of security awareness is the key. If your system is wide open, you'll be hit. There is, in this day and age, no way to avoid that. What you can do is ensure that your controls are in place and robust and that you are prepared for the inevitable. That won't stop the hacker from trying, but it may ensure that you'll avoid most of the consequences.

David Icove, Karl Seger, and William VonStorch, writing in *Computer Crime — A Crimefighter's Handbook,* list five basic ways that computer criminals get information on the companies they attack:[5]

1. Observing equipment and events
2. Using public information
3. Dumpster diving
4. Compromising systems
5. Compromising people (social engineering)

These five attack strategies suggest that you can apply appropriate countermeasures to lessen the chances of the attack being successful. That, as it turns out, is the case. The purpose of risk assessments and the consequent development of appropriate policies, standards, practices, and security architectures is to identify the details of these risks and develop appropriate responses. There are plenty of good books that will help you do just that, so we won't dwell on preventative methods here. However, in the final section of this book, we will recap some key things you can do to simplify the task of fighting computer crime by preparing for it. In that section we will discuss how to be proactive, build a corporate cyber SWAT team, and take appropriate precautions in the form of countermeasures.

Of the five strategies, arguably the wave of the future is number five: social engineering. The professional information thief is a con artist par excellance. These smooth-talking con men and women talk their way into systems instead of using brute force. The Jargon File version 3.3.1 defines social engineering thus:

social engineering n. Term used among crackers and samurai for cracking techniques that rely on weaknesses in wetware rather than software; the aim is to trick people into revealing passwords or other information that compromises a target system's security.

Classic scams include phoning up a mark who has the required information and posing as a field service tech or a fellow employee with an urgent access problem …

Consider the case of "Susan Thunder," a hacker turned consultant who specializes in social engineering. Thunder, whose real name, like many hackers, never appears in public, is one of the early hackers who ran with "Roscoe" and Kevin Mitnick in the late 1970s and early 1980s. When, after a number of exploits that finally resulted in jail for Roscoe and probation for Mitnick, things got a bit too hot for her, she dropped her alias and became a security consultant.

According to Thunder, in 1983 she appeared before a group of high-ranking military officials from all branches of the service. She was handed a sealed envelope with the name of a computer system in it and asked to break into the system. She logged into an open system and located the target and its administrator. From there it was a snap, as she relates the story, to social engineer everything she needed to log into the system from an unsuspecting support technician and display classified information to the stunned brass.[6]

Let's get the technique from Thunder, in her own words, as she posts on the Internet to the alt.2600 newsgroup in 1995:

Social Engineering has been defined as the art of manipulating information out of a given person with a view towards learning information about or from a given EDP system. The techniques are relatively simple, and I will go into greater detail and provide examples in a future tutorial. Essentially, the methodology consists of pulling off a telephone ruse to get the person at the other end of the line to give you passwords or read you data off of their computer screen. Sometimes the techniques involve intimidation or blackmail. Again, I will explore these techniques further in my next tutorial, but first I want to address the differences between Social Engineering (a lousy, non-descriptive term IMHO) and Psychological Subversion.

Psychological Subversion (PsySub) is a very advanced technique that employs neural linguistic programming (nlp), subconscious suggestions, hypnotic suggestions, and subliminal persuasion. Essentially, you want to plant the idea in the subject's mind that it's okay to provide you with the information you seek to obtain.

There is, of course, some question about how much of her exploits are real and how much is in her head. However, there is one important point: social engineering techniques work and they work well. The professional hacker will use those techniques in any way he or she can to get information. When I am performing intrusion testing for clients, I always include the element of social engineering in my tests. It adds the realism that allows the testing to simulate the approach of professional hackers accurately.

Time is the hacker's worst enemy. The longer he or she is "on the line," the higher the probability of discovery and tracing. Most professional hackers will do whatever they can to collect as much information as possible prior to starting the actual attack. How much easier it is to talk the root password out of a careless or overworked technician than it is to crack the system, steal the password file, and hope that you can crack the root password!

PUBLIC LAW ENFORCEMENT'S ROLE IN CYBER CRIME INVESTIGATIONS

Make no mistake about it. If you involve law enforcement in your investigation, you'll have to turn over control to them. That may be a reason not to call in the authorities. Then again, maybe it's a reason to get on the phone to them ASAP.

The abilities of local law enforcement and their investigative resources vary greatly with geographic territory. The spectrum ranges from the ever-improving capabilities of the FBI and the Secret Service to the essentially worthless efforts of local police forces in isolated rural locations. Since computers and computer systems are pervasive, that lack of evenness poses problems for many organizations.

There are times when not calling in law enforcement is not an option. If you are a federally regulated organization, such as a bank, not involving law enforcement in a formal investigation can leave you open to investigation yourself. However, the decision to call or not to call should never wait until the event occurs. Make that decision well in advance so that valuable time won't be lost in arguing the merits of a formal investigation.

There are, by most managers' reckonings, some good reasons not to call in the law. First, there is a higher probability that the event will become public. No matter how hard responsible investigators try to keep a low profile, it seems that the media, with its attention ever-focused on the police, always get the word and, of course, spread it. Public knowledge of the event usually is not limited to the facts, either. The press, always on the lookout for the drama that sells ad space, tends toward a significant ignorance of things technical. But, no matter — facts never got in the way of a good story before, why should your story be any different.

Another issue is that law enforcement tends to keep their actions secret until the investigation is over. While that certainly must be considered appropriate in the investigation of computer crime, it often closes the communications lines with key company staff like the CEO, auditors, and security personnel. Some organizations find it difficult or impossible to live with that sort of lack of communication during a critical incident involving their organizations.

A major benefit of involving law enforcement is the availability of sophisticated technical capabilities in the form of techniques, expensive equipment, and software. The FBI crime lab is known for its capabilities in all areas of forensic analysis, including computer forensics. Recovering lost data that could lead to the solution of a computer crime, for example, is a difficult, expensive, and, often, unsuccessful undertaking. The FBI has experts in their lab who can recover that data, even if it has been overwritten.

However, if you call the FBI there are some things you should remember. If they take the case (there is no guarantee that they will), they will take over completely. Everyone will become a suspect until cleared (more about that in a later chapter) and you can expect little or nothing in the way of progress reporting until the crime is solved and the perpetrator captured.

The FBI doesn't have the resources to investigate every case. First, the case has to have a significant loss attached to it. Second, it has to be within the FBI jurisdiction: interstate banking, public interstate transportation, etc. Finally, there has to be some hope of a solution. That means that it may be in your best interests to conduct a preliminary investigation to determine if the crime fits into the FBI pattern of cases and what you can provide the FBI investigators as a starting point.

Local authorities will, if they have the resources, usually be glad to get involved. They will have the same downsides, though, as does the FBI. The difference is that they may not have the resources needed to bring the investigation to a suitable conclusion.

In most larger cities, and many smaller ones, there will be someone on the local, state, or county force who can at least begin an investigation. It is often a good idea, if you decide to use law enforcement in the future, to become acquainted with the computer crime investigators in advance of an incident. An informal meeting can gain a wealth of information for you. It also can set the stage for that panic call in the future when the intruder is on your doorstep. In Chapter 11 we'll discuss the involvement of law enforcement in more depth.

THE ROLE OF PRIVATE CYBER CRIME INVESTIGATORS AND SECURITY CONSULTANTS IN INVESTIGATIONS

Most organizations are not equipped to investigate computer crime. Although they may have the resources to get the process started, an in-depth technical investigation is usually beyond their scope. It means these organizations have two alternatives. They can call in law enforcement or they can employ consultants from the private sector. Many organizations prefer to do the latter.

Calling in consultants is not a step to take lightly, however. The world is full (and getting fuller) of self-styled security consultants, "reformed hackers" and other questionable individuals who are riding the computer security wave. Finding the right consultant is not a trivial task and should be commenced prior to the first incident.

The first question, of course, is what role will the consultant play. In Chapter 14, we discuss the roles and responsibilities required of a corporate "SWAT team" created to investigate cyber crime. Once you have created such a team, you must then decide what gaps are present and which can be filled by consultants.

One area where some interesting things are taking place is in the business of private investigation. Private investigators, traditionally involved with physical crime and civil matters, are looking at the world of virtual crime as a growth area for their businesses. If you use one of these firms, be sure that they have the requisite experience in cyber crime investigation.

The best general source for investigative consultants is within the computer security community. Here, however, you must use care in your selection, because not all consultants are created equal. The best requirement for your request for proposal, then, is likely to be references. References can be hard to get in some cases, of course, since most clients are understandably reluctant to discuss their problems with the outside world.

Consultants can fill a number of roles on your investigative team. The most common is the role of technical specialist. Most consultants are more familiar with the security technologies involved than they are with the legal and investigative issues. It will be easier to find technical experts than it will to find full-fledged investigators.

The other side of technology is the "people" side. If social engineering is the emerging threat of the 1990s, the ability to interview, interrogate, and develop leads is about as old school investigation style as can be. In this instance good, old-fashioned police legwork pays big dividends, if it is performed by an investigative professional with experience.

Another area where a consultant can help is the audit function. Many computer crimes involve fraud and money. An experienced information systems auditor with fraud investigation experience is worth whatever you pay in cases of large-scale computer fraud.

The bottom line is that you can, and should, use qualified consultants to beef up your internal investigative capabilities. Remember, though, that you are opening up your company's deepest secrets to these consultants. It is a very good idea to develop relationships in advance and develop a mutual trust so that, when the time comes, you'll have no trouble working together. I have told numerous clients that they can get technology anywhere. It's the trust factor that can be hard to come by.

In the next chapter, we'll continue our examination of the nature of cyber crime by exploring the impacts of crime. We'll discuss the theft of sensitive data, the use of misinformation, and denial of service attacks.

REFERENCES

1. Farmer, D. and Venema, W., "Improving the Security of Your Site by Breaking Into It."
2. Garner, R., "The Growing Professional Menace," *Open Computing,* July 1995.
3. Libicki, M., "What Is Information Warfare?" Institute for National Strategic Studies.
4. Stern, D. L., *Preventing Computer Fraud*, McGraw-Hill.
5. Icove, D., Seger, K., and VonStorch, W., *Computer Crime — A Crimefighter's Handbook*, O'Reilly & Associates.
6. Hafner, K. and Markoff, J., *Cyberpunk*, Simon & Schuster, New York.

2 The Potential Impacts of Cyber Crime

In this chapter, we will examine the possible consequences of computer crime. Computer crime is far-reaching. It can affect the personal records of the individual. It can impact the financial resources of a bank, causing confusion and, potentially, affecting customer accounts. Cyber crime can result in confidential information being compromised, affecting the price of the victim's publicly traded shares. It can be an attack on a corporation's marketing information, causing misinformation to be communicated to the sales force. Or, it can bring down an Internet service provider with a denial of service attack.

We will explore each of these aspects — data theft, misinformation, and denial of service — in detail. We will also get a top level look at the elements of these three aspects, as well as a brief introduction to the concepts behind their investigation. Along the way we will begin to form an approach for investigating computer crimes and computer-related crimes, and see some of the ways the intruder covers his or her tracks.

We'll introduce the concepts of *forensic analysis*, *backward tracing* over the Internet, *attack route hypothesis,* and *attack recreation* testing, as well as touching on the role of the experienced investigators working with the technical experts. We'll also begin to discuss some of the general aspects of evidence gathering and first steps in your investigation. Finally, we'll begin the exploration of the important role played by system logs in a successful investigation. This chapter sets the stage for many of the more technical chapters that follow.

DATA THIEVES

Of all of the types of malicious acts which we can attribute to computer criminals, perhaps the most innocuous is data theft. The cyber thief can break into a system, steal sensitive information, cover his or her tracks, and leave to return another day. If the intruder is skillful and your safeguards are not in place, you will never know that the theft has occurred.

Unlike theft of money or paper documents, theft of computer data does not leave a void where the stolen item once resided. If I steal money from a bank, the money is gone. An investigator can view the crime scene and see that what was once there has been removed. The same is true for paper documents. Data theft, however, leaves no such void. If measures to detect the intrusion and subsequent theft are not in place, the theft will go unnoticed in most cases. Therefore, all of the investigator's efforts must be focused on two important tasks: determine that a theft has actually occurred and identify the nature and source of the theft.

Among various types of crime, data theft is unique. Not only can it progress undetected, when it is detected, it may be difficult to establish that it has actually occurred. There are a variety of reasons for this. First, READ actions are not, usually, logged by the computer or server. Thus, we normally need an alternative method of establishing that a file has been accessed.

Second, the accessing of a file does not, of itself, establish that it has been compromised. Of course, if an intruder uploads a sensitive file from our system, we usually can assume that it will be read. However, there are other ways to compromise a file without it being explicitly uploaded. For example, one of the most sensitive files on a Unix computer is the password file. Although today's operating systems have a mechanism for protecting password files (shadowed passwords), there are huge numbers of older machines that don't have such refinements. Compromising a password on such a computer, once the intruder has gained access to it, requires only a telnet (virtual terminal) program with the ability to log the session. Most of today's telnet applications for PCs have such an ability.

The intruder first enters the victim's computer, then, using telnet, he or she performs a READ of the /etc/passwd file. The command is simple. While reading the file, the telnet program on the intruder's PC is logging the session. At the end of the session, the intruder "cleans up" by sterilizing system logs, exits the victim's computer, and edits the log of the session to leave just the password file. The last step is to run a password cracker against the edited log file and make use of any passwords harvested.

Depending upon the file format, other sensitive files may be harvested in a similar manner. For example, any plain text file is subject to this type of compromise. Another use of the telnet log function is recording data mining sessions. The skilled intruder will never take the time to read much of what he or she harvests online. Time is the intruder's worst enemy. The skilled intruder will avoid extensive connection time on a victim machine at all costs. However, even for the most skilled intruder a certain amount of "surfing" is required before he or she actually finds something useful.

When a data thief locates a sensitive database, for example, he or she will simply perform queries and log the results. The logs of the session provide ample resources for later examination. Only under those circumstances where a file cannot be browsed or a database queried does a skilled data thief resort to an actual file transfer. However, there are techniques for file transfers that afford the intruder an unlogged file transfer session. Consider the use of TFTP.

TFTP, or "trivial file transfer protocol" is a method of transferring the information necessary to boot a Unix computer which has no hard drive. The computer gets the information necessary from a server on the computer's network. Since the mechanism to connect to the server and upload the necessary boot files must be kept small enough to fit in a single computer chip, a reduced functionality version of FTP (file transfer protocol) called TFTP makes the connection to the server and collects the boot file. This process cannot use an ID and password, so TFTP requires neither. Obviously, this represents a boon to any hacker who wants to steal files without leaving a trace. Fortunately, most Unix administrators are learning to turn TFTP off if it is not explicitly required for booting. Even then, there are precautions that administrators should take to ensure that TFTP can't be abused.

However, suppose that an attacker has gained root and wants to leave a file transfer "back door" into the system. Once the attacker gains ROOT (becomes the superuser), he or she can modify the /etc/inetd.conf configuration file to turn TFTP back on. Following that with a quick browse of the file systems on the computer to identify desired documents, and a cleanup to eliminate log entries, the intruder can transfer files using TFTP without ever logging into the computer again. As long as the administrator doesn't discover that TFTP is in use (it's supposed to be turned off), this harvesting process could go on indefinitely.

How Data Thieves Avoid Detection During an Attack

We detailed above one of the ways to defeat the logging of a file transfer and its subsequent tracing to an attacker. Now let's take that one step further and investigate some other ways intruders mask their actions. Most of this information comes directly from hacking resources on the Internet. It is available to anyone with the desire and patience to find it. Not all of these methods work all the time on all machines. However, enough of them work often enough so that they offer a considerable challenge to investigators. Also, these techniques apply only to Unix computers.

Masking Logins

There is a log in Unix called the lastlog. This log shows individual logins without much detail. However, the lastlog and the logs that feed it can contain the name of the machine that logged in even if they can't record the username. Although most skilled intruders usually use other machines than their own to attack a victim, the names of computers along the way can be helpful in tracing an intrusion to its source. However, if the intruder masks his or her identity to the victim, the investigator can't get to the most recent computer in the attack chain to begin tracing backward to the source.

The intruder can use a simple method to mask his or her machine's identity to the victim. If, on login to the victim's computer, the hacker sees a notification to the effect that the last successful login by the owner of the stolen account the intruder is using was on such-and-such a date, the intruder simply performs an rlogin and supplies the stolen account's password again. The rlogin program, intended for remote access from other computers (rlogin means "remote login"), also works perfectly well on the same computer. Since the login comes from the same machine, the lastlog will indicate that the login was from "localhost" (the name Unix computers use to refer to themselves), or from the machine name of the computer. While this may be obvious to the skilled administrator or investigator, it shows only that some hanky-panky has taken place. It does not reveal its nature or its real source.

A second trick used by skilled intruders is the shell change. Unix machines often have a history file which saves the commands of the user. An investigator can review the history file, if present, and learn what occurred. Thus, the hacker needs to disable the history-gathering capability of the computer.

All Unix computers use a shell to allow the user to communicate with the operating system called the kernel. There are several different shells available for Unix machines. Usually a few of these different shells are available on the same computer. The shell that a user uses by default is determined by his or her profile. The first command a skilled hacker will enter on logging into a stolen account is, therefore, a shell change. This disables the history process. This works with the c-shell (CSH) and shell (SH) shells. Thus, an intruder will either switch from one to the other or from some other, different shell to another one of them.

Another method of detecting an intruder when he or she is still online is to type who. This gives a list of users currently connected. The display will usually present not only the user but the address they logged in from. A simple shell script (a program similar to a DOS batch file) that performs a "who" periodically, and logs the results to a file for later reference, is an easy way to see if there were unknown users or users who were not supposed to be logged in at the time the *who* connected. If the *who* indicates a user is logged in from a computer which is not normal for that user, there is a likelihood the account has been hijacked by an intruder.

The skilled intruder will, after logging in with the stolen account, login again with the same logging ID and password without first logging off. This opens a second session for the account and shows the origin only as the port to which the intruder is connected as the source of the login. If performed during a time when the owner of the stolen account would normally log in, it is unlikely to arouse suspicion.

Each of these techniques offers the intruder a method of hiding his or her presence. Although the information is under the investigator's nose, it is obfuscated sufficiently to prevent easy detection. The countermeasures for these obfuscations require a different approach to logging, often only available with third-party tools. Logging tools that collect IP addresses, for example, may be far more effective than the normal logging capabilities of unenhanced machines.

The investigator will, of course, be unable to take advantage of third-party tools after the fact. Thus, the question of installing such tools after the first attack and waiting for a possible second foray by the intruder comes up. We will discuss the issues surrounding that decision in a later chapter.

Masking Telnet

Telnet sessions may be performed in two ways. First, you can use the command

```
telnet victim.com
```

This command offers the intruder the disadvantage of information showing up as a parameter in the process list of a Unix computer. If the intruder has taken over a Unix host for the purpose of attacking another computer, the administrator may notice this entry and attempt to stop the intruder. Likewise, the connection may show up in logs if the host is logging completely, especially with third-party auditing tools.

However, if the intruder simply types

```
telnet
```

and then types these commands at the telnet prompt:

```
telnet> open victim.com
```

there is much less chance of being traced. Since a skilled intruder will usually move from computer to computer to cover his or her tracks during an attack, it is important that he or she avoid detection at each step of the way.

There is another technique that an intruder can use to mask a telnet session, or any other for that matter. This technique involves a change of identity, or at least part of an identity change.

When a user telnets from one host to another, some of the environmental variables travel along on some systems (systems that export environmental variables). Skilled intruders will change the environmental variables on a machine used as an intermediate before attacking the next target. This will make it more difficult for the investigator to trace backward through each purloined account on intermediate machines to the actual source of the attack.

How Data Thieves "Clean Up" After an Attack

There are a couple of things a skilled intruder will do before leaving the scene of the crime. The first is to remove any files he or she used as attack tools on the host. The second is to modify the logs on the target to erase any signs of entry.

Many intruders will use the /tmp directory on the victim as a temporary repository for tools. They do this because that directory is there, easy to access quickly (with few keystrokes), and won't be noticed because it belongs there. Also, there are very few reasons to go to the /tmp directory because it is most often used by the system or applications to store information only needed briefly.

Occasionally, an intruder will leave tools or other files in the /tmp directory due a hasty departure or, simply, carelessness. Investigators should examine all temporary directories for evidence, regardless of the type of computer involved.

Modifying the logs requires root access — or, on non-Unix machines, some form of superuser, such as admin or supervisor. It may also require special tools because not all log files are simple text files. However, if the intruder modifies log files, you may find that there are other indications that he or she has been into your system, such as inconstancies with various other logs.

There are several important logs that intruders will try to alter on Unix systems. The wtmp and utmp keep track of login and logout times. This information is used by the Unix finger command, the process (ps) command, and the who command. It is also the source for the lastlog. Altering these logs requires special tools, which are readily available in the computer underground.

Another important log is the system log, or syslog. However, if the syslog isn't configured properly, it won't actually log much of interest. Also, computers should, wherever possible, write their logs out to a central loghost (another computer which collects the logs and is well protected from unauthorized access).

An important logging method, but one which can generate very large log files in a short time, is the Unix accounting function. Actually, Unix accounting is intended for other purposes, such as charging users for time on the system, cpu use, etc. But, because it records every command by user and time executed, it also makes a fine intrusion log. It can be very effective if it is set up properly and purged appropriately into summary files.

The intruder will look for this, even though most system administrators don't implement it routinely. If you choose to use the accounting functions, make sure that you allow reads, writes, and execution only by root. Anyway, if your intruder gets root on your system, the logs will be the least of your worries. The only way to deal with that is to use an external loghost for all of your logs.

Other, non-Unix, systems have similar logging capabilities. However, the number one problem that investigators have where logging is concerned is too little is logged and the logs aren't retained long enough. At minimum, you should log logins, logouts, privilege changes, account creations, and file deletes. Keep your logs for at least six months.

TECHNIQUES FOR DETECTING FILE READS AND UPLOADS

We will cover the details of these techniques later, in Chapter 6. However, there are some techniques that investigators can use to determine that a file has been uploaded. These techniques, requiring access to the intruder's computer, are usually quite successful if performed properly and quickly.

The field of extracting hidden or deleted information from the disks of a computer is called *computer forensics*. We can perform forensic analysis on just about any type of computer disk, regardless of operating system, but it is easiest to perform it on DOS/Windows PCs. This is because of the way the DOS operating system manages file space.

The DOS file system uses unused portions of its disks to store information that it requires temporarily. Also, files are not really deleted from a DOS file system. As anyone who has had to recover an accidentally deleted file knows, if the file space has not been overwritten, the file can usually be recovered. However, even if a portion of the space has been overwritten, there may be enough remnants of the file left to establish that the intruder uploaded it.

If we go back to our earlier discussion of reading a password file during a telnet session, it can be seen that it must have been saved to the intruder's disk during the logging process. During the password cracking process, the password cracker will write a copy of its results to the disk as well. Unless the intruder does a secure delete (a process where the file space is overwritten multiple times with random characters), that information will also be retrievable using forensic techniques.

These techniques have three basic steps. The first is the accessing of the disk safely. This step is critical because, if the investigator does not take precautions to ensure that data is not damaged, the evidence could be destroyed by a booby trap placed by the intruder. The second step is the extraction of the data to a safe place for retention as evidence and further study.

To perform this step, the investigator must perform a *physical* backup of the disk — this is called an *image*. The physical backup copies every sector of the disk to a file. Sectors are copied whether or not they contain the type of data that is readily obvious to users, or, indeed, any data at all. This data, such as active files, will show up in a *logical* backup. This is the type of backup performed routinely to protect ourselves from data loss. Within the sectors of the disk which are not generally visible to the user, we may see the remnants of suspicious files. These are files that have been "deleted" through the DOS delete process, but have not yet been overwritten completely by other, active, files.

However, because the layout on the disk is based upon physical sectors, we may not see an entire file in one place (i.e., in contiguous sectors).

Although DOS attempts to keep files together physically on the disk, when a disk becomes *fragmented,* this is not possible. Thus we must use the third step, analysis, to search and locate the target files. For this purpose we use forensic tools that read the disk image (the file created by the physical backup process), organize the information into logical databases called *indexes,* and allow us to perform efficient searches for both ASCII and binary data.

We will cover the details, including some forensic tools, of the forensic process in Chapter 6. For now it is only important that you understand that it is possible to establish an information theft has occurred. However, your success or failure will depend upon the ability to secure the suspect computer as soon after the theft as possible and upon your skill at extracting hidden data in a manner that allows its use as evidence. Delays or errors in either of these processes will defeat your efforts.

MISINFORMATION

Misinformation is an element of intelligence that has application in the business world. Simply, misinformation consists of altering or creating information to give a false impression about a target's activities, financial situation, or future plans. The simplest form of misinformation is public relations intended to spread negative information about a target. Organizations also use misinformation to misdirect others, away from their real secrets. When an enemy uses misinformation through intrusion into a target's computers, or to manipulate the target's data, the whole thing gets more sinister than bad P.R.

There are several important forms of misinformation that may involve the computer crime investigator. They include:

- Alteration of strategic files, thus misleading employees. An example of this would be alteration of price lists or pricing strategy documents used by field personnel, causing them to produce erroneous quotes or proposals for critical projects or sales.
- Alteration of information used in preparing invoices to produce lower-than-expected revenues. This is especially easy when the raw billing data is collected automatically or is a repetitive billing that doesn't undergo review by a person.

- Alteration of source data in a critical database causing it to produce inaccurate results.
- Alteration of documents such as birth certificates, drivers' licenses, education credentials, or other personal documents to commit fraud. This is sometimes referred to as *document fraud* and has become a very popular use of today's sophisticated desktop publishing and graphics systems.
- Theft and alteration of sensitive documents to embarrass the target or affect a sensitive negotiation.
- Altering sensitive documents or data to affect the outcome of a negotiation, sales proposal, regulatory filing, or other important event.

Misinformation has elements of data theft, intrusion, and destruction or modification of data. When data is stolen and then modified, many of the techniques used to catch the data thief are appropriate. However, when the damage occurs on the victim's computer, trapping and convicting the intruder are much more difficult.

If the intruder attacks a computer and never downloads any data, it may be difficult to prove that he or she was actually the one who did the damage. The problem is that there may or may not be a residue of the intrusion on the hacker's computer. It is possible that a forensic examination of the computer will bear fruit for the investigator, but it is more likely that methods of tracking the intruder over the network will be successful.

In this vein, we should note that most experts have routinely believed that about 10% of all computer crime investigation has to do with the computer, while the other 90% is just plain old-fashioned police work. With the advent of today's computers and their proliferation into every aspect of our lives, however, the computer has become the investigative ground for that old-fashioned police work.

The routine work of detectives investigating today's computer-related crimes may include interviewing people with significant technical knowledge who can confuse the novice and obfuscate facts easily during early interviews. This leads to a longer investigation. It is common wisdom among fraud investigators, for example, that the first seven days after discovering a fraud are critical to its solution and prosecution. In other words, time, in any white-collar crime, is of the essence. In computer-related crimes, this is even more true because evidence can be very easily destroyed by a computer expert.

A key to investigating computer-related crimes involving misinformation is to obtain copies of the "before and after" files. The nature of the alterations must be understood clearly and copies of both found in such a manner as to implicate the perpetrator.

For example, take the case of a misinformation attack that replaces a sensitive document with an altered version. Forensic examination of the computer of the suspected attacker might reveal the original and the altered copy. This is also a good way to establish document fraud. If the work is being done on the victim machine, however, you will likely have to look elsewhere for your evidence. Even so, it is possible that the attacker will have performed some task while logged into the victim's computer, will show up on his or her machine, and can be traced to the victim. For example, a remnant of a directory tree from the victim computer found in the slack (unused) space on the attacker's machine could establish that he or she had gained entry into the victim.

Once the attacker has been identified, it is always a good idea to impound his or her computer and perform a forensic examination. There are, of course, other less technical elements of the investigation. For example, there may be paper copies of altered documents in various stages of alteration. There may be dial-up numbers in the memory of modems that lead to the victim's computer. There may be data on floppy disks that can be extracted or passworded document files that can be cracked, yielding important, incriminating information. A word of warning though: be careful not to violate any privacy laws or other laws stemming from the Fourth Amendment to the Constitution — they prohibit unreasonable search and seizure.

Some dial-up programs automatically keep logs that can be compared with the access times into the victim's computer system. Logs of dial-up gateways should be inspected carefully for clues and associations with other logs. We will examine the whole issue of piecing together parts of logs in Chapter 6.

One good way to catch an intruder engaged in misinformation is to provide a tempting target and then trace the intruder's actions while he or she is online attempting to alter it. There are significant legal and ethical issues here which we will discuss later. However, the use of such devices, called *goat files* or *honey pots,* can sometimes provide enough working time for the investigator to identify the attacker. Remember, in intrusions, time is the attacker's worst enemy.

From a practical perspective, however, you will usually come upon the results of the attacker's work after the fact. This means you will probably not have the opportunity to catch him or her online. In these cases, I prefer a "backwards approach" to solving the matter. This approach is based upon the Sherlockian declaration that when everything that seems logical has been eliminated, whatever is left, no matter how illogical, must be the answer. Begin by eliminating the obvious. The general approach to investigating the technical aspects of any computer-related crime is:

- Eliminate the obvious.
- Hypothesize the attack.
- Collect evidence, including, possibly, the computers themselves.
- Reconstruct the crime.
- Perform a traceback to the suspected source computer.
- Analyze the source, target, and intermediate computers.
- Turn your findings and evidentiary material over to corporate investigators or law enforcement for follow-up.

You can start this process in a misinformation case by eliminating methods of access. Does the victim computer have dial-in access? Is it connected to the Internet? Is it protected from Internet intrusion, if it is? A popular form of misinformation is the alteration of information on World Wide Web pages. Since Web servers are usually outside of any firewall protection, this is an easy thing to do in many cases.

The methods for eliminating access routes vary with the situation, but here, as in other types of inquiries, logs are your friends — if they are detailed enough and retained long enough to cover the period of the incident. Your first effort in such cases should be to procure all logs that could possibly show an access into the victim system. Since access to the victim is the key to the damage, this selective elimination of wrong paths is a critical step.

The second step in my investigations is attempting to reconstruct the crime. Given the remaining paths to the victim, I try to hypothesize how they might be used to gain illicit access. Once I have hypothesized appropriate attack scenarios, I test them.

It is important that you not take this step until you have removed all important evidence from the victim computer. As with all evidence, it must meet the requirements of originality, appropriateness, etc. Don't forget chain-of-custody and other elements of correct evidence gathering. If you are part of law enforcement, there will likely be rules you'll have to follow if you intend to pursue this route. Due to their intrusive nature, these methods are often more appropriate to corporate investigators.

The testing of an intrusion hypothesis involves recreating the crime in as nearly an accurate way as possible. I usually find that such efforts tend to close more of the potential paths into the victim system, narrowing the possible field of attackers. Another important point is that during this phase you may find that more than likely no incident actually occurred. This doesn't mean that the victim is crying wolf. It simply means that statistics have caught up with you. Far more computers fail or succumb to user error than are attacked. This part of your investigation will help reveal if such was the case.

If the attack was especially sophisticated, this part of your investigation will help reveal that as well. However, even the most sophisticated attacks leave their marks. The trouble is that, very often, the marks lead to no one. Establishing the fact of an intrusion and the source of it are very different things. Realistically, both you and the victim should be prepared for that outcome. In most cases, intrusions are the most difficult incidents to connect to an individual.

While you might assume that all computer-related crimes are, at their base, intrusions, when we speak of intrusions we mean those events where the accessing of the computer using a covert communications channel is the primary feature. For example, the theft of data could occur in a variety of ways, some of which involve legitimate access by authorized users. While we could say this of any computer incident, the method of access, while important, will not likely be the primary evidence implicating the attacker.

In an incident where there is no other tangible evidence, the method of access becomes critical. It is often critical, not so much because of its value as irrefutable evidence, but because it can lead us to the attacker where we can use other methods, such as that old-fashioned police work we spoke of earlier, to solve the crime. As we will soon see, denial of access also has this element of the use of the intrusion itself to get to the attacker and further, if not complete, the investigative process.

One final note on traditional investigative techniques in the computer age: there is no substitute for the trained intuition of an experienced investigator. The technical issues we are discussing are, at best, support for that investigative process. However, as we will see in Chapter 8, you should believe your indications.

If the technical evidence, collected properly, tells you that a thing is true, believe it. Computers, contrary to popular opinion, do not lie. It is, of course, possible to make them misrepresent, but they are only doing the bidding of their human masters. Their misrepresentations are, at best, only surface manifestations. In the investigation of computer-related crime there is no adage truer than "look beneath the surface."

DENIAL OF SERVICE

In today's underground it seems that the most popular attacks are *denial of service*. Denial of service attacks include any which denies legitimate users access to a computer resource. That could include data, processors, storage devices, applications, or communications links.

Perhaps we are seeing more of these attacks because of the tenor of the times. Corporate downsizing leads to disgruntled employees. These employees often have excessive access to computer resources and take out their frustration on the computers and their data. Some types of denial of service attacks are:

- Attacks which destroy or damage data.
- Attacks which cause computers to go down.
- Attacks which cause communications devices, such as routers, to go down.
- Attacks which cause access to a computer system to be withheld from legitimate users. Typical of this attack are those which destroy user records, password files, or other functions which enable users to log into the system. An extension of this form of attack are those attacks which have the same affect on databases or applications that require authentication for use.
- Attacks which force a processing, I/O (input/output), or other bottleneck causing the system to slow or, even, stop. A notorious example of such an attack was the "Internet Worm" unleashed by Robert Morris, Jr., in the 1980s. A more current example is the e-mail bomb or "spamming."

Why do denial of service attacks occur? Typically, an underlying reason for these attacks is lack of ability on the part of the attacker to perform one of the other types of attacks we have discussed. If the attacker can't break into the computer, perhaps he or she can achieve the objective by causing it to break down. In this regard, we see young "wannabe" hackers using scripts, found on the Internet or on underground bulletin board systems, which cause a system to fail.

The rewards are bragging rights, revenge on a school or other organization or person they see as wronging them, or the misdirected thrills of seeing a big system crash-and-burn (not literally, by the way — I don't know of a way to burn down a computer system by hacking it). In virtually every case of computer vandalism I have seen, the underlying reason was revenge. And, in most cases, the perpetrator was a person with only moderate computer skills, although often he or she was perceived by co-workers as being far more skillful than they actually were.

The next question, of course, relates to how these attacks work. There are several methods of denying service to legitimate users. We will explore a few of these in more depth in Chapter 4. However, for our purposes at the moment, they fall into a few distinct technical categories:

- **Packet floods.** These cause some aspect of the computer's processing to be overloaded. They include such techniques as synch floods. They are predominantly communications attacks and depend upon the communications process for success.
- **Data floods.** These are attacks which cause the computer's storage space to fill. An example of this type of attack is a log flood, which causes the target system to experience an excessive number of occurrences of a logged event, thus causing the logs to fill using all available space on the storage device. Mail bombs are another example of this type of attack, although there is also a communications aspect to them as well.
- **Critical file damage.** These cause damage to such files as password, configuration, or system files. These attacks generally require the attacker to have the skills to break into the computer and, unless the computer is incorrectly configured, gain superuser access.
- **Data file or application damage.** This is another attack that requires the attacker to gain access to the system. However, in many cases, due to the requirements of an application, the vulnerable files may be written to by normal users. Since no superuser access is required, users or masqueraders with normal access can do significant damage. This is a very tough crime to solve because the attacker may be someone who belongs in the system and whose actions are simply not well logged.

Investigating this type of incident can be very frustrating because the indications often are lost with the damaged files. Attacks which are dependent upon communications may be a bit easier to track because any large data flow usually leaves footprints on the network.

DATA FLOODS AND MAIL BOMBS

For example, a mail flood or other data flood may be traceable even though the attacker used intermediate computers to generate the attack. Mail spoofing (a technique which makes e-mail appear to have come from a source other than its real one) is detectable by expanding the header information in the messages. Many attacks of this type are traceable by sniffing the packets and, through the source addresses, beginning a backwards trace to their origin. The backward trace usually requires the cooperation of the administrators of intermediate sites. However, data floods will also affect their networks and, therefore, they often are willing to cooperate in your investigation.

Your success at tracing the source of computer vandalism may depend upon trapping packets involved in the attack. This has implications with regard to wiretap laws. However, in most cases, you can capture packets if the capture is in your normal maintenance routine and not strictly for the purpose of tracing an attack. Also, you must only use the source and destination address information in the packet.

The contents of the packet usually cannot be used without a court order allowing its capture.

Even so, that limited information can be very valuable because you are largely interested in tracing the source of the attack. There are several good freeware packet-monitoring programs that concentrate on packet type, source, and destination addresses and other "housekeeping" factors without caring about data contents. Routine use of these tools can be a big help should your site succumb to a data or packet flood. Remember, these attacks often occur only once; if you don't capture the evidence when they happen, you probably won't get a second chance.

Investigating denial of service attacks requires essentially the same steps as any other intrusion. Begin by eliminating as many routes into the system as you can, then continue by testing each remaining route until you have narrowed the possibilities as far as you can. In the case of a data flood coming from the Internet, you will need to begin the process of identifying specific sources. Because of the way Internet routers work, packets often pass through many intermediate networks under normal circumstances. If you add intermediate systems used by the attacker to misdirect pursuers, the possibilities get very large, indeed.

If you are able to capture packets that reveal a source address, use the traceroute program to determine where the packets passed between your site and the source. Contact the administrator of the source site and begin the process of traceback if the attack did not originate at his or her site. Often, due to the way an intermediate site has configured its hosts, the traceroute will stop short of the endpoint. This is because the endpoint host is configured to reject the packets that comprise the traceroute.

The intermediate sites discovered by your traceroute may be useful if they can help you marshal additional resources to track the attacker. If the attack crossed state lines, you may have additional help from federal law enforcement. Another reason to perform the traceroute is to determine whether or not the attack crossed state lines. Sometimes, even when the source is in the same state and because of how the Internet routes packets, the route may cross into another state and then back again, potentially making the crime a federal offense. We will discuss all of the above techniques, and some others as well, in Chapter 6 with the topic of cyberforensic analysis.

ATTACKS FROM INSIDE THE ORGANIZATION

Statistically, most attacks against computers, which are not simply user error or failing equipment or software, come from within the organization. These attacks may or may not be easy to trace, depending upon the configuration of the target and any intermediate hosts. The benefit to corporate investigators acting wholly within their own networks is that they can exercise some measure of control on the computers involved and they can compel administrators to cooperate.

Many of the same techniques we have already discussed apply equally to the internal environment. However, you now have the additional advantage of using the system logs on intermediate machines as a resource. The traceback may be more successful under these conditions.

Certain types of denial of service attacks leave very big footprints within the logging systems of other computers. For example, a sync flood on an ethernet segment may have an effect on other computers, aside from the target, on the segment. This may be especially true if there are routers between the source and the destination. There may be remnants of tools on the last computer in the chain (if the attacker used several computers to mask his or her real location) that can lead to the attacker. If the attack started with a PC, there may be forensic evidence on the hard drive that points to use of the PC in the attack.

The early efforts you expend to collect evidence will not always be rewarded, but they are always critical. Be very careful how you probe an attacker's computer. It may be booby-trapped to cause critical evidence to be destroyed at the first sign of tampering. We will discuss search-and-seizure later in much more detail.

The bottom line is that denial of service attacks can destroy data, applications, and configuration files. They can cause networked computers to fail and can interrupt legitimate access by users who need to do their jobs. The fruits of denial of service attacks also have the potential to affect other computers aside from the target.

ATTACKS WHICH REQUIRE ACCESS TO THE COMPUTER

There is a special class of denial of service that requires access to the computer. These attacks may be from legitimate users with a grudge, or they may be more sinister. In any event, they all have one thing in common: access to the target is necessary.

Access can come from several sources, one of which is remote access. This includes dial-in, telnet, remote login, and other methods of connecting from a distance. In these cases, the network is a critical piece of the puzzle. However, an even more critical piece is the configuration of the target computer. Poorly configured machines invite intrusion.

Among other attacks, such things as destroying password files, configuration files, and other critical system files are common approaches that require access to the target. Critical or sensitive Unix hosts should be kept in physically secure areas. Most networked hosts offer up all of their secrets if they are rebooted into single user mode. Older hosts, especially, are vulnerable to this type of attack.

When rebooting a Unix host in the single user mode, there usually is no password required for the root user. The machine comes to life as if root had logged in from the console. From there it is a simple matter to replace the passwd file, add new users (back doors), and erase evidence in the logs.

Novell NetWare servers have a DOS mode, as do NT servers. This can allow similar access if the computers are poorly configured. The hacker's approach will probably be

- reboot the computer into a more convenient mode
- steal and crack the password file OR create some "back door" accounts
- clean up
- return later to do the damage, perhaps misdirecting investigators to another, innocent, user

CHAPTER REVIEW

In this chapter we explored the impacts of various types of computer-related crimes. We looked at these types of crimes in detail and began a discussion of how they are committed and how you can investigate them. We also introduced a general methodology for investigating the technical aspects of computer-related crimes.

In the next chapter we will introduce rogue code attacks. These attacks range from denial of service attacks (such as viruses) to attacks intended to provide access, create back doors, steal or alter files, or allow network connections between computers where no such connections should exist.

3 Rogue Code Attacks

In this chapter, we will examine the technical issues surrounding rogue code. The major types of rogue code which we will discuss are viruses, Trojan horses, and worms. We will describe these types of rogue code, as well as logic bombs, and techniques for examination of systems after an intruder's attack. We also will discuss detection and prevention methods on various types of mission-critical computers.

Because this book is aimed at corporate investigators of computer incidents, we will not spend a great deal of time discussing the internals of viruses, Trojan horses, and other malicious code. However, for the investigator to be successful, he or she must have a clear understanding of how various types of malicious code operate. This includes the mechanisms for doing damage, how the code is spread, and how and why the attacker may leave malicious code in a system after an attack.

As we discussed in an Chapter 2, one of the most prevalent types of computer attack is denial of service. Many intruders, especially those who are not technically capable of performing sophisticated intrusions, choose to cause damage rather than attempt other forms of attack. Relatively speaking, damage and denial of service attacks are simple compared to other more sophisticated intrusions. Therefore, the act of destroying files, causing systems to crash, damaging data on hard drives, and other denial of service attacks are extremely popular, especially with disgruntled employees.

In this chapter, we will cover the types of denial of service attacks that result from the insertion of malicious code into a system or a file. Tracing of malicious code to the perpetrator is often extremely difficult. Viruses can enter a system through legitimate means. A careless, but well meaning, employee may bring an infected file or disk to work from home. Here, the intent is clearly not malicious. However, the malicious attacker will surely use as his or her defense that the virus cannot be traced directly to them. Thus, it is important that the investigator develop techniques for back-tracing the source (sometimes called the "vector") of the code.

Also, disgruntled employees will often do damage to files and then leave a logic bomb to do additional damage at a later time. The investigator must understand how to check a system which has experienced an attack for evidence of such a logic bomb. A major part of any investigation is the "cleanup." We will begin our discussion with top level technical descriptions of various types of malicious code.

VIRUSES, TROJAN HORSES, AND WORMS

We will start our discussion of rogue code with a description of viruses. (The underground use of the plural form "virii" is not correct. However, it does seem to be popular and is certainly one way to distinguish the virus writers from the anti-virus, or "AV" community.) Viruses have two important characteristics. First, they must replicate. Second, they must become part of another executable file. When a virus replicates, it makes a copy of itself in another host. For the purposes of this discussion, we will use the term "host" to describe the executable file that contains the virus.

There are two exceptions to the executable rule. The first is the batch file. While we may consider a batch file to be executable, we may also view it as a text file. Because it is a text file, and not a true executable, it is not possible to infect a batch file with a virus. However, there is a special type of rogue code that can work as part of a batch file. This type of code is called an ANSI bomb.

The ANSI bomb takes advantage of the fact that, in older DOS PCs, there is a device driver called ANSI.SYS which controls certain functions, such as color displays for some older character-based programs. Additionally, however, ANSI.SYS provides keyboard mapping. Thus, by putting control codes into a batch file that ANSI.SYS understands, we can cause the keyboard to be remapped. We can also associate a particular key or set of keystrokes with a malevolent act, such as erasing the hard drive's data.

ANSI bombs usually are disguised in ANSI graphics files. Older bulletin board systems (BBS) use ANSI graphics files because they do not require any special display drivers on the part of the calling systems. The control codes in an ANSI drawing are quite cryptic to the lay viewer. It is easy to embed malicious actions in the code. The code can be part of a batch file that causes the control codes to be read and interpreted by ANSI.SYS. In today's Windows 95 PCs there is very little, if any, reason to use ANSI.SYS.

The other exception is the macro file. We encounter macro files with such programs as Microsoft Word, Microsoft Excel, and Lotus 1-2-3. Strictly speaking, macros are executable files. They are actually executed by another program — Excel, Word, etc. However, during the execution, they behave as if they were the executing program. Thus, it is possible to execute a virus and, perhaps, to replicate it.

Types of Viruses

There are several types of viruses. In general, we see the following:

- File infector
- Resident program infector
- Boot sector infector
- Multi-partite virus
- Dropper
- Stealth virus
- Companion virus
- Polymorphic virus
- Mutation engine

We will discuss each of these virus types in turn.

File Infector

File infectors act directly on executable files. They will generally insert their code at the beginning of the executable files. Each time the program executes, the various codes place a copy of themselves in another executable file. This results in a large number of files eventually being infected. In addition to the replication phase of a virus, there is also an action phase. The action phase is sometimes called the payload. This describes the damage that the virus was written to cause. Once the virus has replicated itself into several different files, it is ready to release its payload.

The payload may be released based upon any of a number of events. The virus may do its damage after it has infected a predetermined number of files. It may do its damage based upon a certain date. Or, it may release its payload based upon some other, preprogrammed, event.

Resident Program Infector

A resident program infector begins by infecting an executable file. When the host file is executed, the virus is placed in memory. From that point on, until the computer is rebooted, the virus will infect every executable file that executes on the computer. With the exception that the resident program infector resides in memory, it is the same as the file infector.

Boot Sector Infector

The boot sector infector infects the hard drive's master boot record. Once it has infected the boot record (which is actually an executable file) it will also infect the boot sector of any floppy disk placed in the floppy drive. Boot sector infectors spread between computers through the vector of the floppy disk. An infected floppy disk will infect the boot sector of the hard drive of any computer it is used in. Some boot sector viruses require that the computer boot from the infected floppy. For others, simply reading the infected floppy disk is enough.

Unlike memory resident viruses, boot sector infectors survive booting the computer. Investigators should always physically write-protect any disks used to boot a suspect's computer and any disks used in a suspect's computer should be scanned before they are used in the investigator's computer.

Multi-Partite Virus

A multi-partite virus combines boot sector and file infector characteristics. It can infect both the boot sector and other files.

Dropper

Droppers are small infected files whose purpose it is to infect the boot sector. Unlike normal boot sector infectors, which infect between disks, the dropper, when executed, replicates its virus code to the host's boot sector. If the dropper's virus also is a file infector, it may be considered to be a multi-partite virus. Droppers are not, themselves, viruses. We may describe them more accurately as Trojan horses (see description later in this chapter) that carry the boot sector virus as a payload. Sometimes they are just a small executable file with no other function than to infect the boot sector. Sometimes the virus is hidden inside a legitimate program. It infects the boot sector when the program is executed.

Stealth Virus

A stealth virus is one which can hide from detection. It does so by one of several methods. One method is to "hook" an interrupt and misguide a scanner around itself. The scanner, therefore, never knows that the code exists. The second method, described by Kane,[1] is to make a copy of the portion of the legitimate program code the virus replaces. It places the copy in another part of the host program and, when scanned, directs the scanner to the legitimate code instead of itself. Stealth viruses are very hard to detect; however, there are several common ones that are detectable by most competent scanners.

Companion Virus

Companion viruses take advantage of the fact that DOS executes files of the same name in a particular order. Since .com files always execute before .exe files of the same name, the companion is simply a .com file with the same name as a .exe file. The .com file is actually little more than the virus embedded in a small executable file. When the user calls the program, the .com (virus) file executes first, infecting the system. It then calls the legitimate program, which then runs as usual.

Occasionally, someone wishing to infect a computer will place a companion virus on the PC to "get the ball rolling." The companion will infect its first file, as described above, and will then delete itself, removing all evidence of its presence or the source of the infection. Investigators should note, however, that the original .com file can be reclaimed in many cases using forensic tools and techniques.

Polymorphic Virus

Polymorphic viruses are able to evade detection by changing or "morphing" them-selves into what appears to be a different virus. However, they don't do this by changing their code. Instead, they use a sophisticated form of encryption to disguise themselves. To understand how polymorphic viruses work, we must spend a moment on encryption.

Encryption is the act of scrambling a string of characters or code using a key and an algorithm. The algorithm performs a mathematical process on the combination of the key (a string of bits) and the data (another string of bits which may represent printable characters or binary code). To unencrypt, we must perform the process in reverse. This is a greatly simplified description, but, for the moment, it will do.

The polymorphic virus generates a pseudorandom key and, with it, encrypts the virus code. When the program executes, the polymorphic virus uses the key to unencrypt itself. Once unencrypted, it can replicate or release its payload. When it replicates, however, it generates a different pseudorandom key. This makes the resulting encrypted form of the new virus (the "child") different from the original one (the "parent"). Scanners cannot predict what the key, and, therefore, the resulting child, will be; therefore, the use of signature scanning (see description later in this chapter) is not practical.

The way to detect polymorphic viruses is to detect the encryption process, intercept it, and run it in reverse to unencrypt the virus. Once the virus is unencrypted, it will exhibit a consistent pattern which can be scanned and identified. Trend Micro Devices, developers of PCCillin, developed this technique which is now used in one form or another by most antivirus products.

Mutation Engine

The mutation engine, purportedly invented by a virus writer calling himself Dark Avenger, is a program which can make any virus polymorphic.

DETECTION METHODS

There are several types of detection methods for finding viruses. The first, and most common, is the pattern scanner. There are also integrity checkers, heuristic scanners, and behavior blockers.

Pattern Scanners

Pattern scanners depend upon knowing a pattern or "signature" unique to each known virus. They work based upon the "dissection" of the virus, isolation of a string of code thought to be unique to the virus, and comparison of the suspected virus with a database of those known signatures. Pattern scanners, by themselves, require a signature database which may or may not be complete. There are several new viruses appearing daily and it is virtually impossible to keep signature files current.

Additionally, it is easy to modify (or "mutate") the code of a virus so that it continues to do its damage but no longer matches the code string the scanner expects to see. Investigators should be aware of lists of signature strings for virus scanners such as McAfee. These signature files appear on the Internet regularly.

Integrity Checkers

Most AV experts believe that the most effective antivirus program is the integrity checker. Integrity checkers produce a database of signatures of files on a PC that represents the files in the uninfected state. The method used to generate the signatures is very complex and will detect symmetric modifications in code — a modification where every bit change has an equal but opposite bit change, intended to fool integrity checkers. Thus, if a virus infects a file, the resulting change in the file's code produces a different signature. The integrity checker scans every executable file, compares its signature with the one in the database and detects differences. A difference indicates a possible infection. There is no need to know the virus, just that the file has been changed. Integrity checkers, used in combination with pattern scanners, also can often identify the virus from its pattern.

Behavior Blockers

The two methods just described may be considered static in that they work on files which are not, currently, executing. However, there is a third type of AV program that must wait for the virus to attempt to replicate. The behavior blocker, pioneered by Trend Micro Devices, doesn't care what virus is attempting mischief. It simply knows that a combination of disallowed events are taking place and it stops program execution and warns the user.

Because there are a limited number of actions a virus can take in the replication phase, the behavior blocker can use an expert system to analyze the actions and determine the possibility of virus activity.

TROJAN HORSES

A Trojan horse differs from a virus in two very important aspects. First, it does not replicate or infect other files. Second, it could stand alone as an independent executable file. The Trojan horse is simply a program disguised as another program. It is usually malicious. An example of a Trojan horse is a program that grabs passwords and forwards them to the attacker. The password grabbing program might be hidden inside of an innocent-looking program, such as a game or utility.

An important source of Trojan horse programs is the disgruntled programmer or industrial spy who has signed on with a company to produce code. He or she might embed a Trojan horse in the code that performs some malicious function, such as mailing customer lists to a competitor. The routines to perform the hidden function would be buried in the legitimate code and might not be easily discovered.

A second important source is the malicious hacker. The hacker will attempt to replace critical system or application files with files that have been "Trojaned," or altered to contain unauthorized functionality. One notorious example of such Trojans is rootkit. Rootkit is a set of critical-system programs which have been altered to allow compromise of the system. If the intruder is able to penetrate the system and replace the correct files with the Trojaned rootkit files, he or she will be able to enter the system undetected and, possibly, gain root (superuser) rights. Rootkit is a Unix attack and, although the original rootkit was for SunOS Unix machines, there are now other rootkits that do the same thing in other Unix operating environments.

Once the rootkit package is on the victim computer, the following programs will be installed SUID root in the destination directory. Their functions are detailed below:

- **z2:** removes entries from utmp, wtmp, and lastlog.
- **es:** ethernet sniffer for sun4-based kernels.
- **fix:** tries to fake checksums; installs with same dates/perms/users/groups.

SUID root means that, no matter who runs the program, it runs as if the root user were running it. That makes any user who runs it the superuser for the function that the program performs.

The following programs will be patched and an attempt at spoofing the check-sums of the files will be made. Also, these files will be installed with the same dates, permissions, owners, and groups of the originals. They replace the original programs:

- **sl:** become root via a "magic password" sent to login. In at least one version of rootkit, the magic password is "D13hh[" (without the quotes, of course). Anyone using this password, no matter what the login name or ID is, will be granted root access with no auditing. The password is very easy to change in the code, however, so you can't count on this one working in every case.
- **ic:** modified ifconfig to remove PROMISC flag from output.
- **ps:** doesn't show the intruder's actions in the process (ps command) list.*
- **ns:** doesn't show intruder's network connections.*
- **ls:** doesn't show intruder's files unless the "/" flag is used.
- **du5:** doesn't show intruder's files unless the "/" flag is used.
- **ls5:** doesn't show intruder's files unless the "/" flag is used.

The Trojans marked with the asterisk (*) can be defeated by having a second, clean copy of the ps and netstat programs. These will still show the actions that the Trojaned files hide.

When investigating an intrusion, especially on a SunOS computer, the investigator should be aware of some of these programs. While it is unlikely that the intruder will make the mistake of leaving tools on the victim computer, a check for z2, es, and fix may prove fruitful. The sl program replaces the legitimate login program with a login program that is the legitimate one plus the additional code to use the magic password. The additional code is the Trojan. Because it is a direct replacement, it will be hard to detect unless the magic password is the one noted.

If you suspect that rootkit has been used in an intrusion, the best way to check is to rename the programs that rootkit replaces, copy legitimate versions of the programs from some other similar machine, reboot the computer, and verify that its behavior is the same as before your test. If you can see files and network connections (ls and ns) that weren't there before, rootkit may have been used. Also, check ifconfig (ic) to see if the promiscuous mode shows up after your reboot. If it does (it should not have earlier, if the old program was the Trojan), you may have been attacked using rootkit.

Don't confuse Trojan horses with logic bombs (which we will discuss shortly). Logic bombs perform a destructive act based upon a trigger event much like a virus. Trojan horses are programs that perform their function when the host program runs. They tend not to be directly destructive, as are logic bombs. Rather, they collect information, open back doors, create unauthorized accounts, etc.

WORMS

Worms are basically viruses that don't replicate within other programs. Instead, they are stand-alone programs that make full, running duplicates of themselves, stealing system resources such as disk space, I/O cycles, and processor cycles. Most worms have bringing down the host system as their intent.

LOGIC BOMBS

Logic bombs, as we mentioned earlier, are programs within programs (like Trojan horses) that perform destructive acts based upon a trigger event. The trigger event may, of course, be the execution of the file containing the logic bomb. The most conspicuous characteristic of a logic bomb is usually its destructive nature.

A typical logic bomb will wait for some event, such as the absence of an employee's name on a payroll list (indicating, perhaps, that he or she has been fired). It will then execute some other piece of code which performs the destructive act, for example, and delete all of the employee records or e-mail proprietary information to the fired employee. The logic bomb is hidden inside an appropriate program. In the example, it might be hidden in the payroll program. Obviously, any system programmer with access to sensitive code and the ability to make changes in it could implant a logic bomb.

Logic bombs are most frequently found on mainframes and Unix machines where system programmers routinely implement new code and changes to existing code. However, with the new generation of PC-based applications, such as Power-builder, SQLServer, Visual Basic, and others that are finding favor in large organizations wishing to develop custom in-house applications, there are plenty of opportunities in the PC environment as well.

MODIFYING SYSTEM FILES

A special type of logic bomb, or, arguably, Trojan horse, is the technique of modifying critical PC system files. These files, most notably command.com, are the heart of the PC operating system. Command.com is the DOS command interpreter. By modifying it you can change the way it executes commands from the keyboard.

Imagine, for example, booting a suspect's PC, typing DIR and watching it delete all information on the hard drive. By changing command.com, that is an easy thing to do. By editing a portion of the command.com file, such that DIR and DEL are interchanged (the code that follows each of those commands remains the same, however), the command DIR actually executes the code for DEL. A bit more manipulation and the DEL applies to the entire disk. This is one of the reasons investigators should never boot the suspect's computer using its own operating system.

Another favorite trick of hackers is to change the order in which DOS files execute. Recall that in our discussion of companion viruses we said .com files execute before .exe files of the same name. Continuing that train of thought, .bat (batch) files execute last. The order is determined in command.com. However, we can edit command.com to change the order. That allows us to make batch files execute first. Thus, we could create a batch file called command.bat. The batch file could run command.com and erase our hard drive, protecting us from having incriminating evidence found by investigators. If the erasure were performed using a secure delete application, we could be sure that our secrets were protected.

This type of logic bomb is easy to create and easy to discover. However, inexperienced investigators often miss this particular trap, boot the suspect's PC, and lose all evidence.

RESPONDING TO ROGUE CODE ATTACKS

Investigators are often called upon to investigate rogue code attacks. Investigating such an attack presents some challenges in terms of setting priorities. Certain types of attacks spread rapidly, affecting computers on a network in large numbers. An excellent example of that problem was the Morris Internet Worm. An error in code caused a worm to spread over the Internet at a rate that infected tens of thousands of computers all over the world in the space of 24 hours. Faced with a spreading wildfire, what are the priorities?

Clearly the number one priority is isolation. Infected computers must be isolated to prevent the code from spreading. Next, however, is where the dilemma begins. It is hard enough to trace the original vector for the code when the system is running with the code intact. When the system is cleaned, however, all evidence may disappear.

VIRUSES

It is a rule of thumb that investigators should not modify the attacked computer in any way, including altering the data on the hard drive, until evidence is collected and a reliable, verifiable copy of the system has been created. Until the mirror is built, the system should not be altered. However, users need their machines. In a rogue code attack, especially a virus attack, it is likely that many computers are involved. You will need to trace the virus through those computers, but how can you take them all out of service to do so?

The answer is that you can't. This is one of those situations where, normally, the priority will be to isolate the affected machines, clean them, and return them to service. Analysis is a secondary consideration in virus attacks. Additionally, it is often very difficult to trace the source vector of a virus on a large network. However, you may have possible options.

The first thing you should do is to save a copy of an infected file. Treat it as you would any crime scene evidence. Make a second copy and save it as a work copy. At some point, if the attack is serious enough, you may want to have an expert dissect the virus and see if it has been modified. If it has, you may be able to track the modified code to the perpetrator. This is very "iffy" and there are few people who can perform this type of testing competently. Later on we'll discuss this type of analysis, called software forensic analysis, in more detail. It is an extreme measure, very expensive, and not very reliable.

If you can identify the first computer to exhibit signs of infection, you may be able to isolate it long enough to investigate the source of the infection. However, even with extended access, it will usually be very difficult to get to the person who introduced the virus. Here, however, are some hints. Remember, depending upon the virus, some or all of these may not work.

Look for the date of last change to infected files. Pick the earliest one you can find. The computer it is on may be the first infected. However, there are several variables here. For one, many viruses don't change file dates. Another problem is that you will have to look at many files in a number of cases to get to an early file date. Even then, there is no guarantee that you have the earliest.

If you can find the first computer infected, look for a nonstandard program, such as a game or utility, that is not part of your company's normal desktop software. Question the computer user about the source of the file and check it for a virus. If it is infected, it may be the program that started the outbreak.

Check floppy diskettes of the users of computers that were infected early. There is a good possibility that the virus was introduced via floppy. Look on the file server for infected files. Compare date and time of last change to any infected files with the log of who was logged on at the time. The same caveats as the first hint also apply here.

TROJAN HORSES AND LOGIC BOMBS

In some regards, these are easier than viruses because they are, usually, confined to a single computer. Here the trick is to avoid triggering the code. However, we usually learn about the existence of rogue code because it triggers and we have a mess to clean up.

If the code has triggered, you'll have a pretty good idea of where it is. If you have a logic bomb hidden in a payroll program, you'll know you have a problem when you run payroll and it does its damage. The only safety net you have, of course, is a complete, properly executed backup and recovery strategy.

If, however, you suspect that there is a logic bomb hidden in a program, you'll need to take some specific steps to prevent it from doing its damage. We'll discuss this in more detail momentarily, but here's the short form. Remember that you don't want to create a situation that will preclude future investigation. So, you should start by taking a full backup of the suspected program and handling it as you would any crime scene evidence. Make a second copy to act as your work copy.

Here, we are very likely to have a unique piece of code. The code often can be traced back to the programmer. As we pointed out above, however, this is not yet an exact science. However, unlike trying to sort out minor changes in an existing piece of virus code, forensic analysis of logic bomb or Trojan horse code may be more rewarding. The reason is that most logic bombs are "custom created" by programmers who probably work for the victim.

There are usually numerous examples of the programmer's coding style available for comparison. You may even find that the programmer has left some of the offending code on his or her own computer. You may need forensic techniques to uncover it, but it may be there nonetheless. Its uniqueness will point an incriminating finger at the programmer.

To verify that the code has been changed, look at the date of last change (although, for several reasons, this is not always reliable). Compare it to the date of last change for the same file on a recent backup. Step backwards through backups, as far as practical, comparing dates. If there is a date change you can't explain, you may have an altered file.

Next make the same comparison using file size. While this is not a 100% certain method (some programs change size for legitimate reasons), it is another step towards determining if you have a problem.

Finally, if you can view the source code (you can for many operating systems), do it the hard way: read the source and look for the rogue code. An easy way to do this, if you have a known good copy of the source, is to do a line-by-line comparison. There are editors that will automate the task for you. Remember, the number one priority usually is getting the application or computer back on line. If you must restore operations, take your copies and restore the original from a backup. But, don't forget to handle your copies properly.

PROTECTION OF EXTENDED MISSION-CRITICAL COMPUTER SYSTEMS

Extended mission-critical systems are those that make broad use of distributed data and platforms. Some even distribute the application. An example of that type of client/server configuration is SAP R/3. R/3 is a very large-scale client/server program for managing core financial information in large organizations. It has a three-tier architecture that includes clients, application servers, and database servers. Depending upon the size of the system, there can be thousands of clients, dozens of application servers, and several database servers. Clearly, rogue code spreading through a system of this type could be disastrous.

The key to protecting a system like this is to protect it from the outside in. If the clients are well protected, you have solved a big part of the problem. However, while most applications like R/3 are fairly secure, the platforms upon which they sit often are not. If a hacker cannot, because of lack of knowledge or the presence of good controls, penetrate the application directly, he or she likely will try to get in through weaknesses in the platform. Rogue code can operate the same way.

Remember, in order to introduce rogue code into a system's files, it is necessary to first penetrate the system itself. Trojans, for example, must replace legitimate files. Logic bombs must be placed inside legitimate code. Viruses must infect the first file in order to begin infecting others. Thus, it is usually the platform that requires primary protection efforts.

The same techniques, then, that we can use to protect the platform from hackers can be used to prevent introduction of rogue code. Those techniques generally revolve around proper configuration of the operating system or network operating system. Secondarily, they may include the addition of stronger, third-party access controls. Here is where the investigator can, before an attack, have some important influence.

Part of the key to protecting a critical system lies in being able to investigate a breach of the system. That means lots of logging. And, it means that the logs have to be well protected. Many third-party access control products provide excellent, well-protected logs. They are complete and cannot be altered without a trace, even by the superuser. If used properly, they will be the investigator's best friend if the need ever arises. The experienced investigator will want to use every means at his or her disposal to ensure that mission-critical systems employ some form of robust logging. At a minimum, the types of events that need to be logged include:

- Logon/logoff
- File deletes
- Rights changes
- All accesses of anything by superusers
- Failed logon attempts
- Unused accounts
- SU (Switch User) in Unix systems
- System reboots
- Remote accesses, in detail (includes dial-in or external network access)
- New user additions

In large systems, such as mainframes, there are other parameters that should be logged as well. Logs should not reside on the computer being logged. They should be spooled off that computer to another, used just for logging, called a log host. The log host should be very well secured and its logging should be robust. Access to the log host should be limited to the fewest persons possible. The log host should be backed up at least daily and the backed up logs stored for a minimum of six months — a year is better. Frequently, we don't find out about the need for an investigation for weeks or, even, months after the event. Often logs for the time period aren't available. That makes the investigation very difficult at best. Usually, it is impossible.

POST-ATTACK INSPECTION FOR ROGUE CODE

If a computer has been the target of a denial of service attack, especially by an insider, the first thing you should do, immediately after performing your backup chores and properly preserving evidence, is to check the computer for rogue code. This is a must before putting the computer back into service. Many attackers will leave a post-attack "gift," which can be as devastating as the original attack if left undiscovered.

Unfortunately, discovering the rogue code can be difficult, time-consuming, and lacking in certainty. The first thing to do is to identify likely targets for alteration. In a PC-based system, the first check should be a virus scan. Perform the scan using two or more different scanners, both of which should have heuristic capabilities.

The next place to look is the next easiest: source code. PC-based systems rarely have source code present, certainly not for commercial products, but on other systems, such as Unix, it's common. The exceptions for PC-based systems are script-based applications, macros, and batch files. Investigators can examine these directly using the simplest of tools, such as text or macro editors.

Inspection of source code is difficult and time-consuming. It requires experienced programmers who can "read" the code and trace execution. The use of a specialized debugger which can execute code a single step at a time is also very helpful. However, never execute suspected code on a production machine.

Next, look at database applications. Database applications often have scripts which underlie the graphical interface. Within these scripts there is the possibility of embedding damaging program steps. Carefully look at how the input forms access the database and what they do with it. Remember, what you see on the input form is cosmetic. The underlying commands may be far different.

On PCs, check word-processing and spreadsheet macros for improper program steps. Also, any scripting language in use should be carefully checked for misuse of commands.

SUMMARY

In this chapter, we discussed the facets of rogue code that apply to the computer incident investigator. We examined viruses, Trojan horses, worms, logic bombs, and procedures to be used to detect alterations to files that could indicate rogue code. The investigator is often called into incidents that include rogue code, and a working knowledge of what it is and how to deal with it is important.

In the next chapter, we'll discuss different types of intrusions, ranging from surgical strikes that damage a finite part of a system, program, or application, to shotgun blasts that take out entire systems. We'll focus on denial of service attacks. However, we'll also discuss the most common form of intrusion: masquerading. We'll look at a couple of case studies: one of a surgical strike on a mainframe and another of a mail bomb program. Finally, we'll examine the most common method of denying service to Internet-connected systems: flooding.

REFERENCE

1. Kane, P., *PC Security and Virus Protection Handbook,* M&T Books.

4 Surgical Strikes and Shotgun Blasts

In this chapter, we will discuss the last of our introductory issues: the nature of denial of service (DoS) attacks. We will examine surgical attacks and global attacks, the two broad categories of denial of service. Because surgical attacks require explicit access to the resource under attack, we will also explore masquerading, the primary method used by attackers to gain access to target systems.

As we mentioned in an earlier chapter, denial of service attacks are on the rise. The reasons have to do with a variety of issues. Basic motivation often is employee dissatisfaction. Employees who feel that they have been wronged by the employer, or have been terminated or laid off, may turn to destructive acts for revenge. Often these individuals have limited computer skills. However, they are able to find resources in "kit" form that let them download a script from an underground Internet site and use it to perform acts of vandalism.

The issue of denial of service is an important one for corporate investigators, both because of its impact on the victim and because the 1986 Computer Fraud and Abuse Act. This update of the 1984 Counterfeit Access Device and Computer Fraud and Abuse Act made it a felony if the damage exceeded $1,000.

We will begin with a discussion of denial of service attacks as an introduction to the details that follow. We will focus on three areas:

1. The specific types of DoS attacks, how they work and how to protect against them
2. The effects of specific DoS attacks
3. Investigative techniques for tracing DoS attacks

DENIAL OF SERVICE ATTACKS

The National Institute of Science and Technology (NIST) Special Publication 800-7, *Security in Open Systems,* offers the following brief discussion of denial of service:

Denial of Service

Multi-user, multi-tasking operating systems are subject to "denial of service" attacks where one user can render the system unusable for legitimate users by "hogging" a resource or damaging or destroying resources so that they cannot be used. Denial of service attacks may be caused deliberately or accidentally. Taking precautions to prevent a system against unintentional denial of service attacks will help to prevent intentional denial of service attacks.

Systems on a network are vulnerable to overload and destructive attacks, as well as other types of intentional or unintentional denial of service attacks. Three common forms of network denial of service attacks are service overloading, message flooding, and signal grounding. It is important for system administrators to protect against denial of service threats without denying access to legitimate users. In general, denial of service attacks are hard to prevent. Many denial of service attacks can be hindered by restricting access to critical accounts, resources, and files, and protecting them from unauthorized users.[1]

SERVICE OVERLOADING

Service overloading is an attack where a particular service, usually TCP/IP, is presented with a flood of packets. When the service has used up all space on its stack, it will attempt to continue processing, even though the stack is full. If the packets continue to attempt communication with the service, it is unable to process them. Eventually, the service times out and becomes useless. Under some circumstances, it then becomes possible to use the services stack to initiate a second, intrusive attack. Often the service is flooded so that it cannot respond to legitimate inquiries, allowing another host to impersonate or "spoof" the legitimate machine, thus receiving all of the legitimate machine's packets.

Service overloading can be used to disable a host for the sake of disabling it (vandalism) or it can be used as part of a complex, multi-step attack that requires host spoofing. This is typical of a portion of IP spoofing, a type of attack that was first reported when Kevin Mitnick attacked a computer at the San Diego Supercomputer Center. Although the attack had been theorized, the Mitnick attack was the first reported example against a victim system.

Service overloading attacks are often referred to as flooding because the service is "flooded" with packets. We will discuss flooding — both of services and of systems — later in this chapter. Now, on to the other type of flooding: message flooding.

MESSAGE FLOODING

Message flooding is an increasing threat on the Internet. Message flooding occurs when some form of message, such as e-mail, is sent to a target host or site in such volume that the target cannot manage it. The result is that the target's resources are used up and the target ceases to function or functions at a fraction of its capacity.

There are two primary types of message flooding: e-mail and log flooding. E-mail flooding is often called "spamming." However, spamming actually refers to the practice of sending the same e-mail message to very large numbers of newsgroups and mail lists. Spamming usually originates with an advertising campaign. Mail flooding and spamming may, under certain circumstances, have the same effect (such as when a particular server hosts a large number of mail lists or when the spam passes through an Internet Service Provider and affects that ISP system). However, mail flooding refers specifically to an attack that consists of huge numbers of the same message sent to the same host or system.

SIGNAL GROUNDING

Signal grounding is an attack that requires physical access to the system. Basically, it consists of interrupting the flow of data in the network cable. The term has been extended to include attacks that cause data to be directed to a nonexistent destination, causing the data to be lost. It is not a particularly common form of attack.

OTHER ATTACKS

There are other types of DoS attacks that are somewhat more complex. These include alteration or destruction of program code; destruction of physical or logical resources, such as system disk drives or memory images; interception of data; alteration or destruction of address space; and overloading of communications resources, disk I/O, or other logical functions.

These types of attack are extremely complex to investigate. By their nature, they require a more sophisticated attacker with the resources and knowledge to cover his or her tracks after the attack. As we will see, surgical attacks under certain circumstances can offer some useful investigative opportunities due to the same complexities that are required to perform the attack. There are, within most organizations, few programmers capable of certain types of highly complex surgical attacks. That offers the corporate investigator a starting point in the event of such an attack.

The primary difficulty the investigator will encounter is collecting compelling evidence that can be easily understood by law enforcement, prosecutors, judges, and juries. As with most of our investigations, this one should start with a careful examination of logs.

Hans Husman, in an underground paper titled, "Introduction to Denial of Service," lists the following specific attacks:[3]

Attacking from the Outside

- Taking advantage of finger
- UDP and SunOS 4.1.3.
- Freezing up X-Windows
- Malicious use of UDP services
- Attacking with LYNX clients
- Malicious use of telnet
- Malicious use of telnet under Solaris 2.4
- Disabling accounts
- Linux and TCP time, daytime
- Disabling services
- Paragon OS Beta R1.4
- Novell's Netware FTP
- ICMP redirect attacks
- Broadcast storms

- E-mail bombing and spamming
- Time and Kerberos
- The Dot Dot Bug
- SunOS kernel panic
- Hostile applets
- Virus
- Anonymous FTP abuse
- Syn flooding
- PING flooding
- Crashing systems with PING from Windows 95 machines
- Malicious use of subnet mask reply message
- FLEX1m
- Booting with trivial FTP
- Malicious use of Internet Explorer
- Attacking Usenet
- Attacking name servers

Attacking from the Inside

- Kernel panic under Solaris 2.3
- Crashing the X-server
- Filling up the hard disk
- Malicious use of eval
- Malicious use of fork()
- Creating files that are hard to remove
- Directory name Lookupcache
- CSH attack
- Creating files in /tmp
- Using RESOLV_HOST_CONF
- Sun 4.X and background jobs
- Crashing DG/UX with ULIMIT
- NETTUNE and HP-UX
- Solaris 2.X and NFS
- System stability compromise via MOUNT_UNION
- trap_mon causes kernel panic under SunOS 4.1.X
- SunOS kernel panic with TMPFS
- SunOS kernel panic with pathconf()

Dumping Core

- Malicious use of Netscape
- Core dumped under WUFTPD
- 1d under Solaris/X86

The details of these attacks are in Husman's paper, included in its entirety in Appendix A. Because English is not Husman's native language, some patience is required from the reader. Also, the descriptions tend to be skimpy and there is an implied assumption that the reader is familiar with Unix. For all of that, it gives a good set of descriptions for investigators who need to be able to recognize the symptoms of particular attacks as a starting point for their investigations.

The corporate investigator often is at a disadvantage in a denial of service attack because he or she does not have the specific technical experience to recognize the attack for what it is. The result is that investigations that should be conducted often are not, because the attack was mistaken for normal equipment failure.

However, equally unfortunate, many normal failures are mistaken for attacks. This can result in embarrassment on the part of the investigator when the "attack" turns out to be a normal occurrence. Understanding the specific nature of the most common DoS attacks can help the investigator to focus on genuine mischief and leave the equipment failures to the network technicians.

SYMPTOMS OF A SURGICAL STRIKE

Surgical strikes all have one thing in common: they occur without warning and without obvious explanation. As such, they often are mistaken for normal systems failures. For example, there are surgical attacks that can force a Unix computer to "panic" (a response to an event that usually causes the computer to reboot) or crash. These attacks invoke actions that the computer views as detrimental to its health, so it reboots, dumping all existing connections. Under certain circumstances, data which was in process at the time of the reboot can be lost.

PANICS

The problem here is that computers panic frequently for a variety of reasons that have nothing to do with an attack. In Chapter 9 we will present a case study ("The Case of the CAD/CAM Cad") where an administrator was accused of causing his system to purposely crash. The truth was much different. Assuming that a panic'ing or crashing system has been attacked is often a bad assumption. However, the use of surgical techniques to cause panics and crashes is hard to do, easy to mistake for normal operation, and difficult to detect and investigate.

On Unix machines, causing a panic is, actually, quite simple. If the code to cause a panic is embedded deeply enough in legitimate code, it may be extremely difficult to locate. The panic command can take up as little as a single line of code. In a huge program, tracing one line of code requires a daunting effort. How does panic work? The best reference available on the subject of crash dump and panic analysis is *Panic! Unix System Crash Dump Analysis* by Chris Drake and Kimberly Brown.[2] Here's what they say about panic:

The Panic"!" Routine

Let's talk about how panic"!" actually works. The panic"!" routine abruptly interrupts all normal scheduling of processes. From the user's point of view, the system is suddenly dead.

Thus, the attacker can embed the panic"!" routine in an application. Select a trap, usually a particular function that occurs periodically, and, when the trap is satisfied, invoke panic"!". The result will be that the computer will, from the perspective of the user, cease to function. However, it will also do some other things that can help the investigator determine the cause of the panic.

When a Unix computer panics, it also produces a dump file. The dump file contains an image of the computer's memory. However, it is not in a format that the investigator can access yet. Usually, panic"!" saves the image to the primary swap device on the affected computer. The contents of the swap device can be retrieved by using the savecore command. Before the savecore command can be invoked, however, there are some preliminary preparations you must perform. These consist of setting up a directory to receive the dump file, setting permissions on that directory, and making some changes to configuration files. Refer to the manual or the man pages for the particular Unix you are working with to get the specifics before you attempt to save the dump file.

Some crashes and panics save the dump file on some machines automatically to a file called *core*. If that occurs, the core contains the memory image at the time of the dump. We will discuss the very complex task of analyzing a dump file later in this book. For more detail, refer to *Panic!* This is unquestionably the best reference on the topic available.

OTHER SURGICAL ATTACKS

Not all surgical DoS attacks occur in Unix. They can be perpetrated against any kind of computer. What they all have in common is that a particular individual function is used to disable other, related functions. For example, if an intruder is able to plant a Trojan horse that waits for a certain user to log in, and then erases all of that user's files and deletes his or her username, that would constitute a surgical attack. The attack has been focused on a single action (deleting the files and username of only one user), and it uses a single function (waiting for the target user to log in and then performing the deletes). A logic bomb can have the effect of a surgical attack if it meets the criteria.

The distinction of surgical attacks from global attacks is important. Investigation of surgical attacks can become as focused as the attack itself. There are specific aspects to the attack that can be discovered. Most important, the victim computer is often the entire crime scene. There may be evidence on the computer that can help the investigator solve the crime. In other, more global, DoS attacks, the investigator will need much more information to arrive at a correct solution, because this type of attack can be directed at the victim remotely. There will be very little evidence left on the victim computer when the event is over.

Although the attacker in a surgical strike may also be remote, he or she must usually gain access to the victim computer and perform the attack on the computer itself. This may leave evidence such as log entries, files that can be recovered using forensic techniques, or other footprints that can help backtrace the attack.

MASQUERADING

Masquerading comes in two broad forms: users masquerading as other users, and computers masquerading as other computers. We will explore each of those separately. The purpose of a masquerade is twofold. First, the attacker wants to divert attention from his or her real identity or the real identity of his or her machine. Second, the attacker wants to focus attention on another user or machine.

In computer masquerades, also called "spoofing," the objective often is to make internetworking components, such as routers, believe that the bogus machine is the one that is being spoofed. By doing this, the bogus machine carries on a communication with other machines that think it is the legitimate one. That action directs packets destined for the victim to the spoofing computer. The packets can be anything from e-mail to authentication packets. One of the most dangerous uses of this type of masquerade is the ability for the bogus computer to become a trusted host. We'll describe that process shortly.

User Masquerades

In order to masquerade as another user, the attacker needs to compromise the victim's ID and password. The most desirable victim, of course, is root. There are all sorts of approaches to harvesting IDs and passwords. The simplest way is social engineering.

Many users invite social engineering by willingly sharing passwords. Many information security experts believe that social engineering is the hacker's tool of the future. Internet Security Systems (ISS) defines social engineering for us in the glossary to their *SafeSuite* technical manual:

Social Engineering

Term used among hackers for cracking techniques that rely on human error and weaknesses; the aim is to trick people into revealing passwords or other information that compromises a target system's security. Classic scams include phoning up a mark who has the required information and posing as a field service tech or a fellow employee with an urgent access problem.[4]

The purpose, of course, is to gather information that can lead to gaining superuser rights on the target system. Investigators should not assume that the intruder gained access through purely technical means. Social engineering is involved in a significant percentage of intrusions. According to phreaker Susan Headley (AKA, Susan Thunder), technology often is not required at all to gain access to IDs and passwords that can lead to a complete compromise of the target system.

In an alleged demonstration of social engineering techniques before officials of the Department of Defense, Headley obtained information that could have permitted access to classified information using no other tools than a telephone, phone book, and her charm. Investigators of computer security incidents should follow up nontechnical leads as readily as technical ones.

Users, when faced with the requirement of remembering multiple passwords for several systems, tend to write the passwords down and put them in easily accessible places. Intruders, masquerading as workers who may have access to the victim's premises, may have acquired these passwords as the first step in accessing sensitive systems. Investigators should consider contract cleaning crews, service technicians, and contractors or consultants as sources of compromised passwords leading to a masquerade.

Of course, there are also technical means of harvesting passwords. There are several tools available on the Internet that can lead to compromise of password files on target systems. Investigators should spend time surfing the Internet for tools and techniques used by intruders. There are several sources of vulnerability information on the Internet that can provide the investigator with information that can help uncover masquerade techniques. Knowing the technique, as we will see in the next chapter, can help reconstruct the incident and lead to the solution.

Once the intruder is able to masquerade as a legitimate user, or as the superuser, he or she may continue to act as that user or may create additional accounts with superuser privileges as back doors into the system. Investigators should always examine user lists and password files for unauthorized accounts.

SYSTEM MASQUERADES

System masquerades are very sophisticated. They have as their objective replacing a legitimate computer with the masquerading computer. The target computer usually is part of a chain of trust with other, more important computers. Sometimes the real targets are inside a protected environment. Sometimes they are repositories of the information the intruder really is after. When the real target is inaccessible, but the intruder can locate another target with a trust relationship to the real victim, a spoofing attack may be the order of the day.

Spoofing attacks require several steps. First, the intermediate machine must be disabled so that the spoofing machine can replace it. Second, the spoofing machine must convince the real target that it is the disabled machine. Finally, the spoofing machine must connect to the real victim and allow the intruder to perform whatever tasks he or she wants. We'll discuss spoofing attacks in more detail next.

If an attacking machine can masquerade as a trusted host, it may be possible for the attacker to gain access to other machines in the chain of trust. Thus, it may be difficult or impossible to backtrace the connection, especially if logs for all affected machines are not adequate. While it may be clear that the trusted machine has been disabled, often by a denial of service attack such as a syn flood, if the disabled (trusted) machine is not logging fully, it may not be possible to trace the source of the DoS attack. Additionally, there is a better-than-even chance that the attacker, especially if he or she is sophisticated enough to perform this type of masquerade, has not launched the attack from his or her computer.

SPOOFING

There are three primary kinds of spoofing:

1. E-mail spoofing
2. Web spoofing
3. IP spoofing

We'll take up each one of these briefly, with our emphasis on IP spoofing. E-mail spoofing consists of masquerading as a user while sending e-mail to the victim. It is difficult in some circumstances to trace forged e-mail to its true source.

E-Mail

Forged e-mail usually is created by telneting to port 25 (the SMTP port) on an Internet or internal host. By conducting a manual dialog with the SMTP daemon, the forger can designate both the sender and recipient of the forged mail. However, an experienced investigator can expand the e-mail header, using a mail system such as Eudora, and see two important clues. First, there will be an entry in the header that says, "Apparently From:." This is likely to be the real source of the message. Second, there may be a series of entries that trace the path of the message. While it's not uncommon for messages to pass through several e-mail servers between source and destination, it is likely that the real source of the message will be at the beginning of the chain of addresses.

You can have difficulties in two situations. First, very old sendmail programs (the application on the Unix e-mail host that actually creates and sends the message via SMTP to the destination) may not provide complete header information, making the real source impossible to trace. Second, if you attempt to trace from inside a LAN-based e-mail system (such as Banyan VinesMail), which strips out "unneeded" header information, the forged message may be altered beyond your ability to reconstruct the header.

Forging e-mail from within an organization that uses LAN-based e-mail and has an Internet connection is also very easy. The forger uses a Web browser such as Microsoft Internet Explorer or Netscape. He or she creates an e-mail return message entry in the configuration menu that gives a different user's e-mail address as the "reply-to" entry. The address must be created to appear to come from the Internet (e.g., jsmith@somecompany.com). Then, the forger will send the forged message to the Internet address of the intended recipient.

In a well-managed Internet mail system, because the Internet address of both sender and receiver is within the local domain, it is likely that the message will never leave the internal network. Rather, it will hit the Internet mail gateway and be turned back to the intended recipient. If the internal mail system uses a LAN-based e-mail system internally, the message will appear legitimate and have no tracing information in the header.

Whether or not you will be able to trace the source of the message depends completely upon how well the e-mail gateway logs message header information. If the gateway logs header information, you may be able to trace the message to the forger. If there are two gateways (one for internal mail and a second one for mail originating outside the internal network) it may, at least, be possible to isolate the forged message's origin to the inside or external network.

Web Site

Web site spoofing is the act of replacing a World Wide Web site with a forged, probably altered, copy on a different computer. A report from Princeton University[5] describes the problem:

"Web spoofing allows an attacker to create a "shadow copy" of the entire World Wide Web. Accesses to the shadow Web are funneled through the attacker's machine, allowing the attacker to monitor all of the victim's activities, including any passwords or account numbers the victim enters. The attacker can also cause false or misleading data to be sent to Web servers in the victim's name, or to the victim in the name of any Web server. In short, the attacker observes and controls everything the victim does on the Web."

The paper goes on to describe the technique: "Web spoofing is a kind of electronic con game in which the attacker creates a convincing but false copy of the entire World Wide Web. The false Web looks just like the real one: it has all the same pages and links. However, the attacker controls the false Web, so that all network traffic between the victim's browser and the Web goes through the attacker.

"You may think it is difficult for the attacker to spoof the entire World Wide Web, but it is not. The attacker need not store the entire contents of the Web. The whole Web is available on-line; the attacker's server can just fetch a page from the real Web when it needs to provide a copy of the page on the false Web.

"The key to this attack is for the attacker's Web server to sit between the victim and the rest of the Web. This kind of arrangement is called a 'man in the middle attack' in the security literature.

"The attacker's first trick is to rewrite all of the URLs on some Web page so that they point to the attacker's server rather than to some real server. Assuming the attacker's server is on the machine www.attacker.org, the attacker rewrites a URL by adding http://www.attacker.org to the front of the URL. For example, http://home.netscape.com becomes http://www.attacker.org/http://home.netscape.com.

"Once the attacker's server has fetched the real document needed to satisfy the request, the attacker rewrites all of the URLs in the document into the same special form by splicing http://www.attacker.org/ onto the front. Then the attacker's server provides the rewritten page to the victim's browser.

"Since all of the URLs in the rewritten page now point to www.attacker.org, if the victim follows a link on the new page, the page will again be fetched through the attacker's server. The victim remains trapped in the attacker's false Web, and can follow links forever without leaving it."

The paper, in its entirety, is included in Appendix B.

There is no effective way to trace the source of this type of spoofing unless the investigator is lucky enough to encounter an attacker who lacks the sophistication of placing the spoof site on a hijacked computer. Of course, the investigator can use traceback tools such as finger, whois, etc. to locate the supposed spoof site. But, if the site is not on a computer owned or controlled by the attacker, the trace will be of little or no use.

The attack can be detected by reading the status line at the bottom of the Web browser, but the user must be skilled and observant enough to recognize that the status line is not displaying what he or she expects. Thus, the investigator is faced with an incident not unlike an intrusion where traceback requires the techniques we have discussed and will discuss later in the book.

IP Spoofing

IP spoofing is a key to attacks that require connection to a victim computer that is part of a chain of trust. There are several steps to the completion of an IP spoofing attack. This is not a simple attack. *Phrack Magazine,* a leading underground "e-zine" (electronic magazine) has one of the best descriptions of the technique available. Briefly:

> IP-spoofing consists of several steps, which I will briefly outline here, then explain in detail. First, the target host is chosen. Next, a pattern of trust is discovered, along with a trusted host. The trusted host is then disabled, and the target's TCP sequence numbers are sampled. The trusted host is impersonated, the sequence numbers guessed, and a connection attempt is made to a service that only requires address-based authentication. If successful, the attacker executes a simple command to leave a backdoor.[6]

The disabling of the trusted host may be accomplished through a sys flood. Sequence number guessing requires a separate routine, available as a script on many underground Internet sites. Sequence number guessing is critical because TCP/IP messages consist of packets which must be reassembled in the original order at the receiving end. Sequence numbers are based upon a pseudo-random starting number, which can be guessed.

Since the real host has been disabled, the spoofing host can take its place and, by assuming the same IP address as the disabled computer, can fool the trusting computer into thinking it is the real host. The key, of course, is that authentication must depend upon source address only. Tracing this type of attack is very difficult and, often, is impossible.

CASE STUDY: THE CASE OF THE CYBER SURGEON

What happens when a critical program running on a mainframe abruptly stops running and crashes? At the best, time and resources are wasted trying to get the application back up and running. At the worst, irreparable damage may be done due to the nature of the application. Causing a crash of an application without detection is a sophisticated problem. It can be more difficult, depending upon the operating system.

This case study describes just such an incident occurring on an IBM mainframe running a mission-critical application. On such mainframes, the application may be compiled at runtime. The compiled image resides in memory on the computer, as on any other computer, including PCs. Because the image is not always placed at the same memory location, an intimate knowledge of the computer, the application, and ways of compromising the memory image are requirements for causing the application to crash by damaging the image.

Of course, a Trojan horse or logic bomb would cause the same effect, but the damage would have to be done to the source code. This leaves tracks. An attack upon the image while it is executing in memory, however, leaves no tracks and may be mistaken for a natural failure. In the case of this particular attack, the attacker was able to determine the base address of the application in memory (the address location where the application's image is loaded at runtime). The attacker then located a small block of memory which, if altered, would cause the application to crash, zapped (a command that turns bits to zero) the block of data, and caused the crash.

Because the computer was protected by a security program, the intruder had to bypass security. It would seem that the intruder would be very easy to identify based upon an obvious high level of skill and access rights. In fact, another system programmer (the suspect was also a system programmer) turned the suspect into authorities. However, because logs, as delivered to investigators, had been altered (unknown to the investigators at that time), even computer experts believed that there was no way to say, without a doubt, that the suspect had committed the crime. The case was dropped.

Some months later, the same system programmer, who had "discovered" the incident, reported a repeat of the event and, again, pointed to the original suspect as the perpetrator. This time, however, other system programmers came to the aid of the suspect and, at a meeting of all of those involved and investigators, revealed a second, more complete copy of system logs. When the system programmer who had reported the incident was faced with a set of obviously contradictory logs, he admitted that he had performed the attack and altered evidentiary logs to implicate the suspect.

This case history has several important lessons for investigators. First, logs must be protected from alteration, even by superusers. Second, although skill levels can point to a short list of potential suspects, they are, by no means, the end of the investigation. Finally, logs may provide the most important evidence available. But there are usually multiple sets of logs (in this case there are system logs, security application logs, and the logs of the damaged applications), and they need to be used together to develop a full picture of the evidence. When one log contradicts another, the investigator must examine all of the logs to learn what actually happened.

SYMPTOMS OF SHOTGUN BLASTS

Shotgun blasts have several things in common, symptomatically. They typically result in the entire system crashing. Surgical strikes, on the other hand, may be directed at a single application, as in our case history above.

Shotgun blasts are usually obvious for their existence, if not for their source. An e-mail bomb, for example, is hard to miss. Logs, if they are reasonably complete, will show the existence of floods of most kinds. Surgical strikes, on the other hand, may go unnoticed. Shotgun blasts are quite likely to affect systems related to the target while surgical strikes generally are quite localized. Finally, shotgun blasts are hard to mistake for a natural occurrence (although it does happen), while surgical strikes usually are viewed as natural system or application failures.

Investigators should be careful to differentiate between natural failures and real attacks. There is a tendency to view any failure that seems out of the ordinary as an attack symptom. Statistically, most such incidents are not attacks at all.

"UP YOURS" — MAIL BOMBS

Late in 1996, a hacker who calls himself AcidAngel developed a mail-bomb program called "Up Yours." According to the Up Yours Frequently Asked Questions (FAQs)

> Up Yours is a program developed by AcidAngel of Global kOS to mail-bomb specific users on the Internet. The present version is 100% completely anonymous and uses random headers and subject lines and even uses random servers. It implements a HELO spoofing technique that is next to impossible to trace ... and is capable of sending mail using one server at the rate of 20 e-mail messages in around two seconds (tested on a 28.8).[7]

Up Yours is, at this writing, entering release 4. AcidAngel has clearly stated that he will not make the source code available so that there is no easy way to develop countermeasures. Tracing mail bombs originating from Up Yours, while difficult, is not impossible. Up Yours depends, for its anonymity, upon use of anonymous servers.

There are some general tips for tracing e-mail bombers. These tips take advantage of the expanded headers we've already discussed plus a couple of other techniques. Christopher Reagoso, a systems analyst whose World Wide Web home page is http://www.webscaper.com, gives a list of hints based upon his experience tracing a mail bomber:

"1. Attempt to determine the true e-mail address of the offender by reading the extended headers of the mail bomb.
2. Discover more detailed information about the mail bomber through the use of a WWW Finger Server.
3. Discover more detailed information (such as phone number and mailing address) of the offender's Internet service provider. This is done by mutating the offender's e-mail address to the address of a WWW URL (Netscape address) and using Netscape or other browser to view their home page.
4. Gather motives and other evidence by using the cost-free DejaNews Research Service and searching on his full e-mail address. Prepare these for forwarding to his system administrators.
5. Forward the entire mail bomb with extended headers, detailed information about the offender, and all evidence gathered to the system administrators. It is a good idea to send a courtesy copy to your system administrators, who may be able to assist you further."[8]

This approach will not work with Up Yours if the server used by the mail bomber is truly anonymous. The purpose of the anonymous server is to obfuscate the address information that would be present in the e-mail header. When the server is not used properly, however, it will be possible to use header information to trace the source.

There are a couple of techniques alluded to here that bear additional discussion. First, the use of a finger server, or the finger utility, may or may not get information about the individual mail bomber. It will, however, get information about the server the attack originated from if you were able to expand the header.

The use of Deja News is an investigative twist that helps you learn about the offender so that you can understand why he or she attacked. Hackers at this level (sometimes called "ankle biters") usually brag about their exploits on mail lists and newsgroups. Deja News will help you locate their braggadocio and track them down.

FLOODING ATTACKS

We have mentioned syn flooding and alluded to other flooding attacks throughout this chapter. We won't go into much more detail here except to characterize some of the more popular flooding attacks.

Syn flooding is the best known of the generic class of attacks referred to as flooding attacks. When two TCP/IP hosts attempt, initially, to communicate, they exchange synchronization packets, or "syn" packets. These packets are intended to establish communications, including the housekeeping that such computers must do to exchange packets correctly and reassemble messages. However, if one of the machines continues to send syn packets without waiting for an acknowledgment from the target host, the target will, eventually, become disabled due to an excessive number of packets in its queue. It will not be able to continue to receive data and will, essentially, go off line.

Message flooding can be the result of e-mail messages or, in some cases, log messages. The attacking machine performs repeated instances of attacks that will cause the victim's system logs to respond with a log entry. The victim becomes bogged down recognizing and processing log entries and filling up available disk space and cannot continue to process. Flooding attacks leave footprints and, with patience, usually can be traced.

SUMMARY

In this chapter we have discussed denial of service attacks and masquerading as a technique to avoid detection. We have examined both broad-based attacks (shotgun blasts) and focused attacks (surgical strikes). We contrasted these two approaches based upon techniques, results, and investigative procedures.

In the next chapter we will complete the first section of this book by proposing a specific protocol for investigating a computer-related security incident. We will also describe the overall process of intrusion management, which consists of avoidance, testing, detection, and investigation.

REFERENCES

1. Barkley, J., "Security in Open Systems," NIST Special Publication 800-7, 7 Oct 1994.
2. Drake, C. and Brown, K., *Panic! Unix System Crash Dump Analysis,* Prentice-Hall, 1995.
3. Husman, H., "Introduction to Denial of Service," t95hhu@student.tdb.uu.se, copyright 1996.
4. *Users Manual for NT Version of SafeSuite,* Internet Security Systems.
5. Felten, E. W., Balfanz, D., Dean, D., and Wallach, D. S., *Technical Report 540-96,* Department of Computer Science, Princeton University.
6. "daemon9," "route," and "infinity" *Phrack Magazine,* 7: 48, June 1996.
7. Up Yours v 2.0 Frequently Asked Questions.
8. Reagoso, C., webmaster@webscaper.com.

Section 2

Investigating Cyber Crime

5 A Framework for Conducting an Investigation of a Computer Security Incident

In this chapter, we will describe a framework for conducting an internal investigation of a computer security incident. Because the focus of this book is the corporate investigator, rather than law enforcement, we will skip discussions of search warrants, subpoenas, and other issues with which law enforcement must deal. We point out, however, that you will not, in all likelihood, have decided whether or not to request assistance from a law enforcement agency when you begin your investigation. For that reason, you must treat every investigation as if it will become a criminal proceeding.

The approach we will outline in this chapter is appropriate to internal investigators or private investigators you may hire to assist with an investigation. We will draw from experienced law enforcement professionals and the criminal justice system for suggestions because we may find ourselves in a position to support them as they take over an investigation and subsequent prosecution. Throughout the remainder of this book, we will refer to this framework and use it as we discuss specific investigative techniques.

Our first topic will address the overall issue of managing intrusions. We will introduce the intrusion management process which includes avoidance, testing, detection, and investigation. The appropriate application of intrusion management can have the effect of limiting intrusions, due to a combination of robust safeguards and early warning of intrusion attempts. Additionally, when an intrusion does occur, this process ensures that you will have the best chance of tracking and resolving the intrusion.

We will continue our discussion by exploring the need for an investigative process. Next, we will see what such a process should offer. Then, we will look at a process that is used by law enforcement and is suggested by experts in the criminal justice system. As part of that, we'll see why, as corporate investigators, we may have somewhat different needs, and will probably not have the resources at our disposal that are called for in criminal proceedings. Finally, we'll propose a generalized approach that fits the style of an internal corporate computer incident investigation, whether you are conducting it with company staff, or being assisted by consultants or private investigators.

MANAGING INTRUSIONS

Intrusion management is a four-step process. The steps are avoidance, testing, detection, and investigation. Intrusion management has, as its primary objective:

> Limiting the possibility of a successful intrusion through effective preventative, quality management, and detective processes, and facilitating successful investigation of an intrusion, should one occur.

The primary goal of intrusion management is to prevent intrusions entirely. We can address that goal by implementing a program of effective security controls. Those controls should be present at every interface point within an information management system. Effective controls grow out of effective information security policies, standards, and practices. Organizations should impose controls aimed at mitigating functional areas of vulnerability at each interface point. There are six such functional areas of vulnerability:

1. **Identification and Authentication:** Functions intended to establish and verify the identity of the user or using process.
2. **Access Control:** Functions intended to control the flow of data between, and the use of resources by, users, processes, and objects. This includes administration and verification of access rights.
3. **Accountability:** Functions intended to record exercising of rights to perform security-relevant actions.
4. **Object Reuse:** Functions intended to control reuse or scavenging of data objects.
5. **Accuracy:** Functions intended to ensure correctness and consistency of security-relevant information.
6. **Reliability of Service:** Functions intended to ensure security of data over communication links.

Using appropriate tools, we can test our systems for these vulnerabilities and, through proper configuration or use of third-party products, we can ensure that appropriate steps are taken to reduce or eliminate them. Tools we should use are of two types: preventative and detective.

Preventative tools include those that we use to perform initial evaluation and configuration. Detective tools are intended to ensure that any change to the configuration is detected. An example of such a suite of tools is the Enterprise Security Manager (ESM) from AXENT Technologies, Provo, UT. ESM allows us to evaluate the configuration of a computer against a predefined security policy. Once the computer's configuration has been adjusted to comply with the policy, the ESM monitors for changes to the configuration. In broad terms, we may consider that monitoring to be an audit function. Thus, we see that auditing is an important part of the intrusion management process.

Another example of testing tools is the SafeSuite scanner from Internet Security Systems (ISS) in Atlanta, GA. SafeSuite is a TCP/IP attack simulator. Used against hosts, routers, servers, and firewalls in a TCP/IP network, SafeSuite can perform over 100 different attacks typical of hacker attacks. SafeSuite uses the same exploits that the hackers do, and ISS expends considerable effort to keep the scanner current with the state of the hacker's art.

The third step is detection. This is somewhat different from the detective controls present during the avoidance and testing steps. In this case we are talking about detecting an intrusion attempt in real time. The real-time aspect of detection is important. Knowing that an attack is in progress, and being able to take immediate action, greatly improves the odds of successfully terminating the intrusion and apprehending the perpetrator.

Real-time detection depends upon having a "watch dog" system that sits in the background and oversees all activities involving the device under surveillance. The watch dog also must be able to interpret what constitutes an attack. Two examples of real-time attack detectors are Intruder Alert (ITA), from AXENT Technologies, and RealSecure, from ISS. ITA works on a platform basis, detecting attacks against the platform. The platform's administrator configures the ITA, using a set of scripts, to interpret an attack against the computer. RealSecure monitors for communications-based attacks, similar to those simulated by SafeSuite.

Finally, intrusion management defaults to investigation when all other measures have failed to prevent an attack. However, investigation, as you may have already gathered, may be futile unless luck and circumstances are with you. By integrating your investigation process into the intrusion management process, you improve your odds markedly because you have gathered significant and important information along the way.

For example, tools such as the ESM and the ITA allow extensive, robust logging, protected from tampering. They also allow for responses from the system under attack that may be able to gather information about the attacker that can assist you during the investigation. In my experience, the leading hindrance to a successful investigation is lack of complete, timely, and reliable information about the attack and the attacker.

Attacks often are not discovered until well after the fact. That problem constitutes strike one in the intrusion management ball game. Strike two comes when the attacker has been clever enough to cover his or her tracks effectively. If the logs are not complete, protected from tampering and retained long enough, it's strike three and your investigation never gets to first base. Good intrusion management mitigates against all of those problems and ensures you a chance to start around the bases. Whether you get an eventual home run, of course, depends upon many other factors.

WHY WE NEED AN INVESTIGATIVE FRAMEWORK

Is there anything in business that can be successfully accomplished without a formal process? If we could examine every major corporation, we would find that, except for minor, departmentalized projects, every undertaking has a formal process. The process begins with a business plan; is managed according to a project plan; is completed according to a schedule, including timelines, budget, and manpower forecasts; and is audited at the end to ensure it progressed and completed according to plan. There are very good reasons why major companies operate this way.

Big companies spend big money. In times of tight budgets, they want to ensure that they are getting the most for their dollars. Hence, they manage everything that costs money very carefully. When we investigate a computer crime, our currency is information. As you will see, every resource we apply to an investigation either costs us or gains us information. When we solve the crime, we are able to do so because we have accumulated enough correct and accurate information to describe what happened, who did it, why they did it, what they gained, what we lost, and how the act was accomplished. In turn, we are able to explain the event and, hopefully, convince a jury that our suspect committed the crime.

If we get the wrong information, inadequate information, or tainted information, we will not reach our objective of solving the crime. Crimes are not solved until they can be successfully prosecuted. Many times I have said something like, "I know he did it; I just can't prove it." That is a statement about an unsolved crime. If "he" did "it," I should be able to gather the information required to prove it. However, when investigating computer-related crimes, there is a small problem with that reasoning. Technology that may be required to solve the crime, by our definition, may not exist.

Even so, there is something we should remember about cyber crime: everywhere the intruder goes, he or she leaves tracks. The tracks may be extremely hard or nearly impossible to discern and follow, but they are there. Until we have technology to help us see all of those tracks, in some cases the final solution may elude us. No matter. More often than not, computer-related crimes are, with enough knowledge and patience, solvable. The key is in collecting more of our information currency than we spend, squander, ignore, or corrupt.

We should emphasize here that this process is neither simple nor is it speedy. If you are not prepared to take the time and spend the money to ensure success, don't bother with the investigation. Take your licks, call your insurance company, plug your security holes, and get on with your life. Investigating and prosecuting computer-related crime is expensive and time-consuming. It will take otherwise productive individuals, with high levels of skills much in demand, and become a vampire, sucking the resources out of them and their investigation teammates.

That, in simplest terms, is why we need a formal process. We are protecting our valuable currency just as the large corporations protect theirs: by taking a structured approach to our investigation. That structured approach is our step-by-step framework.

The investigative process is not a simple one and it is not the same for all types of crimes or all types of investigators. However, there are always some commonalities. All types of computer-related incident investigations need a structure. They need professionals who understand related technologies, as well as professionals who understand the investigative process. Both of those skills rarely are found in the same individual.

All types of computer-related incident investigations are like good newspaper reporting. They answer the five Ws: Who, What, Where, When, and Why. According to Rosenblatt,[1] the initial investigation of a computer intrusion has six goals, in the following order of importance:

1. To understand how the intruder is entering the system.
2. To obtain the information you need to justify a trap and trace of the phone line the intruder is using.
3. To discover why the intruder has chosen the victim's computer.
4. To gather as much evidence of the intrusion as possible.
5. To obtain information that may narrow your list of suspects, or at least confirm that the intruder is not a current employee.
6. To document the damage to the victim caused by the intruder, including the time and effort spent by the victim in investigating the incident and determining the amount of damage to its computer.

Rosenblatt (an assistant district attorney at the time of this writing) seems to be talking to law enforcement personnel here, but much of his advice is directly applicable to corporate investigators as well. In fact, the only glaring exception is number two: trap and trace. Trap and trace usually requires law enforcement intervention. Thus, we might add a special objective for corporate investigators:

Gather enough information to decide if law enforcement should be involved.

Also, remember our general rule: Until you know how you are going to use the results of your investigation, treat it as if it will end up in the criminal courts. Even when you decide against criminal action, and determine not to call in law enforcement officials, you will need solid evidence in a civil action. You may even have to defend yourself against such actions by your suspect as wrongful termination, invasion of privacy, or discrimination. So, proceed with care.

WHAT SHOULD AN INVESTIGATIVE FRAMEWORK PROVIDE?

The simple answer to this question is that a framework should provide a process for conducting a computer incident investigation. If that were all there is, we could list the steps and be done with it. However, no investigations or, at least, few investigations, are quite that simple. As we will see later in this book, there are a multitude of factors complicating the investigative process. The more clearly you define your investigative process, then the more likely you are to be successful, if you ever need to use it.

An investigative framework, properly thought out and constructed, should give us a step-by-step process for conducting an investigation into a suspected computer intrusion. It should let us determine early in our investigation that an attack actually has occurred. And, it should lead us to a final conclusion. That, by the way, does not imply that all such conclusions are successful. A disturbingly large percentage of investigations end with the conclusion that the victim was attacked, but the source of the attack cannot be determined.

Therefore, an important part of the intrusion management process is the plugging of security holes we discover in the course of an investigation. If we view the intrusion management process as a circle, avoidance requires testing and detection that, if unsuccessful, lead to investigation, the results of which, if properly applied, help us achieve a higher degree of avoidance. Our investigative framework should provide for improving our system's resistance to attack.

ONE APPROACH TO INVESTIGATING INTRUSIONS

Rosenblatt offers a generalized approach to investigating intrusions. The approach is aimed at law enforcement, but it provides some good food for thought for corporate investigators as well. Rosenblatt's approach is step-oriented. Each step leads to the next, and he provides checklists of actions within each step.

- **Step 1:** Initial investigation
- **Step 2:** Tracking down the intruder
- **Step 3:** Closing in on the intruder
- **Step 4:** The arrest

The key steps for the private sector, of course, are the first three. The actions within those steps, generally, are applicable to corporate investigations. At the very least, they show us an approach to the details of an investigation. Moreover, they help us meet the goals that Rosenblatt sets for the initial investigation of the incident.

For our approach, we have expanded upon Rosenblatt and added detail. We also have expanded the importance of his six goals to encompass the entire investigation, instead of the preliminary work. Icove, Segar, and VonStorch[2] have a somewhat different view of the investigative process. They developed their approach for the Federal Bureau of Investigation. Thus, it is focused primarily on the needs of law enforcement and the criminal justice system. Their process consists of:

- Checking records, such as system documentation and logs, as well as information about suspects
- Interviewing informants
- Conducting surveillance
- Preparing a search warrant
- Searching the suspect's premises (executing the search warrant)
- Seizing evidence

You will note, perhaps, an emphasis on traditional investigative techniques. Like most police agencies, the FBI is most comfortable doing investigative tasks that involve people. Interestingly, there is a very important role for this "old-fashioned police work." Computers and technology notwithstanding, it is people who commit intrusions, not computers. Thus, at the end of the day, solving the crime may come down to legwork and people-oriented investigative techniques.

The FBI, and a few state and large local law enforcement agencies, as well as the Secret Service, have come a long way in the past few years with regard to computer crime investigative skills. However, their forte is still dealing with witnesses and suspects. There is a very important lesson here: Current and former police officers and federal agents have a lot to offer in a computer incident investigation.

Corporate investigators should make an effort to partner with these specialists. If the investigative team is properly manned, each participant's talents and skills will contribute to the success of the investigation. There are no superstars in the investigative process. Each participant has a task to complete, consistent with his or her skill and experience.

It is important, however, that the corporate investigator be aware of the approaches used by law enforcement and the requirements of the criminal justice system. Although there are differences in the approaches of criminal and civil proceedings, the basics are the same. There are rules of evidence, issues of privacy, and burdens of proof that remain consistent. If your incident ever finds its way into a court of law, whether civil or criminal, you'll need to be sure that you've satisfied all investigative requirements if you want to win your case.

DRAWBACKS FOR THE CORPORATE INVESTIGATOR

For all of that, however, there are drawbacks to this approach for the corporate investigator. First, the corporate investigator will not be preparing search warrants. Second, he or she cannot extend the investigation outside his or her organization without the explicit consent and cooperation of other, outside, parties. Certainly, the corporate investigation cannot invade the privacy of the home of a suspect. Some cooperation may come from owners and administrators of intermediate sites, but, lacking that cooperation, the investigation stops at the victim's borders. Thus, approaches intended to culminate in an arrest may not be appropriate for the corporate investigator.

Second, the approach taken by law enforcement is one that takes into account the solving of the crime and little else. Corporate investigators are burdened with internal politics that can hamper or aid in the investigative process. The people-skills needed by the corporate investigator are typical of those needed in corporate America, not of those needed by the local police.

Third, the corporation is increasingly at risk from employee lawsuits for everything from invasion of privacy to wrongful termination. Corporate investigators must consider corporate culture, policies in place to aid them or protect the employee, privacy act requirements, even-handed enforcement of policies prior to the incident, and a host of other business and private sector concerns. Law enforcement has a clear set of guidelines that generally apply to the criminal investigative process. They can exercise those guidelines without regard for the personality of the organization.

Finally, corporate investigators must be wary of bad public relations. News of a successful intrusion can have dramatic consequences for the organization, ranging from loss of customer confidence to investor lawsuits. The corporate cop must be sensitive to all of these restraints, while conducting an effective investigation, the results of which can be turned over to corporate lawyers for civil action or to law enforcement from criminal prosecution.

What is needed, then, is a methodology that addresses the unique requirements, personality, legal restrictions, and environment of the private sector organization, while it prepares for any potential legal or criminal action. The approach should not restrict the effectiveness of the investigative process. It should fully support intrusion management within the organization. And, it should fulfill the requirements that might be imposed by either the civil or criminal law systems. It should address completely the technical nature of computer-related crimes, and it should allow for the quirks of technology that cause benign incidents to masquerade as hostile actions. It should do all of this while maintaining a comfort level for investigators of varying experience — from technologists to police and federal agents. A big order, indeed!

A GENERALIZED INVESTIGATIVE FRAMEWORK FOR CORPORATE INVESTIGATORS

With the foregoing in mind, we have developed an investigative framework that addresses the needs of the corporate investigative team while preserving civil and criminal legal options. This approach has been used successfully and it takes full advantage of resources available in both the criminal justice system and corporate America. In broad terms, we have structured our process into seven discrete steps as follows:

1. Eliminate the obvious
2. Hypothesize the attack
3. Reconstruct the crime
4. Perform a traceback to the suspected source computer
5. Analyze the source, target, and intermediate computers
6. Collect evidence, including, possibly, the computers themselves
7. Turn your findings and evidentiary material over to corporate investigators or law enforcement for follow-up

Combine these steps with Rosenblatt's six goals to get a full picture of the overall process. Finally, recall that we are trying to answer the "five Ws": Who, What, Where, When, and Why. To those, of course, we want to add "How." Let's take up each step of the process so as to prepare ourselves for the detailed tasks and techniques.

ELIMINATE THE OBVIOUS

It was Sir Arthur Conan Doyle, speaking through his character Sherlock Holmes, who taught us that ...

> When you have eliminated the impossible, whatever remains, however improbable, must be the truth.[3]

With that in mind, our first objective in any computer incident investigation is to begin the process by eliminating the obvious. The most important first step in this objective is to determine if a security incident actually occurred. As we will discuss later, many suspected attacks are actually benign, natural (though occasionally unpleasant) occurrences. Computers fail for a variety of reasons, not all of which are denial of service attacks.

If, for example, there is no modem connected to the victim computer, and there are no modem connections to the network containing the computer (including connections to networks that connect to the victim's network), then it is probably safe to say that the attacker did enter via direct dial-up. If, additionally, there is no Internet connection or, likewise, any connection to an outside network (e.g., the victim's network is completely self-contained within the victim's organization and touches no outside resources), we can conclude that the attack came from within the organization. We can further assume that it came from a computer attached to the network or from the victim computer itself.

To paraphrase Doyle, we have eliminated external access as the source of the attack and, although we may trust our employees implicitly, it is probable that one of them (or, perhaps, a contractor, and, less likely, a visitor) committed the crime. Many times I have heard: "He (or she) could not have done it. I've known him (her) for years. He (she) wouldn't ever do such a thing!" To that I generally answer, "You'd be surprised what people might do under the right circumstances." Stress, such as impending layoff, disciplinary action, failure to get a raise or a promotion, or personal problems can make a usually trusted and reliable person do bizarre things.

In general, our elimination step relates specifically to technical issues. For example, we need to evaluate the routes to the victim machine very carefully and analyze the access controls in place. Especially when investigating Internet-originating attacks, the potential universe of sources is nearly unlimited. Without some method of narrowing the field of possible attack vectors, you haven't the slightest hope of tracking the real source of the intrusion.

However, we must also consider human factors. For example, I investigated an intrusion into a complex system. We were able to narrow the field of sources to the system administrator accounts, of which there were four. Obviously, the next task was to eliminate the system administrators themselves as suspects, allowing us to focus on the compromise of one or more of the accounts. One administrator was easy to eliminate. She had been hiking in the mountains when the attack occurred. Without access to electricity, telephone, or computer, it was unlikely that she had perpetrated the attack.

An important part of this first step in our framework is learning what events surrounded the incident. We can do that best by conducting some interviews to gain background information. All of the information we gather at the beginning is intended to tell us as much about the incident itself and the climate in which it occurred as possible. Rosenblatt gives us a good set of parameters for conducting preliminary interviews:

- Gather background information about the victim environment.
- Gather the details of the incident from the victim's perspective.
- Collect evidence of the incident — note that we are not referring to evidence surrounding suspected source or intermediate computers — this step refers to the evidence on the victim computer itself. Part of this step is intended to verify that an incident actually occurred.
- Track and document damage caused by the incident — attach a dollar value, if possible.

HYPOTHESIZE THE ATTACK

The next step is to figure out how the attack occurred. We will try to address Rosenblatt's first goal:

- To understand how the intruder is entering the system.

Hypothesizing the attack requires two important steps. First, analyze the attack theoretically. This includes mapping all possible attack vectors (access routes to the victim computer), analyzing access controls on the victim, analyzing the victim's logs, and evaluating known exploits involving the same type of computer and operating system.

Sources for exploit details are present on the Internet at a variety of security sites. One of the best collections of security documents resides at the COAST Project at Purdue University. COAST is *Computer Operations, Audit, and Security Technology*, a multiple project, multiple investigator laboratory in computer security research in the Computer Science Department at Purdue University. You can locate the COAST Archive on the World Wide Web at URL:

http://www.cs.purdue.edu/coast/#archive

You can also search the *BugTraq* archives (http://www.geek-girl.com/bug-traq/search.html), the *8LGM Security Advisories Index* (http://www.8lgm.org/advi-sories.html), or *Underground.org* for Unix vulnerabilities (http://www.under-ground.org/bugs/). There are, of course, many other sites such as CERT (the Computer Emergency Response Team) and CIAC (the U.S. Department of Energy's Computer Incident Advisory Capability). However, these last two sites do not provide adequate exploit detail to reconstruct the exploits.

The second step in hypothesizing the attack is to test the hypothetical routes to the victim and users with access to ensure that they are reasonable for hypothesized attack. This includes analyzing access controls present at each required step of the way to the victim and analyzing access control lists for lists of users and superusers, while considering who, if anyone, within the organization had legitimate access to the victim, as well as the requisite skills to perform the attack. It also includes determining details about the attack, such as time, date, circumstances, what was done by the attacker, etc.

At this point it is extremely important that the computer not be powered up (if it is not already) or powered down (if it is currently turned on). No changes should be made to the victim computer and it should not, if possible, even be operated, especially if it is a PC running any version of Microsoft Windows. There may be valuable evidence still residing on the computer's hard drive that could be damaged or destroyed under improper operation. You should strongly consider disconnecting the victim computer from the network and any other external access. You do this simply by unplugging the network or modem connector from the computer.

Once you have hypothesized one or more possible attack scenarios, move on to the next step, testing your hypothesis by reconstructing the attack.

RECONSTRUCT THE CRIME

Computer-related crime is unique in that we can, unlike a murder or robbery, recreate the crime. Here, we will continue to address Rosenblatt's first objective, this time by actually testing our hypothesis to see if it results in the same kind of access as the intrusion itself.

We will learn, hopefully, what route or routes the attack took to the victim, how he or she defeated access controls, and what level of logging we will have available. It is important to perform this testing on a different, but similar, computer, if possible. Reconstructing the crime on the real victim computer could wipe out important evidence which could help lead you to the perpetrator.

We will also begin to address two more of Rosenblatt's objectives:

- To obtain the information you need to justify a trap and trace of the phone line the intruder is using.

and

- To obtain information that may narrow your list of suspects, or at least confirm that the intruder is not a current employee.

We reconstruct the crime by performing the actions we have hypothesized in the previous step. We want to make sure that the test "victim" is configured as closely to the real victim as possible. That includes its internal configuration, logging, network connections, and access controls. If the computer is a PC, we may boot the PC with a floppy disk running DOS without Windows and take a physical image of the hard drive, using a program such as SafeBack (Sydex). You can then restore the physical image to a test machine and will have an exact mirror of the victim to test. We'll discuss imaging drives in more detail later in the book.

If we are able to obtain the same results as the attacker did, we can begin to understand the "How" of the attack. That may or may not lead us to the perpetrator, but it will certainly help us narrow the universe of possible attack sources.

It is important to realize that, at this step, we will not, usually, solve the crime. It would be a rare case indeed where simply reconstructing the crime led us right to the intruder. The best we can usually hope for is to understand clearly the methods and routes used in the attack, as well as to narrow the field of possible attackers somewhat.

Perform a Traceback to the Suspected Source Computer

This can be the toughest part of your investigation. If the previous steps lead you to suspect that the attack originated outside of your network, you may be faced with tracing back over the Internet. We'll discuss that in more detail later in this book. But, suffice it to say, at this point, the Internet traceback is a daunting task which requires patience, skill, and a clear understanding of how the Internet functions.

In this step we are addressing several of Rosenblatt's objectives:

- To understand how the intruder is entering the system.
- To obtain the information you need to justify a trap and trace of the phone line the intruder is using.
- To gather as much evidence of the intrusion as possible.
- To obtain information that may narrow your list of suspects, or at least confirm that the intruder is not a current employee.

and our added corporate objective:

- Gather enough information to decide if law enforcement should be involved.

The second objective, trap and trace, as we have said, implies the need for law enforcement. However, there is some tracing we can do within our own organization or over the Internet. When we need to involve the telephone company and tracing of calls over the phone system, a warrant or court order usually is necessary. We'll discuss the details of tracing in a subsequent chapter.

Experienced intruders do not attack their victims directly from their own computers. Rather, they establish a "collection" of intermediate computers under the control of organizations with whom they have no connection. In a university environment, for example, it may be another department's computers, or computers at a different university or organization with whom the university's computers have a trust relationship. It may include computers which are administrated poorly, enabling the intruder to enter surreptitiously and establish clandestine accounts from which to launch other attacks.

The intruder establishes "back doors" to these intermediate computers and uses a chain of those accounts to reach the victim. There will usually be no geographic relationship between the intermediate sites or between the sites and the intruder. Finally, the intruder will attempt to alter logs along the way to cover his or her tracks over the full path of the attack. Internal intruders may attempt to do the same thing, either within the internal network or, if possible, by leaving the network and returning from a remote site.

Therefore, traceback requires that you have road signs along the path that the intruder took to get to the victim computer. In simple terms, it means you need to establish when the intruder entered each computer, terminal server, telephone switch, or router along the way. For this, you need logs.

The problems you will encounter when tracing back to a source include:

- No logs for the period of the attack
- Inadequate logs for the period of the attack
- Altered logs for the period of the attack
- Intermediate stops between the real source of the attack and your victim computer, which hide the attacker's route
- Lack of cooperation from administrators of intermediate systems
- IP address spoofing or, simply, false IP addresses
- Direct console access to the victim computer covered up by log alteration
- Alteration of victim's logs or other cover-up tricks
- Only a single call, via phone lines, with no further opportunity to trace

Traceback over computer systems depends upon logs. If multiple computers are involved, you'll need to compare logs from each computer. There are issues of the veracity of the logs to deal with. The issues come on two levels. First, the logs may have been altered by the intruder to mask his or her actions. That is a problem for the investigator because it presents misleading information.

Second, the logs could have been altered by the investigator or other interested party (more about people issues in a later chapter). That presents a problem for the court. When you pull logs off a computer, be sure to take two original copies. Treat one as evidence and the other as a work copy. Never work on the copy, whether it's a file or paper copy, which you plan to present as evidence in a legal action.

Also, if you turn your investigation over to law enforcement, remember they will have the same requirements and potential pitfalls as you. Make sure you are able to hand over pristine copies of original logs, complete with a valid, documented chain of custody, which you can swear to, if necessary.

ANALYZE THE SOURCE, TARGET, AND INTERMEDIATE COMPUTERS

Now we get down to the remainder of Rosenblatt's objectives. Analyzing the computers involved in the attack should reveal most of the required information. Don't, however, forget that you can never have too much evidence. Also, there's a big difference between evidence and proof. Proof irrefutably establishes the facts. It can take a great deal of evidence, depending upon its nature, to constitute proof. Also, proof is often subjective. At some point, there is enough evidence to satisfy people that you have proved your case.

Evidence, on the other hand, is objective. A log entry is a log entry. You may depend upon it as long as you can show it has not been altered. Whether the entry *proves* anything may be another issue entirely. As you consider the evidence you uncover during this step, following are some useful tips.

First, believe your indications. In the absence of evidence to the contrary, believe what your testing tells you. When you put all of the pieces together, look for inconsistencies. Until then, accept what you see; don't try to rationalize it.

Second, if you obtain conflicting evidence, step back and try to understand what you are really seeing. It may not conflict at all. It may simply require a clearer understanding of the facts or the technology involved. However, again, don't try to rationalize a conflict to make it come out the way you think it should. Work out the nature of the conflict. It often means that some information has been altered to be misleading. If that seems to be the case, scrap the conflicting evidence and look elsewhere.

Do not, under any circumstances, do anything to alter any of the computers you are examining. It is best, especially if you uncover the computer that you believe is the source of the attack, to work from reconstructed physical mirror images. Remember, if you do discover the source of the attack, you may be called upon to produce it in a legal proceeding. If that happens, you can be sure that the "other side" will analyze it and attempt to rebut your theories of how the owner used it to attack your system.

When you analyze a computer involved in an intrusion, here are some of the things you'll need to do:

- Boot the computer from a known-good floppy disk. You should prepare a diskette that boots DOS (not Windows) for this purpose. I have a special bootable floppy disk that contains SafeBack and the drivers necessary to attach an Iomega Jaz drive with the Traveler option to the target computer's parallel port. That allows me to make physical images of target drives on 1 GB disks without altering anything on the target's hard drive. Problems with the integrity of physical backups on the Jaz drive have been reported. I have never experienced any. *Caveat Emptor.*
- Take a physical image of the hard drive. Restore the image to a test computer and protect the image. Work on the test computer.
- Examine all logs.
- Look at last date of change on critical files. This may or may not yield results, because these dates are easy to change.
- Examine configuration and start-up files for anomalies.
- Look for hacking tools.
- Compare critical files with known-good examples. This, too, may prove fruitless because there are Trojaned versions of many critical files that have checksum, file length, and creation date spoofing built in.
- Examine the password file for unauthorized accounts.
- Search the hard drive mirror for keywords appropriate to the incident. Include hidden areas, slack space, and caches.

- Examine communications connections and configurations.
- Look for changes to files, critical file deletions, and unknown new files.

At this point, you're simply examining the computer image. In the next step you'll begin the evidence collection process. Your previous steps have led you to computers you suspect as being involved, in one way or another, in the incident. This step allows you to examine these computers and decide what evidence may be present and worthy of saving.

COLLECT EVIDENCE, INCLUDING, POSSIBLY, THE COMPUTERS THEMSELVES

If you can do it, impounding the computer is your best bet if you suspect (from the previous step) that it contains critical evidence. Failing that, you will need an original mirror image of the computer's hard drive(s). From that image you can create a test computer's hard drive that is an exact physical duplicate of the "real" computer. If you can't impound the computer into a chain of custody, treat the disk or tape containing the mirror image as evidence and maintain a documented chain of custody.

If you believe that the attack came from outside of your system, you'll probably need to involve law enforcement. You don't have the legal right to enter the suspect's residence and seize the suspected computer or search for evidence. If the attack originated from another organization, you may succeed in getting the local administrator to allow you to work with him or her to pursue the investigation. Whenever you seize a suspected source computer, however, be sure to protect it from compromise. More about those techniques later.

At the time of this step you won't know, at least with certainty, what evidence to collect. There are some rules of thumb, however, that can help you. First, collect everything that supports your hypothesis of how the attack occurred, from whence it originated, and what was done to the victim. Then, collect everything that contradicts your theories. You will need that to refine your explanation (or refute it completely) and prepare you for the efforts of the opposition to discredit your investigation. In many instances, competent law enforcement specialists will also want to know the "downside" of your evidence before they take on your case.

In most cases, especially criminal proceedings, both sides are required to reveal "exculpatory evidence." This is evidence that suggests that the opposition is correct in its assertions. Responsible investigators will be as diligent in ferreting out exculpatory evidence as they are in revealing evidence of their theories.

Take physical mirror images of all involved hard drives. If you forget something, or if the other side throws you a curve in court, you'll have a reliable image of the computer to test. Collect all floppy disks in the locale of the involved computers and analyze them as well. I use a program from Sydex called Anadisk for analyzing floppy disks. Also, impound any printouts, handwritten notes, backup tapes, CD-ROMs, WORMs, or other related items that could shed light on your intrusion.

Make drawings or take photographs of the computer and its peripherals. If you impound the computer, keep all peripherals and cables with it. Label cables so that you can reconnect the system in the lab exactly as it was connected when discovered.

If there is a dot matrix or impact printer attached to the computer, remove the ribbon and replace it with a new one. Examine the original ribbon for evidence. If there is a display on the computer's screen, photograph it.

The subject of powering down an involved computer is a touchy one. The victim computer can, usually, be powered down in the conventional manner (which varies with different operating environments) without fear of booby traps, which could delete evidence. However, the suspect's computer is an entirely different matter. It is very easy for the suspect to rig the attack computer to destroy evidence if it is powered down in the conventional manner.

Here's where the controversy enters the picture. Some kinds of computers will experience significant file damage if they are not powered down properly. For example, this problem is typical of Unix machines. We'll discuss booby traps in a later chapter, but, for the moment, believe that they are easy to create and can destroy evidence completely. So, we have the dilemma: damage files by improper power-down or risk triggering a booby trap and destroying evidence. Here is where the investigator must use judgment.

> Use a technical expert in the specific operating system and platform if you don't completely understand that system at a technical level. Before you let the expert take any action, however, be sure that you explain the issues of evidence preservation to him or her completely. Most technical experts are inexperienced in investigative issues.

If you determine, often from your preceding analysis of the computer, that there is a possibility of a booby trap, you're probably safer to pull the computer's plug and take your chances with file damage. Of course, there are computers with which you can't do this. Mainframes and minicomputers, for example, can't simply be shut off. Work with your technical expert in these cases to defuse any bombs hidden in the affected system.

When you reboot the computer, never use the computer's operating system and command interpreter. Boot from an external source, such as a floppy disk or CD-ROM image of the operating system. Be sure that the floppy boot disk, if you use one, is physically write-protected to shield it from viruses. Once you have rebooted, your first order of business is to take a physical mirror image. Then you can move on to collect the rest of your evidence, and analyze what you have collected.

The best way to store images is on optical media. This preserves it from damage by environmental or magnetic conditions. It also cannot be erased in most cases — WORMs and rewritables act as if they are erasing, but, in reality, they are creating new copies and voiding the old ones.

If you impound the computer, be sure you store it in such a manner that it is protected from access by anyone you have not specifically authorized. Remember, you may have to swear you knew, for a fact, that the computer could not have been tampered with outside of your knowledge — from the moment it was impounded until it was produced in court or officially turned over to someone else.

Also, be sure that it is in an environmentally friendly storage area. It may be months or, even, years before a case comes to court, if that is the eventual outcome of your investigation. Computers don't like hot, humid, or dirty storage areas, especially for long periods of time. The same holds true for any magnetic media you are preserving as evidence. Be especially wary of magnetic fields. They destroy information on disks and tapes.

TURN YOUR FINDINGS AND EVIDENTIARY MATERIAL OVER TO CORPORATE INVESTIGATORS OR LAW ENFORCEMENT FOR FOLLOW-UP

It's decision time — but it's probably not your decision. Will your organization pursue the investigation, drop it, or turn it over to law enforcement? The best you can do here is to prepare your report of findings carefully and completely, document your evidence, and make your recommendation.

I generally use one or more large, three-ring binders, carefully indexed, to collect copies of evidence. I place the "real" evidence in evidence bags or envelopes and mark them carefully. I then sign and date the envelopes, using an evidence label that contains a complete description of the contents. My label has room to pass the envelope on to other recipients, collect their signatures, and preserve chain of custody. I place the label over the envelope's flap after sealing so I can demonstrate that the envelope has not been opened.

When you save a file as evidence, you need to be able to establish that it has not been altered since it was saved. I use an MD5 hashing program from NTI (New Technologies, Inc.) called CRCMD5. MD5 is an encryption algorithm that yields a hexadecimal "signature" when run against a file. The signature is unique to the file and any change to the file, no matter how trivial, alters the signature. This program creates a file that contains the MD5 hash signature.

I then encrypt the CRCMD5 signature file using my PGP public key. Pretty Good Privacy (PGP) is a public key encryption program widely available on the Internet and from commercial sources. I can then unencrypt it at any time, rerun CRCMD5 against the original file, and compare the signature to the one just unencrypted. If they match, the file's integrity is intact and chain of custody has been preserved. If they are different, someone has altered the original file, and its value as evidence is lost.

It's a good idea to refer to pieces of evidence, in your binder, by item number directly into your report. This makes it easier for readers to locate the evidence that supports a conclusion. Make sure that the titles and numbering schemes you use for your evidence binder items match the originals in their evidence envelopes. One piece of evidence to an envelope, please. Also, separate items in your binder with dividers to match the evidence envelopes.

I generally start my reports with an Executive Summary. This section describes the incident, my method of investigation, and general conclusions. I place the conclusions in a bulleted list, and then create a separate detailed section for each conclusion, after the Executive Summary. The detailed sections start with the finding or conclusion. I then describe how I arrived at the conclusion, point out any exculpatory evidence that may prove contradictory to my conclusion, and list the evidence that supports the conclusion.

Timelines are excellent ways of reaching a conclusion. If you can collect log entries that show a distinct, clear chain of events that culminate in the incident, you have taken a giant step towards proving your case. However, time lines often are considered circumstantial or are disputed on the basis of the ease with which logs can be altered and file times spoofed. You'll probably need more to support them.

The bottom line is that your results usually will determine whether your management will continue the investigation, escalate it, turn it over to law enforcement, or terminate it. How they read your results will depend in large part on how you present your conclusions and how well your evidence supports them. Make certain that your conclusions are technically sound, your evidence solidly in support of them and properly preserved, and that you have considered any exculpatory evidence that may have been found. Then, prepare your report clearly, simply, and be certain that your evidence is easy to access. Complete your report with recommendations for preventing a recurrence of the incident, including the root causes, if any, that permitted it to occur.

SUMMARY

In this chapter, we introduced a methodology for investigating computer incidents in a corporate environment. We compared the methodology with similar approaches largely used by law enforcement and criminal justice investigators. We discussed, at a general level, some of the techniques available to investigators for pursuing an investigation. We will expand upon these introductory discussions as we continue through this book. We wrapped up with some suggestions for preparing investigation reports and preserving evidence.

In the next chapter, we will begin our detailed discussions of investigative techniques. We'll start with the basics: human aspects of computer crime, determining the motive, means, and opportunity as part of the process of focusing on a suspect, and some of the human factors that can trip up the perpetrator.

REFERENCES

1. Rosenblatt, K. S., *High Technology Crime — Investigating Cases Involving Computers*, KSK Publications, San Jose, CA, 1995.
2. Icove, D., Segar, K., and VonStorch, W., *Computer Crime, A Crimefighter's Handbook*, O'Reilly & Associates.
3. Conan Doyle, A., *The Adventures of Sherlock Holmes*.

6 Look for the Hidden Flaw

In this chapter, we will discuss some of the human aspects of computer crime. We will start with an FBI profile of different types of computer-related crimes and the typical perpetrators. Computer-related crime is not much different from other forms of larceny or vandalism. And, while the perpetrators of computer-related crimes may possess skills lacking in other criminals, many of the human aspects are quite similar.

There are a few unique aspects of some types of personalities that engage in computer crime, however, and these can help us ferret out the source of a computer-related theft, vandalism, or other break-in. Finally, we can apply some basics of investigation to help us find the likely perpetrator in a field of suspects.

There is a very important point to be made here. How involved you will get in the actual investigation of individual suspects depends upon several factors. Remember that, unless you are tasked with the "people" part of an investigation, most of your work will be technical — involving machines, far more than people.

Investigating individuals is fraught with pitfalls, especially for the inexperienced investigator. Wrong or unfounded accusations can subject your organization to lawsuits for invasion of privacy, wrongful termination, or harassment. Even so, careful application of tried-and-true investigative techniques will help you more effectively focus the technical portions of your investigation. We will discuss some investigative techniques later in the book. Here, we are concerned with overriding issues. We begin with a discussion of what types of crimes are committed by which types of people.

THE HUMAN ASPECTS OF COMPUTER CRIME AND THE FBI ADVERSARIAL MATRIX

People, not computers, commit crimes. People who commit computer crimes do so for a reason. Different types of crimes attract different types of criminals. The FBI has developed an "Adversarial Matrix" that describes computer-related incidents in terms of several factors centered around the perpetrator. The full description of this matrix is available in *Computer Crime, A Crimefighter's Handbook*.[1] Here, we will summarize and apply the information in the matrix to our investigative resources.

The categorization of computer crimes and the offenders who commit them is far from simple. However, there is a certain logic about it. For example, vandals tend to be disgruntled employees or disturbed individuals who want to make a statement, and can't find a socially acceptable way to do so. In today's World Wide Web-based cyber society, we can add individuals who, for political or social reasons, spread their activism to online graffiti by altering the Web pages of their adversaries.

However, not all vandalism is targeted at serious targets. Often, the vandal feels that he or she is simply committing a harmless prank. The other end of the spectrum includes terrorists. A story in a national news magazine hypothesized that an attacker could sit in a hotel room, focus his or her attack on a target on the other side of the globe, and watch the chaos on CNN. Unfortunately, that's a fairly accurate scenario.

The FBI categorizes computer criminals into three distinct groups: crackers, criminals, and vandals. Although hacking, or, if you prefer, cracking, a system is certainly part of any, or at least, most, attacks, those individuals that hack systems for the sheer pleasure of it generally fit into the cracker group. These offenders tend to attack systems for knowledge, entertainment, and bragging rights among their peers. They are also what we might refer to as "cyberpunks."

Are these perpetrators harmless, as they would lead us to believe? Maybe, and maybe not. The fact is they are breaking the law by attacking our systems and they may do damage without meaning to. Most organizations have as little tolerance for the cracker group as they do for criminals and vandals.

Criminals are engaged in acts that would be criminal acts with or without the computer. They steal secrets, both national and corporate; they commit fraud; and, along the way, they add computer-specific crimes, such as violation of the Computer Fraud and Abuse Act. Vandals destroy files and systems or alter data, such as Web pages or databases.

Along with the individuals themselves, the FBI adds some other characteristics, including the type of organization the offenders are involved with (e.g., espionage, organized crime, or small groups of crackers); why the offender is motivated to commit computer-related crimes; and connections to international organizations. Other characteristics explored by the FBI include: how the criminal goes about planning and executing an attack; the level of expertise and training of the perpetrator; support he or she receives from the sponsoring organization, if any; the minimum equipment required to commit the offense; and personal characteristics, including personality traits, which could be used to compromise the intruder.

CRACKERS

Crackers are unstructured in terms of the groups they belong to. Occasionally, they seek membership in small, "elite" groups of three or four other crackers with grandiose names like Legion of Doom. They interact on bulletin boards, private mail lists, and Internet chat channels. They are usually young, outspoken, and sometimes type in alternate upper- and lower-case characters, referring to their exploits as "kewl" or "rad." They often replace the letter f with ph, as in phun for fun, and s with z, as in philez for files.

Security professionals often categorize this level of cracker as an "ankle biter" or "knob twister," implying that they can't do much real harm to a system. In reality, that's a naive approach. These individuals are often able to use tools readily available on the Internet to gain access to poorly protected systems or to launch denial of service attacks.

Crackers, regardless of the groups they appear to participate in, are, by their nature, true loners. The less they participate in organized cracking or "elite" groups, the more dangerous they are likely to be. Crackers often are antisocial misfits who only feel comfortable online, or with computers, instead of people. They may be in very poor physical condition due to bad eating and sleeping habits. They often have difficulty relating socially to other people. Many feel persecuted by society or their bosses, teachers, or parents.

Serious crackers also often have a very high degree of expertise and can cause serious damage or loss. The notorious hacker Kevin Mitnick would probably fit in the cracker category (although he is viewed by many as a criminal). Mitnick is a very talented cracker who grew up with the computers he attacks. His attacks usually are successful and often are innovative. Crackers, as a group, should not be underestimated. Also, crackers often, if the motivation is high enough, evolve into full-blown criminals.

Crackers tend to be very intelligent and curious. The "Hacker's Manifesto" makes it very clear that the true hacker craves knowledge. They often are not very well equipped, using low-end computers (or high-end PCs supplied by parents for other reasons) with modem connections. Their software tends to be pirated or freeware. Their knowledge is usually self-acquired. "Try it, that's how you learn" seems to be the cracker's training credo. More and more, however, crackers are college students. This doesn't seem to get in the way of being self-taught, though. Most crackers believe that they can learn faster on their own than from an instructor. Knowledge and information are the cracker's gods.

Crackers share information about targets and may search randomly for vulnerable systems. They rarely, except when bent upon revenge, target specific systems for any reason beyond their knowledge of it. For example, having picked up a list of interesting targets from a bulletin board (BBS), the cracker may try several of the systems out of curiosity. They rarely have a specific goal in mind beyond exploring the system.

Crackers are vulnerable to detection because they do not believe they are doing anything wrong, and talk freely to their peers about their exploits, often on public forums, such as Internet mail lists and newsgroups. They also tend to keep notes, disks with lists of passwords and stolen accounts, and other incriminating information. Tracking a cracker requires a good understanding of the computer underground and its resources, as well as acceptable means of participating in underground discussions, such as an alias.

CRIMINALS

Criminals, to keep it simple, are "in it" for the money. They may also have some ideological or political motivation, but most criminals are after cold, hard cash. Computer criminals often are the mercenaries of cyberspace. Many are also accomplished criminals in noncomputer areas, such as fraud, sabotage, and industrial espionage. The computer simply adds a new dimension to their acts.

Computer criminals may work independently, be "contractors" to organized crime, or part of international terrorist organizations. Competent computer criminals are very skilled, often having a detailed understanding of computer networks, tools, and hacking methods and techniques. Criminals usually have specific targets and objectives in mind and will use traditional intrusion techniques. The best technicians will program their own tools and steal tools from experts, as well as modify existing tools to their purposes.

A "good" computer criminal is very much like a "good" professional burglar. He or she will view computer crime as a profession, and will strive to be effective and competent. That, of course, means garnering the most gain while avoiding detection and capture. Unlike traditional criminals, computer criminals can steal information without leaving tracks or other indications of his or her presence. It has not been uncommon over the years for me to ask a client, during a risk assessment, whether their system has ever been compromised, only to hear that they don't know. I once naively commented to another security professional that my system had never been compromised. "That you know of," was his reply. Sadly, too true!

Today, computer criminals may gain access to targets using modems, direct connections to the Internet, or from inside the target. Competent computer criminals may also be experts at social engineering, even going so far as to obtain jobs or consulting engagements with target companies. From that vantage point, the criminal can gain intimate knowledge of the target system and information or money available on it, as well as its vulnerabilities. It is remarkable the level of unsupervised system access that organizations offer to computer consultants without checking them out thoroughly prior to engaging them.

Occasionally, criminals will "subcontract" crackers to assist in information-gathering about a target. Professional computer criminals may be very well funded and have access to sophisticated equipment. Their downfall, however, is likely to be greed. Many years ago, evangelist Billy Graham asked a very rich man how much money it would take to make him truly happy. "Just a little more," was the reply. That attitude is, often, typical of criminals of all types. However, in the case of computer criminals, the overriding belief that they are invulnerable to capture adds to the dimension of greed.

And, unfortunately, it's small wonder. The FBI estimates that fewer than 10% of all computer crime results in a successful investigation — most aren't even reported. Approximately 10% or less of that number are prosecuted, and only about 10% of that number are actually punished. That means the typical computer criminal has over a 99% probability of getting away with his or her crime. Those are good odds in any endeavor. They're frightening in this venue.

VANDALS

Vandals are crackers, usually without the cracker's skills. They also seek to do damage to the target, a motive exactly opposite that of most crackers. The vandal's motive is revenge or disgruntlement. In today's environment of downsizing and layoffs, disgruntled employees are an ever-increasing threat. Vandals may also have political motivation, such as the vandals that modified World Wide Web pages belonging to the CIA, companies that sell fur coats, or other targets of activists.

Vandals often have very limited technical skills. They do, however, have access to the victim system. They also often have access to vandalism tools, such as mail bombs or programs to generate syn floods or other data flood attacks. Whether or not the vandal understands the technology he or she is using is irrelevant. They use the tools and obtain results. In PC-based systems, viruses often are the weapons of choice. Live viruses (called "virii" in the underground) are readily available from BBS and virus sites on the Internet.

Vulnerabilities of vandals include the same as those of crackers; plus, their lack of sophistication often results in leaving audit trails on victim systems that lead back to them. It is important to note that vandalism is a crime under the Computer Fraud and Abuse Act and, if damage costs are high, may also be covered by other, more mundane, laws not specifically intended for computer systems. If the computer or system is a "federal interest" machine, the FBI will certainly want to hear about the attack. We will discuss the involvement of law enforcement and the criminal justice system later in the book.

MOTIVE, MEANS, AND OPPORTUNITY

In proving any crime, the investigator usually wants motive (why?), means (how?), and opportunity (when?). The idea is to match the logical motive, means, and opportunity of the crime (why would someone do this, how was it done, when was it done) to the motive, means, and opportunity of the suspect (why would he or she do this, how did he or she do it, did he or she have the opportunity to do it). In computer-related crimes, this is often more easily said than done.

Motives vary, as we have seen above. They can be anything from curiosity to money, power, or revenge. In today's work environment, we find an increasing number of disgruntled employees, both still employed and laid off or terminated. However, that can sometimes be misleading. Often the most disgruntled employee won't even consider vandalizing his or her employer's computer systems. However, if we stop with motive, we might be tempted to single out the individual for further investigation.

Means, in computer-related crimes, often translates to skill level. Does the suspect have the required degree of computer expertise to commit the crime? Reconstructing the crime can tell us a great deal about means. By performing the same acts we believe are required to cause the observed effect, we can judge, to some degree, what types of skills the perpetrator must have had.

Opportunity is much tougher. It is often hard to pinpoint when the crime was committed. Delayed-effect viruses, logic bombs, and altered logs may give us a false picture of when the act actually occurred. Here it is important not to attempt to tie the time of the crime to the time it was discovered. Unless you are fortunate enough to be able to match a login time to an event, or can catch the offender online, you can't be sure you know when the act took place.

Even if you can match a login time to an event, or logs correspond in ways that lead you to pinpoint a time, you can't be certain that the logs weren't altered. Unless special precautions have been taken to protect the logs from being rewritten, even by the superuser, this is a difficult match.

Corporate investigators of computer incidents tend to be at a disadvantage, as compared to their law enforcement counterparts. Law enforcement professionals usually were investigators long before they became involved in computer crime. Many came from investigating other forms of white collar crime. They have had time to learn and hone their investigative skills.

Corporate computer incident investigators, on the other hand, tend to be auditors, security professionals, or other noninvestigative specialists. If you find yourself in this group, and are called upon to investigate a computer incident, get some help from professional investigators. You may have just the person you need in your corporate security department. These departments often are made up of retired police officers and FBI agents. We'll discuss the investigative partnership in more detail later.

Recall what we said earlier: most computer incidents result in lots of (potentially) *circumstantial* evidence. Circumstantial evidence is little more than a collection of incidents, clues, recollections of witnesses, and other bits and pieces of facts that fit together, if we're lucky, like a puzzle. The good news is that circumstantial evidence is just as much evidence as a smoking gun in the hand of a killer. The bad news is that no one piece holds that much authority in the final proof of your case.

In order for your circumstantial evidence to become the proof you need, it must either cause your suspect to confess (rare, but it does occasionally happen) or build up such a huge pile that it's irrefutable. We have touched on evidence earlier, but let's digress a little and expand upon what we already know.

EVIDENCE AND PROOF

It takes, I once heard, a "heap of evidence, to make one small proof." Before we move into that discussion, let's define evidence the way professional investigators and lawyers (and, of course, courts) do. There are formal rules of evidence that offer guidance. Beyond that, however, there is also case law. Case law covers definitions and expected outcomes based upon decisions of other courts. Basically, case law serves to tell us how judges and juries have interpreted the law as it's written in the statutes. Case law is at least as important as, and sometimes more important than, the underlying statutes themselves.

Computers have brought us some special problems with evidence. For example, the rules of evidence tell us that anything the witness does not experience directly is "hearsay." That means if I tell you that I know George did it because George's sister told me so, my testimony can't be used because I have no direct, firsthand knowledge of George's participation. All I have is hearsay from his sister.

With computers, we can make a case that anything coming out of the computer that we don't directly see could be hearsay. The fact that logs can be altered, file dates changed, documents erased or changed leads us to believe that only the person who creates the information, using the computer, has direct knowledge of it.

However, we can use computer records as evidence if we are very careful, and meet some specific criteria. These criteria, as we will see in our discussion of forensic analysis, are critical to our ability to amass enough of that circumstantial evidence to get to the status of proof. Because virtually all of the evidence we, as technical investigators, will gather is circumstantial, we want to be sure we're not wasting time.

For computer evidence to be admissible, it must first be probative. That means it must be beneficial in proving our case (or, perhaps, disproving it). If it is unrelated to the incident or in showing that our suspect committed the incident, the court won't let us use it. Telling a jury that we know George crashed our server because he has a bad attitude and drinks a lot won't prove our case, unless we can show that his attitude gave him motive and his drinking presented him with an opportunity (perhaps he attacked our server while he was in a drunken rage). Even then, we'll certainly need a great deal more to be successful.

The second thing we need is proof that the records being used were produced in the normal course of business. Special logs, created for no other reason than to trap an offender, won't be acceptable by themselves. We might add them to other logs or records that are created in the normal course of business to corroborate the other records. For example, we may have logs and witnesses that swear that George was online when the server crashed. They know because they were working on the system as usual and the logging process that is normally in place was working.

That might be enough for law enforcement to get an order for a pen register which monitors the phone line. The next time George calls in and attempts to crash the server, the pen register will corroborate the log evidence with evidence that the call came from George's phone line.

Computer evidence must be authentic. It must be shown by experts to be pristine and unaltered from their original state. This, you will find, is of critical importance when we discuss forensic evidence. How the evidence was collected, handled, preserved, transferred, and protected from alteration will be key elements in accepting or discrediting the evidence. Usually, the pristine state of evidence must be established by the testimony of experts and of those individuals who collected, preserved, and handled it.

Finally, computer evidence must meet the best evidence rule. That means, while it need not be the original, it must be the best copy available. If the original is available, a copy will not do. Sometimes, a copy, taken under controlled circumstances and treated and handled properly, will meet the best evidence rule, even if the original is available. This can happen when we print a log from a file that has been properly collected, preserved, and handled if the printout is also properly handled and the original file can be made available for comparison. An expert would usually have to testify as to how the printout was made and to the other details of handling the file and the printout.

The handling of computer evidence requires a special discussion. Evidence is preserved in what is called a chain of custody. That means it is possible to establish positively the possession of an item of evidence from the time it was collected until the time it is used in court. Such things as dated signatures on evidence envelopes, protection in locked safes or file cabinets, and preservation from access by unauthorized individuals will help to preserve chain of custody.

When you have collected your evidence, be sure you can protect it from damage by the elements (heat, cold, water, magnetism, etc.), as well as from other individuals, without your knowledge. When I collect a file of any kind, I always immediately create a duplicate. I then run a program against it that creates a digital fingerprint of the file using a program from NTI called CRCMD5. CRCMD5 creates a secure hash. The hash is a number that the program derives from a very complex algorithm applied to the bits in the file. Courts have accepted MD5 hash signatures as evidence that a file is in its original state.

I then save the signature to a text file and encrypt the text file with my PGP encryption key. Only I know the pass phrase. If called upon to prove that the file in my custody is unaltered, all I need to do is run the CRCMD5 program against it, unencrypt my text file, and compare the two signatures. Since the hashing program date-stamps the signature, I can prove that the file is unaltered.

While it might be argued I could have recreated a bogus hash by resetting the computer's date and rerunning the program, such an argument is purely speculative and, without evidence supporting it, would probably be ignored.

Not only do witnesses and experts need to be reliable, software must also be reliable. In general, test programs, forensic tools, auditing programs, and other detection utilities should be commercial products which can be shown to be reliable examples of tools intended to perform their evidentiary tasks.

Tools that are freeware, unsupported, unknown to the courts and to experts in the field, or are homegrown may be open to challenge. While you may have come to rely upon your favorite freeware tool (I have several that I use in daily practice), when it comes to establishing evidence in court, it's best to stick with the real thing. What's real is what's known to be real by an accepted practitioner of the art.

While you may be able to explain why your unique tool is okay and reliable, remember that your audience will usually be struggling to keep up with the technology being presented in the normal course of the case. Adding highly technical discussions of the internals of a freeware tool will, certainly, cross their eyes and put them to sleep.

Evidence is a sword that can cut two (or more) ways. There is evidence that you will not be able to use. Generally, that is evidence covered by the exclusionary rule. That rule covers evidence that was improperly or illegally collected. This is usually more of a problem for law enforcement because they function under the strict rules of search-and-seizure. However, it can affect corporate investigators as well. For example, your suspect may claim that you violated his or her privacy in the gathering of evidence. You may have to show that you haven't violated the wiretap laws by using a sniffer. Any of these could cause your evidence to be thrown out.

Evidence can be protected by the accused using protective orders. These orders are granted if the court is satisfied, for example, that the evidence contains information that is a trade secret that could considerably cost one party if revealed. It could be granted if the court believes serious harm to its possessor could result in its revelation. In fact, anything that satisfies the court that more harm than good will be done by revealing the evidence will usually get it suppressed.

Evidence includes the act of establishing that something illegal actually occurred. This could mean showing that the perpetrator actually broke into a system. To do that you will want to establish proprietary rights to the system, files, or other software accessed or damaged. There is an urban legend about a case involving IBM and a hacker. The hacker's defense was that the IBM computer had a welcome banner that said "Welcome to IBM ... please log on." The hacker contended that there were no proprietary rights to the system or anything on it because IBM welcomed him to the system and invited him to log in. True story? Who knows. The fact is that a point is being made here: If you can't prove it's yours, you can't accuse someone of stealing it from you.

Some of the things that establish proprietary rights are password requirements (where the password is kept secret), encryption, other types of access controls, hidden files, warning banners, and other acts that clearly state "this is mine — stay out without my explicit permission."

Now that we've pretty well covered evidence, let's turn it into proof. First, we need that "heap" of evidence. Second, it must be real evidence, as we've described above. Third, it must not be excluded for any reason. Fourth, and this is where we are now in our discussion, it must dovetail and interlock so as to establish a seamless blanket that covers our conclusions completely. That's the hard part. Or, perhaps, it's the two hard parts: the seamless nature of our proof and the ability to cover our explanation completely.

Remembering that I am not an attorney (so this isn't legal advice — get that from your corporate lawyers), here is one approach to building a proof. First, be sure that you can define the incident clearly. Put the incident into its proper perspective. What really happened? What was lost? Crimes have what are called elements. These elements must all be present to establish that a crime took place. The elements are defined in the law that defines the crime. One element of most crimes is usually that some damage must have occurred and a loss of some sort was suffered by the victim. Further, the loss may have to reach a certain amount before law enforcement can pursue it. This is the starting point in your investigation.

Next, you will want to establish that, based upon your clear understanding of what happened, a security-related incident actually occurred. That may sound silly (we'll cover it in more detail later), but there are a great many things that happen with and to computers and their data which are the results of normal operation and failure of systems or errors by innocent users. Don't get caught up in the hysteria that usually accompanies a computer incident. Keep your objectivity.

Your next step is to hypothesize the incident and attempt to recreate it. As you recreate it, collect your evidence. We'll discuss crime scene investigation shortly, but, for now, recognize that you will probably only have one chance at the evidence: your initial investigation. You may choose to impound systems, which improves your odds of collecting evidence later, but the incident is now fresh in your mind. Be methodical, take your time, and collect your clues.

Now, mentally reverse the recreation process. Using your clues, go back over the incident, as hypothesized, with a critical eye. How would you refute the evidence gathered if you were on the opposing side? Think of every reason why your evidence is no good or you've missed some important fact. You may have conjectured a step in the incident for which you have only a hunch — no real evidence. Where can you look for the evidence needed to fill the gap? What if you can't find it? At this point in your investigation, it is as important to disprove your theory as it is to prove it. As you will soon see, one common defense is that the incident never occurred. It was just a computer anomaly.

And, of course, don't stop with the evidence you *think* you'll need. Collect everything that seems out of place, plus everything that could possibly indicate what happened. I generally have a list of files and logs that I go after even before having any idea what happened. The idea is to get every file that might contain evidence before it either disappears or is altered.

Once you have gathered everything you can think of in the way of evidence, step back from your investigation for a while — not a long while, time is usually of the essence in these things. Because you probably didn't have a fully developed hypothesis when doing your preliminary investigation, it's likely that you missed some important evidence. If possible, go back for it. That's a very good argument for impounding the computer. Of course, it would be nice if we had everything needed to explain the event fully, and prove it completely the first time we see the crime scene … that just about never happens.

Don't forget our rule: treat everything done in an investigation as if it will end up in a criminal action. That means you won't decide what evidence is important and what is not. You'll just preserve and handle it all as if it is critical to your case. Who knows … it might be. Finally, start the process of building the blanket of evidence into a mountain of proof.

LOOK FOR THE LOGICAL ERROR

How many times have you heard that the bad guys always screw up? In computer crimes, that happens a lot. But, sadly, it also doesn't happen a lot. There are some very skillful — and lucky — criminals in the computer crime business. But, there are some things that trip up even the best occasionally. That's where you may have an advantage in your investigation.

Computers themselves leave tracks. It takes a very knowledgeable computer expert to know where every track is being left. As you will learn in our discussion of forensics, there are many hidden areas of a computer disk that even most so-called experts don't know about. The reason is actually pretty simple: Many computer "experts" usually are little more than very accomplished programmers. While that in itself is no mean accomplishment, there is a great deal more to a complex computer system than the code.

An understanding of underlying operating system functions, the hardware, the hardware/software/firmware/operating system interface, and the communications functions inside and outside the computer offer a wealth of investigative opportunities, and, possibly, traps for even the most accomplished hacker. Even as we will show, the code a programmer writes may contain clues to his or her identity. All we, as technical sleuths, need to do is find them.

In this chapter we will not delve deeply into the methods required to find these obscure clues. Rather, we will discuss the process of hunting for them. This will prepare us to pursue the techniques discussed in later chapters. Also, this book will not teach you much about operating systems. You will need to get your underlying technical knowledge in other ways, from other sources. What it will show, however, is how to apply that knowledge to your investigation.

Computers are supremely consistent in how they process data. They behave very predictably. I'm joking, right? Not really. When computers don't do what you expect, it's always for one of two reasons, whether we as experts like to believe it or not. Either someone or something has altered the computer's behavior, or we didn't understand the expected behavior in the first place. Those two, rather obvious, conclusions can be of huge help to us in the technical aspects of an investigation. They can also lead us directly to the human aspects.

If, for example, we completely understand, at every level, how an application processes its data, and, at some point, it processes the data differently, that understanding can lead us to a conclusion. Let's take an example. In an earlier chapter we discussed the case of the Cyber Surgeon. The perpetrator altered a small block of memory so skillfully that the result appeared to be anomalous behavior of the computer itself. Then, in trying to cover up, our offender altered logs. The alteration was caught, you'll recall, by other system programmers. Let's examine that whole case in a somewhat different light than in our earlier chapter. In this examination, we'll look for the logical errors in the clues turned up during the investigative process: the hidden flaws that lead to an incorrect conclusion on the part of the investigator and the correct conclusion for the system programmers.

First, we had an anomalous event: the application crashed. That by itself may not have been particularly strange. However, in an effort to localize the problem (no crime was suspected at this point), technicians analyzed logs for the period. When I saw the logs, they had been annotated by the system programmer, who eventually confessed to the crime. At that time, of course, I had no idea they had been altered.

What I did note, of course, was that the small block of code had been altered and a particular programmer was logged on at the time. Naturally, that leads to a conclusion: the programmer is a suspect. At that point, I left the case to work on a different problem associated with the client's network, my specialty area. Another investigator, a specialist in mainframes, picked up the investigation. Although all fingers were pointing to the programmer in the logs, the investigator could not say with certainty that he really was the offender. The investigator refused to accuse the programmer because it would have been almost impossible to prove in court. Here is our first hidden flaw.

Logically, if the logs pointed directly at the programmer, there should be other, corroborating evidence to support the logs. There wasn't any. Although there was a security shell running on the mainframe at the time (Top Secret from Computer Associates), there was no direct evidence in its logs either. The investigator wrote that off to incomplete configuration of Top Secret. That was the second hidden flaw. The security shell should have added to the evidence, even if, by itself, it couldn't prove the case. It didn't. The investigator gave up.

Later, the real perpetrator performed the attack again and, again, altered the logs. This time, however, other system programmers had examined the logs and, due to a more in-depth knowledge of the system and the application, noticed the third hidden flaw. The logs, as presented, didn't match the logs the programmers analyzed.

The investigator had not interviewed the suspect directly. The suspect, however, had no real reason to attack the computer. Rumors said that he had been disgruntled over changes in his department, but all of the rumors were hearsay. That was the fourth hidden flaw: the suspect did not have a real motive.

Also, nobody could place him at his console at the time of the attack — opportunity, then, was lacking — the fifth hidden flaw. And, finally, the case was being based largely on the word of a system programmer (who turned out to be the real offender) and the means: the accused's skill with the target system. The investigator was absolutely correct: as presented, it would have been impossible to prove the case.

Analyzing a computer security incident is not just technical. However, the technical aspects must make sense. Ignoring an anomaly can lead to an incorrect conclusion. There are old saws about this type of situation that seem to fit here. If a thing seems too good to be true, it probably is. If the solution is too easy, it may be the wrong solution. If there are obvious contradictions, it may be the wrong solution. If it makes no sense, it may be the wrong conclusion.

Why are we discussing things that, on the surface, seem obvious? Computer incident investigations are complex and, often, emotional. It is important to develop that solid, ordered process we discussed earlier in order to ensure that, in the heat of the moment, you don't miss or misinterpret something important.

VANITY

When we deal with the cracker group of computer misanthropes, we get a great investigative tool given us for free: vanity. Young crackers, such as those we've characterized as ankle-biters, can't keep quiet about their exploits. In fact, bragging rights are one of their chief motivations for cracking systems. We can use this personality quirk to our advantage, both in gathering information and in focusing in on a suspect.

A second quirk is that, by their nature, many crackers are loners. They share their information in public and semi-public forums, such as BBSs and Internet chat rooms or newsgroups. It is not hard to access these forums. Investigators should spend a reasonable amount of time wandering about the computer underground, gathering information and getting the flavor of its inhabitants.

Another benefit of surfing the computer underground is a greater understanding of tools and methods. Crackers have patterns of behavior that are often identifiable to them as individuals. Tools and viruses often bear the marks of their makers. Text files and text headers in cracking code may contain direct references to the creators of the code. While this by itself usually doesn't mean a great deal in typical corporate attacks, it may help the investigator to understand the attacker, his or her technical approach, and motivation better.

Of course, there is a real probability that the code wasn't created by the person who used it to commit the offense. This type of program is so available in the underground that virtually anyone can get hold of it. But, tracing code to its creator is not usually necessary. What can help is that the code often can be traced to its *user*.

Using forensic techniques, we often can find the residue of the code on the suspect's hard drive. Then, by backtracing to the source, we may be able to establish that the suspect obtained the code and used it to commit the offense. Because underground programs often undergo alteration from user to user, finding identical versions of a destructive program or hacking utility at a source site, on the suspect's computer, and at the crime scene begins a very satisfactory process of evidence gathering.

If we suspect we are dealing with an outside cracker, we should begin to learn where he or she "hangs out" in cyberspace. There is a very good possibility that the suspect will share his or her newly found knowledge of your system.

Security administrators at large ISPs, universities, and large corporations spend a fair amount of time using aliases in the underground. They will usually be willing to help track a cracker if their system is involved. Also, local law enforcement computer crime specialists often have a wealth of knowledge about the denizens of the computer underground. Even if they are not involved in your case, they may be able to offer some unofficial assistance in terms of underground information. The time to develop your underground contacts is now — not when the event occurs. By then, it's far too late.

SUMMARY

In this short chapter we briefly explored the human aspects of computer incident investigation. Much of what we introduced here isn't particularly tangible. It's not even always accurate, people being as unpredictable as they are. However, it's food for thought as you try to untangle the web of a possible computer-related crime.

We also took a much closer look at what constitutes evidence and how to handle it. We saw what doesn't constitute evidence, and how to avoid it. Finally, we returned to our examination of the human aspects and introduced vanity as an investigative tool. We also pointed out the logical process of evaluating evidence and how to avoid being the victim of hidden flaws, or logical errors.

In the next chapter, we'll begin to chew on some of the real "meat" of this book: analyzing the remnants of a security incident. You might think of this chapter as the techniques of a back room computer system pathologist examining the corpses of dead, damaged, and corrupted computers, data, and networks. In fact, we refer to this science as computer forensics.

In our virtual forensic lab we'll explore computer forensics — gathering hidden information off of computer disks — and we'll introduce a couple of new terms: cyber forensics, gathering hidden information from a network, and software forensics, determining who wrote software code.

We'll wrap up the chapter by expanding our earlier references to system logs, their usefulness, their limitations and how to tie several together to create a picture of an incident.

REFERENCE

1. Icove, D., Seger, K., and VonStorch, W., *Computer Crime, A Crimefighter's Hand-book*, O'Reilly & Associates.

7 Analyzing the Remnants of a Computer Security Incident

In this chapter, we will discuss the field of computer forensics. We'll subdivide the field into three parts: computer forensics, cyber forensics, and software forensics. There is a purpose behind this subdivision which, as far as I know, is new to the computer forensics discipline. While the overall definition of forensics seems to be generally agreed upon, the subfields which relate to the computer are not.

Recently, I attended a conference on computer crime. There were at least four speakers who touched on the issues surrounding computer forensics. Each gave a slightly different definition. While all four definitions got the job done and were similar, it was clear to me that the science of computer forensics was well understood only within the ranks of computer forensics specialists. Since this book is intended for the general security, information security, or audit specialist, it is probably appropriate that we posit a definition (or set of definitions) for the disciplines we are discussing. We'll do that each time we discuss a particular computer forensics discipline.

We'll begin this section by setting the stage. We'll define a security incident and discuss the number one problem of all investigators: timeliness. Then, after we expand on the problem, we'll discuss the solutions. Finally, we'll go into the single biggest asset or liability, depending upon their condition, system logs. The logs, or audit trail, constitute the investigator's leading potential asset. Without them, the investigator has a much more difficult task. Also, we will look at the limitations of logs and what you can do about them when they are not complete enough. Let's set the stage ... .

WHAT WE MEAN BY A COMPUTER SECURITY INCIDENT

A user bolts out of her office, into the hall, shouting with panic in her voice, "I've got a virus!!!!!! My computer's down!!!!! It's going to kill the network!!!!!" Fifteen minutes later, the system administrator determines that the problem has nothing to do with a virus. It was just a sick PC. A fantasy? A war story conjured up to add interest to this book? Not on your life! I experienced that precise scenario at a major Department of Energy national laboratory in 1994. Trust me ... it still happens.

The point is that not all computer incidents are security incidents. Responding to a security incident costs money. I did an investigation that cost my client over $50,000 and our conclusions were not satisfactory enough for the prosecutor. You can save your company (and the criminal justice system) a lot of money if you are able to identify, with believable certainty, the source and reality of the incident.

Many of my clients have created specific definitions of security incidents, and a few have subdivided those definitions into classes of incidents. The latter approach is the one I strongly recommend. It allows you to set up appropriate responses to various degrees of threats. For example, "calling out the militia" may not be appropriate to a minor incident, such as an isolated virus, but it certainly would be if your firewall is being attacked in earnest by a well-equipped, determined hacker.

Two to three categories of security incidents are appropriate for most organizations. A category one incident might be an incident that doesn't pose a major global threat to the enterprise. A category two incident may be one that could cause the whole enterprise to shut down, or could compromise a core system — financial, operational, marketing trade secrets, or development trade secrets, for example. It is important that we make a distinction between what requires immediate attention and what can wait. Medics in hospital emergency rooms call this approach *triage*. We need a triage system for security incidents if we are to maintain the credibility and appropriate responses to protect the enterprise. How can we do that?

Our first step must be a formal risk assessment of our system. We need to know what is at risk, where it is at risk, and what could compromise it. Then, we need to evaluate countermeasures. Finally, we need to assume the worst: nothing was successful in protecting us. We were penetrated, a loss was sustained, or damage was done. What is the impact? What is our potential loss?

By ranking risks in this manner, we can determine the appropriate response to an incident. As part of a formal intrusion management program, this is probably the most beneficial return: we know what can hurt us, we know where it can hurt us, and we know what it will cost us if the hurt is successful. Knowing these elements will help us to define three things: appropriate countermeasures, appropriate recovery priorities (part of a business or disaster recovery plan), and response priorities to incidents exploiting the identified vulnerabilities.

Using the example above, a class two incident should get immediate response. It should be reported to the proper authorities (depending upon your response plan) immediately. The response team should take immediate action, as defined in your response plan. The response team should be convened and the true nature of the event should be analyzed to determine the next appropriate response.

Some of the types of incidents that could spell disaster are:

- Successful, or potentially successful, attack on your Internet firewall
- Successful, or potentially successful, attack on core financial, marketing, production, or development systems
- Successful, or potentially successful, attack on your protection or security systems at any level (information, logical, or physical, such as security or protective systems)

- Compromise of any critical or sensitive data — especially incidents that are not or do not appear to be isolated — this includes attacks on laptops that appear to be global against your organization, rather than attacks of opportunity (referred to as *distributed, coordinated attacks*)
- Any attack on your monitoring, logging, or auditing systems or data

By defining what we mean by a security incident, and defining the required response, we can significantly simplify our task of intrusion management. We also can require, by policy or corporate procedure, a particular response from users, administrators, or system managers. Without such a set of definitions, we may or may not be able to respond appropriately.

Remember that we have emphasized, throughout our discussions so far, the requirement that all incidents be investigated using techniques that would allow our investigation to stand up in a criminal proceeding, if necessary. No investigation can withstand the attacks of the opposition in a courtroom unless it has been conducted with care, professional due diligence, a proper procedure, and with proper attention to the issues we have already discussed. These include preservation of evidence, chain of custody, and adherence to the rules of evidence.

WE NEVER GET THE CALL SOON ENOUGH

It is a trait of human nature: we try to solve problems ourselves before we report them. Nowhere is this trait more evident than in the arena of corporate politics. Managers and supervisors go as long as they can before they report security incidents. There are a few cases where reporting, of course, is rapid:

- Where the damage is so evident that reporting cannot be avoided
- Where there is potential damage or compromise that would spotlight the person responsible, if he or she did not report it properly
- Where it would be politically expedient to report the incident

As you can see, reporting a security incident often is dependent upon the political benefits to be accrued by the reporter. By making reporting incidents a part of corporate policy you may bypass these potential pitfalls assuming that your organization has a policy of enforcing policies.

No matter what your policy is, there is a high likelihood that the incident will be, at least to some extent, "cold" by the time you begin your investigation. Logs, then, are critical. However, there is a nearly equal likelihood that they either will be incomplete or nonexistent for the period of the incident. We'll discuss logs in more detail later. For now, it is enough to realize that that bad, incomplete, or missing logs will certainly add to your investigation headaches.

Given that you are faced with one or more machines that may or may not have participated (either as perpetrator computers or victim computers) in your incident, along with very limited log evidence, what will you do to follow our stepwise technique for investigating incidents? You have two avenues open to you: you can follow tried-and-true police investigative techniques of interviewing witnesses and interrogating suspects — good old-fashioned police work — or you can use forensic science to reconstruct the crime. I recommend that you use both.

We've discussed the "touchy-feely" approaches to psyching out potential evidence, tracking the "bad guys" and, generally, doing the "Sherlock Holmes" approach. Now, we'll take the other tack: employing forensic science to help reconstruct the crime. If you can use both approaches successfully, you'll usually get very close, if not right on, to a solution. Investigation of computer-related incidents is multidimensional. Never assume (unless, of course, the solution falls into your lap) that any one avenue of investigation is going to take you to the answer.

One of the great benefits of forensic science is that it allows us to reconstruct events that have already passed. We no longer need to observe the crime in progress. We no longer have to depend upon developing witnesses, although we should continue to do so as part of a total investigation — courts don't like to make decisions based entirely upon forensic evidence. We no longer need to recreate events through interviews — again, we should not neglect this important aspect of a full investigation.

Now we can add the dimension of scientific corroboration. We can also develop leads that will help us in the conventional part of our investigative tasks. We can tell when a suspect is lying or omitting important details. We can develop lines of questioning, both for our investigation and for our legal counsel to use in court. We can create solid, irrefutable evidence that will stand up to scrutiny because of its solid scientific basis. In short, we can mitigate the fact that the call to investigate may not have been timely.

COMPUTER FORENSIC ANALYSIS — COMPUTER CRIMES AT THE COMPUTER

We'll begin with the most accepted branch of computer forensic science: the branch that deals with extracting evidence from the computer itself. AuthenTec International, a data recovery and computer forensic company in the U.K., discusses the need for prompt, accurate action when investigating computer fraud in their pamphlet, *The Enemy Within*.

> Once the fraud is discovered, speed is critical. When the fraudster suspects discovery, he will redouble efforts to hide assets. Information discovered in *the first seven days* is shown to be critical in terms of successful recovery. Leads that are not followed in the early stages, perhaps because they appear minor at the time, can prove to be far more difficult, if not impossible, to follow later.[1]

Of course, one problem we encounter when attempting to gather evidence is that we cannot interview a computer. Or, can we? I'm sure all of us have said at one point or another in our lives, "If only that [insert name of inanimate object here] could talk." With forensic analysis, computers can talk. And, they can tell us plenty!

DOS, that operating system which evokes a mixture of strong emotions from users of various skill levels, is at one time the investigator's friend and the bad guy's enemy. Left to its own devices, DOS forgets nothing.

Every time you type any character at the keyboard, you place that character in memory. DOS, then, places it on the local drive. Here's how that works. DOS maintains space in memory for all keyboard input. This temporary storage space, called the keyboard buffer, is dumped to disk when it is either full or the user is finished with it. We will discuss, in a moment, where this information actually ends up. However, we can say at this point, that those keystrokes could make up passwords, incriminating phrases, or other information that we would like to capture. This is the information that the perpetrator would like to keep secret.

As most people know, DOS never erases a file. When the user deletes a file, the entry for the file, appearing in the DOS directory, is removed. If we use a tool such as the Norton Utilities, we will see the directory entries for all deleted files, with only the first character of the file name changed. The only time a file is deleted from a hard disk (or, any DOS disk, for that matter) is when it is overwritten.

Because DOS disks become fragmented, it is likely that a large file will be spread over several different sectors of the disk. Thus, it is likely that a disk write action would overwrite only a portion of a large file, leaving other portions open to discovery. We must use special tools, however, to discover both the existence and the contents of these fragmented files.

DOS Disks — A Brief Tutorial

Let's get a couple of definitions under our belts before we continue. It's helpful to understand how a DOS disk works. You can think of a DOS disk as a phonograph record — if you're old enough to remember phonograph records, that is. The major difference between the disk and the record is that the grooves on the record are a spiral, tracking from the outer edge of the record to the center. Disks, however, are made up of concentric circles of data written magnetically onto the disk's surface.

At the same time, the disk is logically broken up into wedges that look like pieces of pie. The result is that there are blocks of data logically written together on each track of the disk. These groupings of data on a single track are called *sectors*. A sector usually contains 512 bytes of data space. The concept of data space is an important one, as we will soon see.

Hard drives usually have multiple platters or disks. These platters all rotate together on a spindle so that a point on one platter lines up consistently with the same point on all the rest. Put another way, if, while the drive was turned off, we drilled a hole down through all of the platters, neatly aligned one below the other, the holes would remain aligned when the drive was turned on and the platters started spinning.

Platters also usually are read and written on both sides. Thus, when we have a drive that has ten platters, we have twenty disk surfaces upon which to store data. Sectors are grouped together on a single platter to form *clusters*. Clusters vary in size depending upon such variables as the operating system version and disk data capacity. Clusters on hard drives are typically 32 K in size. If we follow a sector down through all of the platters, both sides, they form a *cylinder*. Data is written to DOS (which, by the way, includes MS Windows, Windows 95, and NT, for our purposes) in clusters. DOS writes data until it fills a cluster, then it seeks another cluster. It continues this process until it has completed writing out the file that it is storing. The clusters do not need to be contiguous.

When a disk is newly formatted, however, files tend to be written onto contiguous clusters. Over time, the disk begins to fill up. Not all files are large. Some, such as batch files, may not even fill a single cluster. Eventually, there may not be enough contiguous clusters to hold a large file, so DOS breaks up the file and spreads it around the disk, taking advantage of available clusters. When that happens, we say that the disk is *fragmented*. Fragmented disks do not perform as well as unfragmented disks, because the read heads must jump from cluster to cluster, instead of tracking sequentially through contiguous clusters.

Something else happens when DOS writes to a disk. If the file being written is not exactly the same size as its final cluster (e.g., is not big enough to fill the final cluster to the end), the leftover space in that cluster is available to DOS for other purposes. One of those purposes is *not* adding another file, however. A cluster may contain only one, or part of one, file. The file allocation table (FAT) doesn't know how to locate more than one file or file fragment in a cluster. But DOS still has a use for this empty space, called *slack* space. That use makes finding evidence on a DOS disk potentially easy. Here's why.

SLACK SPACE

Remember that we said earlier that everything that gets typed on a DOS machine ends up on the disk somewhere? The somewhere, among other places, is in the slack. Additionally, every time DOS closes a file, it tries to write that file to the slack space. It does this in much the same manner that it dumps the keyboard buffer. Basically, DOS is clearing its memory, and it puts the "garbage" on the hard disk in file slack. When it runs out of slack, DOS simply writes over slack that it has already written.

Slack is not visible to the computer functions that keep track of files. Thus, it is not possible to see the slack without special tools. We'll get to them in a moment. Let's go back, for a moment, to the statement that files, when closed, dump to the slack. That is a very important, potential security breach. Suppose, for example, you want to encrypt a very sensitive file. You encrypt and, as far as you know, the file is secure. However, using forensic tools, we can look in the slack, and a couple of other places we'll discuss in a moment, and we might find all or part of the original plain text file. Why? Because it existed in DOS memory during the encryption process. When the encryption was completed and the file was closed, DOS dumped its memory which contained the original file. That dump ended up in the slack.

Typing IDs and passwords can result in the same unprotected information. Word processors don't save directly to the filename we tell them to either. They first save to a temporary file, going to the final file only when we close out the document. That's how they can recover when the system crashes or goes down, ungracefully, while we're working on a document. Of course, the word processor often clears the temporary file (often, but not always), but that doesn't, as we have just seen, mean that the file is really gone.

Most of the data in file slack is from the current session, according to research conducted by New Technologies, Inc. (NTI) of Gresham, OR. Data found in slack may include directory entries which, according to the NTI research, can aid in determining when a file was updated or deleted. Directory information saved to slack space on a floppy disk can be used to tie the disk to the computer it came from, because the directory structure of the computer will be recorded on the floppy. DOS selects its slack from the disk currently active when it closes a file. If the floppy is the active disk — drive A:, for example — its slack will get whatever DOS just finished doing when it dumps its memory.

The NTI research also shows that file slack is not affected by fragmentation. That means that defragmenting a disk will have no effect on slack. Another interesting result of the NTI research is that the file slack attached to a particular file will stay intact as long as the file itself is not altered. However, if the file is moved, or a changed version is saved, the slack changes and any data hidden in it is subject to alteration or loss. Experiments have shown, however, that moving a file has no effect because the file doesn't really move. Only its directory entry is changed. You can move a file only within the same DOS volume.

Unallocated Space

We have discussed unallocated space. We just didn't call it that. Unallocated space is the space taken up by the "real" file when you erase it. Of course, the file is completely intact, assuming that the space has not been used to save a current file, and includes its former slack space.

Unallocated space can be a gold mine of forensic information, as long as we have the tools to view it. There are some issues involved in viewing these hidden spaces (slack and unallocated) that we'll discuss when we get to our section on forensic tools. For that discussion, we'll use the innovative tools from NTI as our models.

Windows Swap Files and Web Browser Caches

The swap files created by all flavors of MS Windows are a potential bonanza for forensic investigators. There are two types of swap files: temporary and permanent. Permanent swap files continue to exist even after we shut down Windows. Temporary swap files "collapse" when we close Windows. We need to treat these two types of files differently, as we'll see in the next topic.

First, remember that the swap files are being changed constantly. These are files that Windows uses for everything from a scratch pad to temporary memory. When Windows needs to multitask, it actually places a portion of the inactive program in memory. Thus, we get the impression that several programs are running at once. They really aren't. They're being swapped back and forth in memory so fast that they continue running. During the time that they are not actually running, a small portion of the program, called a *stub,* continues to remain in memory, holding everything together until its program's turn to run returns. If Windows doesn't have enough memory for swapping, it turns to the swap file on the hard drive. Thus, anything may be written in the swap file; it's all there for the investigator to discover.

Swap files are tricky, though. They change without warning and there is no way you can affect that. Windows operates under the surface and out of the user's direct control most of the time. That means it is writing to the swap file constantly which, of course, is changing that file's contents. When you do an orderly Windows shutdown, some of the shutdown process gets written to the swap file, overwriting potentially useful (for the investigator) data. We'll address some solutions to that problem momentarily. Worse, the process of starting Windows creates and deletes many temporary files, some in the swap file.

Web browsers, such as Netscape and MS Internet Explorer, create cache files to improve performance. These cache files are hard to view, but there are freeware utilities called "UNMOZIFY" that will allow you to see their contents. Browser cache files are prime targets for investigators of inappropriate Web usage, visits to cyberporn or child pornography sites or, in the case of hacker investigations, visits to hacking sites where tools were obtained to hack the victim.

PROCESSING FORENSIC DATA — PART ONE: COLLECTION

There are two major dangers in collecting computer forensic data: loss and alteration. If we are not careful, we can overwrite important data, losing it completely. Or, we could overwrite part of it, changing its meaning or erasing critical pieces such as characters in passwords. Finally, computer forensic data not handled appropriately will attract significant rebuttal in court. The bottom line is that proper collection of forensic evidence is critical.

The key aspects of forensic data collection are:

- The tools you use to collect the data
- The techniques you use to collect and preserve the data
- The tools you use to analyze the data
- The techniques you use to analyze the data

Let's take each of these aspects in turn. We'll start with collection tools. There are some important requirements:

- They must not alter the data as a side effect of the collection process.
- They must collect all of the data we want, and only the data we want.
- We must be able to establish that they worked properly, e.g., as advertised.
- They must be accepted, generally, by the computer forensic investigative community.
- The results they produce must be repeatable.

NTI produces several useful collection tools as part of its suite of forensic tools:

- GETSLACK — collects data in the slack space of a disk
- GETFREE — collects data in the unallocated space

- FILTER_I — collects and processes data hidden in slack, unallocated, swap, or cache spaces, including binary data. Collection is based upon filtering of binary information, collection of words and probable words, and the use of fuzzy logic to "guess" possible useful information that may be hidden in binary data.
- TEXTSEARCH PLUS — collects data based upon text search strings

Additionally, Sydex, another Oregon company, produces SafeBack, a physical backup tool used to collect a mirror image of a hard disk. It also produces Anadisk, a utility for analyzing floppies. All of these programs, plus an early version (4.0 is good) of the Norton Utilities, should be in the investigator's tool kit.

COLLECTION TECHNIQUES

Now that we have our tools, let's move on to using them. We have earlier discussed collecting evidence, but now would be a good time to review some important points. First, treat all of our evidence as if it will be used in criminal litigation. Second, never work directly on the evidence itself. Collect it and work on a copy. We have a couple of ways to do that, as you will see.

Third, once you have collected your evidence and made a copy, store the original safely and maintain a chain of custody. Finally, label everything, catalog carefully, document your findings, and use a technique that lets you establish when the evidence was collected, by whom, and that it hasn't been altered since its collection. Now, on to specific techniques.

Let's assume you have just arrived on the crime scene. You see a computer that may have been used to attack your payroll system. The computer is still turned on. What do you do? The first thing you will want to do is nothing. Clear everyone from around the computer, examine it for such things as network or modem connections, check any other connections to it, and carefully observe the screen display.

If there is a modem or network connection, unplug it from the computer. Do not turn the computer off. Do not turn the modem off. You should disconnect the modem from the telephone but do not use the telephone for making a call. The modem and the telephone may contain the last number dialed, a list of commonly called numbers, or other information that you can use to establish if the computer was used to attack your system. Disconnecting the devices from the computer, however, ensure that the owner of the PC cannot dial in or come in through the network and destroy evidence.

If your observation of the screen display indicates that there is a currently running remote session, it is probably even more important the you cut the connection at once. If the computer is a file server, you may want to get someone who knows the operating system to issue the command that lists currently connected users. Remember, however, that in doing this you run the risk of altering data in the hidden areas of the hard drive.

If you can do so, it is a good idea to redirect lists to a floppy disk and never display it. By not displaying, you won't write to the hard drive when the DIR command completes. Instead, by redirecting to the floppy, you'll capture on safe media and, when the command closes, the residue will be written to the slack space on the floppy. Label the floppy and write-protect it.

Next, document the connections to the PC. If you encounter a Unix computer, instead of a PC, the process is the same, for the moment, anyway. You can document by sketching or taking a Polaroid snapshot. Then take labels and label all connections so you can reassemble the system exactly as you found it. Now, we're ready for the most controversial step: turning off the computer.

Some computers suffer painfully if you simply pull the plug. Unfortunately, doing an orderly shutdown exposes you to several potentially catastrophic possibilities. The worst, of course, is the possibility of booby traps. Hackers often rig their computers to destroy evidence or, even, the computers themselves (by formatting the drive), if a secret sequence is not used to shut them down. In DOS computers, this sequence can even be embedded in the command interpreter. In Unix, there are several files involved in the shutdown process that are easily altered.

Just because you're investigating the victim computer, don't assume that it hasn't been booby trapped. Hackers often need to leave evidence of their efforts on the machine if they intend to come back. If necessary, they may rig the computer to destroy that evidence. The other part of this argument is that some systems, such as Windows, alter files as part of the shutdown process. The files they alter, sadly, are among the most valuable to our investigation.

In general, my decision, based upon a great deal of experimentation, is that PCs, regardless of whether they are running DOS, Windows, or NT, can be shut down ungracefully without much permanent damage. Most important, when we go to start them up again, as we will discuss next, we can be fairly certain that their data is waiting for us intact. When the investigation is over, if we need to rebuild the computer, we'll have a physical mirror that we can use to put it back to its original (or nearly original) condition. In every case I've observed, the system could rebuild during initial bootup after we finished with it.

The possible exception is older versions of Novell NetWare servers. These will probably require some effort to reconstruct, but they, too, can be brought back to life. The important point is that pulling the plug on PCs is no disaster. Pulling it on a Unix machine may be. Let's stick with PCs for the moment.

Once you have determined that it's time to get "into" the PC, simply pull the plug. Don't turn it off — some systems have a graceful shutdown built into the power-off circuits. I have a Unix machine configured for use as an Internet gateway for our network that has a built-in battery power supply. When you turn it off, it automatically goes into its graceful power-down cycle. If you pull the plug, the battery takes over until the shutdown process cycles correctly and the power-down is complete. There isn't much you can do about this type of system. One possibility is a reboot with an alternative boot device, such as a CD-ROM or emergency floppy.

Now, you need some of the tools we discussed above. Before you can use the tools, however, a little preparation is in order. I have a full set of prepared forensic tools, on disks of various sizes, ready for use. Let's begin by listing the steps we'll need to take in general terms. That will help us understand what our tool kit should look like, all prepared for the field.

- Shut down the computer.
- Reboot to DOS (NEVER Windows) from a floppy.
- Make two physical backups of the hard drive.
- Use one physical backup to create a mirror of the machine under test; save the other for evidence.
- Analyze the mirror machine.

To make your physical image you will need an external drive, such as an Iomega Jaz, Zip, or other large capacity drive. I use the Jaz drive, but, a word of warning, they are tricky to set up. The Jaz drive wants to connect to a SCSI port, but it will use the parallel port, if necessary. To use the parallel port, you will need the Traveler option. Jaz Traveler is a pair of special adapters that convert the drive's SCSI input to accept parallel ports on the source PC. You will also need a full set of Jaz drivers, including the GUEST driver, on your boot disk.

I have prepared a disk that boots DOS 6.22, loads the Jaz drivers, and sets me up with the Jaz drive on the target PC, all ready to back up with SafeBack. SafeBack is also on the disk. I selected DOS 6.22 because it is fairly stable and pretty plain vanilla. If you want the most stable, unadorned DOS, however, use DOS 3.X. I have boot disks for 3.X, 4.X, and 6.X. Do not use Windows 95 for booting. Never boot from the computer's operating system.

By using the GUEST driver for the Jaz drive, I never need to write anything to the target computer. DOS 6.22 is comfortable with the Jaz drive, so it just takes a few minutes to get set up. It will take much longer for the backup, especially if you use the parallel port. If the computer has a SCSI port, use it. SCSI is much faster than parallel and the GUEST driver will happily discover the SCSI port and your Jaz drive. One final word about the Jaz drive: There have been reports that it is occasionally unreliable. I have not personally observed that, but a word to the wise, etc.

The next step is to use SafeBack to create the physical backup. A physical backup backs up everything on the disk — even empty sectors. When you restore to the test machine, you will have an exact physical mirror of the original disk. The mirror will be correct sector by sector. All hidden, unallocated, slack, cache, temporary, and swap files will be located on the mirror exactly as they are on the original. Analysis of the mirror is identical with analysis of the original. The results will be precisely the same.

Once we have a physical backup on our Jaz (or other) media, we can restore to the test machine. SafeBack is very simple to use. It is a DOS character-based program. Never try to use forensic tools from inside Windows. The changes Windows will make to the swap file will damage any evidence that may have been there. Also, Windows creates and deletes files. There is no way to predict the effect that will have on evidence in other hidden areas. In short, working from within Windows will make all of your forensic efforts worthless.

You now have the original machine, a physical copy of the drive, and a restored test machine. It's time to start analyzing.

ANALYSIS TOOLS AND TECHNIQUES

We will use several of the same tools for analysis that we used in collecting our data. The difference is that we will use them somewhat differently. For example, we can use GETSLACK to collect all of the information from the slack space and save it to a file on a floppy, which we will use FILTER_I to analyze. We could also use FILTER_I to analyze file slack right on our test machine. Because we are interested in following leads, hunches, and anything else we can to get started, we might simply dig right in with FILTER_I.

The text search tool has an advantage for us if we want to explore the physical backup. SafeBack creates a single file that contains all of sectors of the original disk. This means that buried in the file we may find keywords that could lead us to evidence. However, there is also the strong possibility that information is scattered all over the disk, making it hard to collect. There is an advanced technique, which we will discuss shortly, called *chaining*. Chaining consists of following fragmented files from sector to sector to reconstruct the file. Generally, however, NTI recommends the following steps when using their forensic tools in an investigation:[2]

- Make a mirror image bitstream backup using SafeBack — restore to your test machine.
- Catalog the disk contents using the NTI FILELIST utility. This produces a file level directory listing of the entire disk.
- Create a keyword list that is appropriate to your investigation. Use your own ideas and leads developed from interviews with witnesses. You can also run FILTER_I to use its fuzzy logic to help develop keyword leads.
- Use TEXTSEARCH to search for your keywords in all of the hidden areas of the disk (slack, unallocated space, etc.)
- Manually evaluate the results of your searches.
- Rerun FILTER_I using the binary filter.
- Document your results.

Here's a quick word about the last step: documentation. There are two issues you'll need to face when dealing with documentation. First, is it an accurate representation of what you actually found? That means you can swear to the way you gathered your information and documented it. The second issue is the need to prove that what you are presenting as evidence has not been altered since it was collected. We briefly mentioned this earlier. Here's the documentation process. We'll use the example of cataloging the disk.

First, we run our FILELIST utility to get a catalog of the files on the disk. This will be a logical catalog, containing only what the DOS directory structure can recognize. It will not contain anything from the hidden areas of the disk. The output of the utility is a text file with directory details. It is date-stamped.

Now, we run another NTI utility, called CRCMD5, against the file. CRCMD5 creates a unique fingerprint of the file. Any change, no matter how trivial, will alter the fingerprint indicating that the file has been altered. It is virtually impossible to guess what the change in the fingerprint would be if you made an alteration in the file. We redirect the output of CRCMD5 to a text file.

Finally, we encrypt both files using a public key encryption program and either our own public key or the key of a trusted third party, such as your company's attorney or a law enforcement or criminal justice official. When it comes time to attest to the unaltered state of the catalog, all you need to do is unencrypt the files, rerun CRCMD5, and compare the results.

You can use the same technique to preserve and certify any files you wish to keep for future evidence. The encrypted nature of the files says that the only person who could have accessed the files after encryption was the person who owned the secret key corresponding to the public key. The CRCMD5 fingerprint says that the file hasn't been altered since it was fingerprinted.

One of the problems with computer forensic techniques is the huge amount of data you may have to analyze. Today's computers typically use drives in excess of a gigabyte in size. That's a lot of space at 32 K per cluster. The ability to process large amounts of data rapidly is one of the benefits of automated forensic processing, such as we find with the NTI tools.

Chaining

Chaining is a very complex approach to recreating a large file from slack or unallocated space on a fragmented disk. The technique requires a couple of tools. First, to see how the sectors are arranged, you will need a copy of a program such as the Norton Utilities. Because we want to work in DOS — never Windows — an older version of the Utilities is best. I like the old DOS version 4.0. We will also need to be able to find a starting point for our file. For that, any of the NTI search utilities will do. Use the search utility to locate the keyword you want on the rebuilt mirror. Select a phrase in the area of your keyword that is unique.

Go to the Norton Utilities and examine the disk. Do a search on the phrase or keyword (if the keyword is unique) to find the portion of the file that you found with your NTI search tool. Note the sector number. That sector will have a sector that connects to it and/or that it connects to. Let's expand on that a bit.

Recall that we said only a single file can occupy a sector of a disk. Any leftover space will be used by DOS. Let's begin with a legitimate file, not a fragment that DOS saves to slack. The sector you found will be part of a collection of sectors that makes up the whole file. By finding any sector you can find the rest, even if they are not contiguous. Norton will tell you the previous sector, and next sector, if any. You can save each sector separately to a floppy disk and, after you find all of the sectors, recombine them to see a whole file.

If the data you want is in slack, it is probable that you have all there is. Remember that slack for a given file is continually overwritten until DOS has dumped its memory completely. If this is a result of closing a program or document, DOS will try to use the slack for the original file.

UNIX AND OTHER NON-DOS COMPUTERS

We've discussed DOS computers. There is really only one difference between a DOS computer and a Unix computer for the purposes of forensic analysis. We need to get the Unix equivalent of SafeBack to get a physical image. Because there are various types of Unix, there is more than one approach to analyzing Unix disks.

In this section we will discuss three different approaches. The first uses SafeBack and is the preferred approach. The second and third use Unix utilities, available with most Unix versions. We won't go into the details of these two because they are not consistent in their results. They merit a brief mention, though, if only as a warning to avoid them. We'll begin with the preferred approach.

Start by removing the Unix drive from the computer, if the computer is not an Intel-based PC. Some versions of Unix, such as BSD and Linux, run in an Intel environment. This allows you to boot to DOS from your prepared SafeBack floppy, just as you would with a DOS PC. If your Unix is not running on an Intel platform (for example, Sparc or RISC platforms), you will need to place the Unix disk in an Intel PC. For Intel-based Unix, keep the disk in the Intel machine for the moment.

Use great care to ensure that, when you boot this machine, you boot from your floppy. If the CMOS is set to boot the hard drive first, you may corrupt the Unix disk. When you boot, the PC may not, immediately, recognize your Unix disk. Go to SETUP, using whatever mechanism your PC provides during boot, and configure the CMOS to recognize the new drive. Generally, it is a good idea to remove other drives and make your Unix drive the primary hard drive. Remember that you must set the jumpers on the drive itself to make it the primary master drive. You may need a reference from the manufacturer to know how to set the jumpers of the drive correctly.

Once you have the PC recognizing the new drive, reboot to the DOS floppy containing SafeBack and any drivers needed to run your Jaz or other backup device. Perform your physical backup exactly as you would on a DOS PC. This creates the bitstream backup that you can use to create a mirror.

You can also perform a direct physical copy using SafeBack, bypassing the bitstream backup. The result of this disk-to-disk copy is that you create a mirror in one very fast step. I don't recommend using this process until you have a good bitstream backup on separate media to use as evidence, in case something goes wrong later in the process.

Performing a direct copy can be tricky because of the quirks of drives and PCs. The rule of thumb is that you must configure the CMOS to recognize a primary master drive and a primary slave. The drives themselves must have their jumpers set accordingly. The source drive contains your original data. The destination will contain your mirror. The destination must be at least as big as the source. Bigger is okay. We use 10 GB disks for mirrors. Most DOS machines will only recognize the first 8.3 GB without special drivers. Forget the drivers. If the mirror needs them, it will get them from the source disk.

Another caution, when performing a direct mirror, is that you can sometimes become confused as to which disk is the source and which is the target. Be sure you know which disk is which. The consequence of not knowing is that you overwrite your original disk. Perform your mirror using the SafeBack COPY selection. You may have to set the ADJUST PARTITIONS selection to "NO" to get the mirror to work. If "AUTO" works, however, that is your best choice. You can use this same direct mirror technique on any disk, not just Unix.

Once you have a mirror of the Unix disk, you'll want to begin analysis. Because the concepts of slack and unallocated space differ on different Unix versions, we'll look at analysis two ways. First, we'll assume we have an Intel, compatible Unix, such as BSD or Linux.

There is about an even chance that your mirror will boot. Unix uses several different drivers to boot the machine. These drivers must be compatible with the hardware devices on the computer running from the disk. If your disk contains a boot sequence using drivers that are not compatible with the computer into which you placed the disk, the machine may not boot. In this case, your best bet is to have a bare bones version of the same Unix on another disk and boot from that disk. Let's examine that a bit more carefully; we will use this technique again if we must analyze a non-Intel Unix.

First, we need a bare bones version of the same Unix on a hard disk set up as the primary master. Free BSD and Linux are easy to get and set up. I keep backups of these two Unix variants available to restore to a machine in my lab so that I can perform this procedure. Set up your mirror as the primary slave. Boot from your good Unix disk and configure the device drivers to recognize your mirror as a second (or other) volume. For example, if your boot disk is set up using the device driver /dev/hda1, you would set up (assuming that there are no other volumes, such as a swap volume, in use) your mirror as /dev/hda2. The exact procedure varies with the distribution of Unix you are using.

Once you have rebooted and your mirror is being recognized, you can wander through it and analyze it as if it were on its original computer. If your Unix is not Intel-based (such as Sun, IBM, or H-P), use the same procedure as above but load your mirror as the second (or greater) volume in a platform with which it is compatible. For example, if you have mirrored a Solaris disk, place it in a Sparc computer as a second (or greater) volume. Make sure that the computer is using the same Unix to boot from.

If your Unix is Intel-based, you usually can perform slack and unallocated space analysis exactly as you would with a DOS PC. Always run your tools from a bootable DOS floppy. When you use the NTI Text Search tool, you must use it to examine *physical* space. If you boot from a DOS floppy, you will not be able to see the logical Unix drive. Text Search will see the physical sectors and will include all slack and unallocated space. You can also take your mirror of non-Intel-based Unix variants, place it in an Intel PC, and use Text Search in the same manner as if you were looking at DOS. Again, use the physical search because DOS will not recognize the Unix formatting.

There are other ways to examine Unix computers. For example, Unix machines use swap space on hard drives in much the same ways that Windows uses swap space. Swap files must be recovered, if available, by booting the machine from an image of the kernel. This is usually done from a CD-ROM distribution of the operating system, or an "emergency" boot disk. The swap file must then be offloaded to an external device to avoid causing any change to the actual disk.

Some analysts suggest the use of the CPIO or DD utilities to create images of Unix disks. While those approaches can work, we recommend against them since results can be inconsistent and testifying about the procedure difficult. Because these two utilities vary somewhat in their functionality from Unix to Unix, your best bet is to control your environment using tools you know. Law enforcement specialists have successfully used the SafeBack approach and it has a history of acceptance in court cases.

The contents of Unix memory can be of additional use to the investigator. Unix memory can be accessed by causing a core dump and analyzing the resulting file. We discuss core dump analysis in more detail later in this book. Another way to get an image of the memory is to take a copy of the kmem (kernel memory) file, or its analog, on Unix versions, which do not use kmem. The only drawback is that kmem may not have in it the most current memory information.

Remember that the image offers us three sets of test possibilities. First, it is an environment that we can examine as if it were the original machine. Second, we can actually operate the system to see how it responds without damaging the original environment. Finally, we can examine the ASCII portions of the file prior to restoring it to a test machine. This allows such analysis as keyword searching in an open ASCII environment.

We can treat NetWare machines similarly. As long as we have a DOS partition, we can run our tools and see, if not use, the NetWare partition. NT, using a non-DOS partition, may offer some challenges. Booting DOS and then trying to see the NT partitions is not successful unless the machine has been set up using a standard DOS file allocation table (FAT).

We can, of course, still create a mirror image, but we may not be able to do much with it in terms of restoring to a test machine. We can, however, still analyze the ASCII image file to some extent. This is where smart keyword search engines, such as TEXTSEARCH, shine for us. We can also run the TEXTSEARCH tool against the *physical* sectors of the mirror.

If the NT machine has been configured using NTFS (the NT File System), as most NT computers are, there is a freeware utility called NTFSDOS that allows us to read the disk as if it were DOS. We boot the NT computer from a DOS floppy containing NTFSDOS and our TEXTSEARCH tool. Once we have booted, we run NTFSDOS. It will assign a virtual drive letter to the DOS representation of the NT file system. On a simple machine, with just an A:\ (floppy) and C:\ (hard drive), the virtual DOS disk representing the C:\ drive will be D:\.

Once we have that representation, we can run TEXTSEARCH on the physical sectors and retrieve a great deal of information. However, remember that NT does not, even with NTFSDOS, use slack and unallocated space the way DOS does; therefore, limitations exist on what you can see.

Another hint: the NT passwords are contained in the c:\winnt\win32\config\sam file. If you boot DOS and run NTFSDOS, you can access this file, copy it to your floppy, and run a password cracker, such as L0phtCrack, against it to recover passwords.

CYBER FORENSIC ANALYSIS — COMPUTER CRIMES INVOLVING NETWORKS

Backtracing on a network, especially one such as the Internet, can provide significant challenges. It can be a very slow process and, usually, the intruder must be online in order for a search to succeed. Additionally, you often will need the assistance of telephone companies and Internet service providers (ISPs) that might require a warrant. This means that law enforcement will need to get involved, unless you can get the cooperation of intervening system (the systems between you and the intruder) managers.

There are several things you can look for when backtracing. The obvious ones are source IP addresses in your logs, source IP addresses in packets you capture using a sniffer, and information gathered by using tools, such as reverse finger, nslookup, and whois. Sadly, if your intruder is a real pro, most of these will be pretty worthless in and of themselves. But, at worst, they can provide a starting point for your backtrace.

The most important thing for you to do in catching an online intruder is to catch him or her in the act. Of equal importance is extensive logging. You need all of the information you can get about the intruder and his or her activities while online. The time to start logging is not after an intrusion. However, it seems to be a fact of life that we never have complete enough logs. We'll discuss logs in more detail later, but, for now, let's look at how, in general, they can help us backtrace.

It is likely that any competent intruder will have jumped to a site other than his or her own to launch the attack. This, whether you like it or not, is where you'll need to start your backtrace. As starting points, look in your Unix logs for the following:

- Times of login and logout — use the LASTLOG.
- Anomalies in the LASTLOG — use a log analysis tool, such as CHKLASTLOG.
- Source IP address — use SYSLOG or any other logs you have that record IP addresses. SYSLOG must be configured for this type of information. It may produce any of several MESSAGES files. Other logs may be from TCP wrappers installed on critical services.

Similar information exists in NT logs. However, Windows95 and NetWare offer between little and no logging.

Once you have established the nearest site to you, you'll need to work with the administrator of the site to jump back to the next step in the attacker's path. If the attacker is still online, you can use tools like reverse finger to find where he or she is located. Reverse finger will take you back to the site from whence the intruder is attacking you. With luck, you'll be able to get a source address for the next jump back. However, the intruder may be using a site which does not respond to the finger service. That could stop you.

Remember, however, that the intruder had to establish an account on the attack site. He or she could not simply "pass through." That may mean that the intruder has broken into the site, which should be of interest to the site administrator. It may also mean that the intruder is a legitimate user at that site. Examples are ISPs, universities, and large corporations. If that is the case, you have a legitimate complaint against the site administrator because he or she is usually considered to be responsible for monitoring the actions of the site's users.

We had an experience with a large ISP which was the source of an attack against our system. The ISP security department took immediate action to identify the perpetrator. We were able to identify the source of the attack through the use of TCP wrappers on our telnet service. We prohibit telnet access except from very specific addresses. The wrappers log every attempt, legitimate or not, and reject attempts from disallowed addresses.

It is important to note that your logs may not reveal the actual user attacking you. You may have to be satisfied with the machine that is the source of the attack. In order to be successful at backtracing, you'll need a very precise time of the attack, the machine from which the attack occurred, and the victim's IP address.

If the attack is repeated, you may be able to capture it with a sniffer. Sniffers can be set to trigger on an event, such as a packet's source address. Once triggered, they can record every transaction involving the IP address. Sophisticated sniffers may even allow you to set up attack scenarios that record all of the attacker's actions in detail. An example of this type of program is RealSecure from Internet Security Systems. RealSecure depends upon attack profiles to identify suspected attack attempts. It can then take specified actions, including detailed logging. The logging is of sufficient detail to recreate the attack and can be used as evidence if the resulting logs are properly preserved.

Some intruder alert programs accomplish the same thing by reading logs in real time and applying action scripts. An example of that type of alert mechanism is ITA from AXENT Technologies. These programs are more focused on the hosts under attack, while sniffer type programs focus on the activity on the network. We usually install both types when we are tracing a repeat intruder.

In all cases, we are usually attempting to gather enough evidence to turn the attack over to law enforcement. It is likely that the intruder is, ultimately, accessing the first host in his or her string of sites via phone lines. Trap-and-trace over phone lines requires a warrant. This means involving law enforcement.

The first site used by the intruder is especially important if the intruder is using phone lines to access it. If the site is an ISP, there will usually be good records of the modem receiving the call. Most ISPs use modem pools with terminal servers that assign IP addresses randomly to callers as they dial the pool. However, given the time of the attack, there usually are logs that will tell what line the call came in on. From those records, the phone company can determine where the call came from. That's the good news.

The bad news is that there is a subset of intruders who are very good at hacking phone systems. These crackers, called *phone phreaks,* or just *phreakers*, may start their attack by breaking into PBXs or independent long distance carriers to steal phone service. They will jump from one to another before beginning to jump around computer networks. In these cases, finding the call into the first ISP, university, or corporation may just be the end of the phone trail. You may have to backtrace the phone activities just as you had to backtrace the network connections. For this, again, you will usually need law enforcement. Corporations are usually glad to help where they can. Long distance carriers may or may not be interested in helping, depending upon the size of the breach.

SOFTWARE FORENSIC ANALYSIS — WHO WROTE THE CODE?

This is the most arcane area of computer forensics. It is highly theoretical at the current state of the art. Some excellent work in software forensics is being done at Purdue University. We will spend just a short portion of this book discussing software forensics, because the average reader will have neither the intensive computer science background nor the tools with which to perform software forensic analysis. However, a limited understanding of the process is useful because there may be times when software forensic analysis is appropriate, and the reader may wish to engage the services of a trained analyst.

According to Eugene Spafford and Stephen Weeber, writing in a Purdue University Technical Report:[3]

> The keys to identifying the author of suspect code are selection of an appropriate body of code and identification of appropriate features for comparison.

The obvious problem, of course, is that the author probably took pains to hide his or her style. There are other problems, not quite so obvious, that make software forensics difficult.

The first is that source code is rarely available. Compiled code, when reverse-engineered, yields source code that is affected by the compiler used to compile it. The same code revealed during decompilation may have had any of several different original source statements. Simply put, there are many ways to write a statement in just about any computer language. The compiler will treat all of them similarly, and, when reverse compiled, will return only one, not necessarily the original.

However, according to Spafford and Weeber, there may still be features in executable code that can prove useful to investigators. For example, data structures and algorithms may be unique to the preferences of a programmer and can, therefore, suggest his or her identity when taken with other factors.

The compiler used and other originating system information may be embedded in the compiled code. The level of the individual programmer's expertise may point to a particular individual or subset of potential perpetrators. Programmers may have a preference for particular system calls that may lead to identifying them from their code. Finally, programmers will normally make errors and those errors may be consistent with the individual programmer.

Availability of the original source code may be useful — certainly more useful than the compiled code. Some of the identifying characteristics identified by Spafford and Weeber include the language selected, methods of formatting, comment styles, variable names, spelling and grammar, use of language features, execution paths, and bugs.

While programmers that fit into the cyberpunk category often will add their pseudonyms and other "hacker" comments into their code, the professional intruder usually will not. The writers of viruses generally fit into the cyberpunk category, while those who write logic bombs and their own intrusion tools usually do not. However, even professional programmers generally exhibit a programming style that may point back to them as the creator of a piece of code.

Another area of difficulty arises when a piece of code is modified by the actual perpetrator. Forensic analysis of the code would, then, lead back to the original programmer, not the intruder.

If you are contemplating using software forensic analysis to track a piece of malicious code to its author, it will be helpful to have narrowed the field of potential suspects to a manageable list of known possibilities. Next, you will want to collect as many samples of code written by the suspects as possible. Remember, you'll need to eliminate some external source as the programmer. This means that, if the code appears to be something that the suspect may simply have modified, software forensic analysis may be useless. The technique only is useful on the suspect's original or highly modified code.

For more information on software forensic analysis, I recommend the following documents available from http://www.cs.purdue.edu/coast/coast-library.html (the COAST project at Purdue University):

- *Authorship Analysis: Identifying the Author of a Program,* I. Krsul, Department of Computer Sciences, Purdue University, M.S. Thesis, CSD-TR-94-030, 1994.
- *Authorship Analysis: Identifying the Author of a Program,* I. Krsul and E. H. Spafford, Department of Computer Sciences, Purdue University, CSD-TR-96-052, 1996.
- *Software Forensics: Can We Track Code to Its Authors?* E. H. Spafford and S. A. Weeber, 15th National Computer Security Conference; pp. 641–650, Oct. 13–16, 1992.
- "Software Forensics: Tracking Code to Its Authors," E. H. Spafford and S. A. Weeber, *Computers & Security,* 12(6), pp. 585–595, Dec. 1993.

THE LIMITATIONS OF SYSTEM LOGS

Throughout this section, and, indeed, the whole book, we have emphasized the use of system logs to track and provide evidence of network and host intrusions. The problem, of course, is that logs have some important limitations that we need to be aware of if we are to use them appropriately.

First, logs must be shown to be unmodified to be of any evidentiary use. Logs are easy to modify. Earlier, we pointed out a way to ensure that they had not been modified because we collected them, but what about before we discover the intrusion and collect the appropriate logs?

If logs are in a location on a victim machine that is accessible by the system administrator, or any other superuser, you probably will need to explain how you know that they could not have been tampered with by the intruder, or another user with superuser rights. This is usually impossible to establish because the intruder will, likely, have gained superuser status in the course of the attack. As we have learned, cleaning up and sterilizing the system logs is a priority of any competent intruder.

Your only option in this case is significant corroborating evidence that shows that the logs are accurate. This can be in the form of other, applicable logs that were not subject to corruption. It may be in the form of direct witnesses who can testify that the events shown on the logs occurred as shown, and that no others occurred that are not shown.

Your best bet is to ensure that logs are protected from tampering. Since this may not be possible before the first attack — due to the way the victim is configured — you should make provisions for secure logs immediately upon notification, in the event that there is a follow-up attack.

Logs may be secured in a variety of ways. My preferred method is to spool the logs off of the victim immediately to a machine (log host) intended for capturing logs. Access to the loghost machine should be extremely limited. Certainly, there should be no trust relationship between the two machines that would allow the attacker to access the loghost from the victim. Once the logs are spooled to the loghost, they should be backed up to nonvolatile media (such as optical drives) or tape backup. The backup should be preserved as evidence.

Another limitation of logs is their completeness. To be useful, logs should show when an event occurred, the source of the event, and the nature of the event. Completeness is a two-edged sword, however. The most complete logs are also the largest. Additionally, creating these large, detailed logs uses enough system resources to affect performance. Logs, then, must be a compromise between completeness and practicality.

We recommend that logs showing the important information above be created for at least the following events:

- All superuser access
- Login and logout
- Attempts to use any controlled services (e.g., ftp, telnet, the "R" services, etc.)
- Attempts to access critical resources (password files, the kernel, wrappers, etc.)
- E-mail details

TCP wrappers and other specialized wrappers usually write their logs to the syslog in Unix systems. In NT systems, there rarely are specialized programs like wrappers. However, the security logs can be adjusted to provide a greater or lesser degree of detail, as required. It is often appropriate to install wrappers on a victim Unix machine and allow attacks to continue long enough to gather appropriate information about the attacker.

Another way to overcome the limitations of logging supplied with the operating system is to use a third-party product. Programs mentioned earlier (ITA from AXENT and RealSecure from ISS) can provide good logging and can protect their logs from modification.

THE LOGS MAY TELL THE TALE — BUT WHAT IF THERE ARE NO LOGS?

This is the single biggest barrier to successful investigation of an intrusion. Logs that are not retained or do not include critical information are of no use to the investigator. You are left with very few choices for investigation. All of them are complicated and time-consuming and may or may not yield results. The cost of recovering critical information when logs are not present may exceed the loss by the intrusion. You may be well-advised to write off the current intrusion and take immediate steps to correct the logging deficiencies. However, here is an approach that may, if the circumstances permit, yield at least limited results. The results may be of more use in tracking the intruder than in proving your case. *Caveat emptor.*

In order to gather information that doesn't appear in logs, either because the logging was incomplete or because there are no logs, we can use computer forensic techniques such as those discussed earlier. The objective is to collect information that has been left on the disk. This might take one of two forms.

The first possibility is that the event was logged and the logs rolled over before we could collect them. There are many potential problems with this approach, beginning with the potential damage to the log files left as residue on the disk. Because the logging program is rolling the same information over, it is constantly overwriting the older information, first in–first out (FIFO). There is a pretty good chance that any useful information has been overwritten by the time you get to it. Most programs will continue to write in the same physical sectors as they roll over the logs. However, if you are going to analyze the disk anyway, it doesn't hurt to try to reconstruct the logs. You may get lucky and be able to extract a temporary file with the information you need.

The second possibility is that there never were any logs because the machine wasn't logging. Believe it or not, this offers the best possibility of recovering useful information. Our approach will be considerably different from what we would use if we were analyzing logs. Now, instead of looking for events that we know would be logged — potentially limiting — we will look for any event that we need to establish. That means a detailed forensic analysis of the disk.

There are still limitations, of course. The first is that you probably will not be able to use this method directly to establish when an event occurred. Unless there is a program, such as a logging program, time-stamping events, there will be no time associated with them on the disk. This is true even if the event is visible on the disk under forensic analysis. The second potential problem is that not all events leave imprints on the disk. For example, any actions performed by the kernel or command interpreter probably will not leave any imprint. Thus, commands such as COPY will likely not show up.

For all of the limitations, however, there may be valuable information that can lead you to just as much detail as many logs and more than some. Additionally, you'll get information such as IDs and passwords, which can help lead you to compromised accounts and can help you track activities performed under the guise of stolen accounts.

Typically, we include forensic analysis of the victim computer's fixed disks as part of the incident analysis, if our client's budget permits. If it is your system that you are analyzing, perform the forensic analysis if you have the time and trained resources.

There is another approach that may be useful in the case of a network intrusion. Look for other devices that may have been included in the intrusion that are logging more completely than the victim. For example, if you experience an intrusion from the Internet, you may get some benefit from examining logs of the firewall or, if the breach was through a mail host or other device that communicates with the inside through the firewall, check logs on that device.

If you have been able to access a computer that you suspect may have been involved in the incident, check logs on that computer. You always will want to use logs from other, involved, computers as corroboration to the victim's logs. However, in this case, you will probably need to depend upon those logs as your primary evidence.

Finally, the logs of the attack machine may prove to be very important to you. Whenever possible, you should, of course, impound the attack machine if it is within your control (it's probably a law enforcement issue, if not), and perform forensic analysis of its disks. That includes extracting logs and corroborating information. A very clever attacker will probably find a way to avoid obvious evidence of his or her actions appearing on the attack machine. However, most attackers are unaware of the power of forensic analysis. That opens the whole hard disk up to your examination.

MULTIPLE LOG ANALYSIS

We have alluded to the subject of multiple log analysis several times, both in this chapter and earlier. Now it's time to look at the subject in more depth. Multiple log analysis has two primary objectives. First, we can use multiple log analysis to provide corroboration. Second, we can use it to fill in gaps. We'll take these in reverse order — the gap-filling first.

Let's assume that we have the logs from the victim computer. Those logs, as we have said before, may or may not be complete. We can run tools such as CHKLASTLOG (Unix) against some of them to see if they have been altered. But even these tools can't guarantee that we've found every, or, for that matter, any, instance of log tampering. There are very efficient tools in the underground that can effectively alter all of the logs that contribute to the lastlog. Altering the syslog is a piece of cake. So, our objective in multiple log analysis is, in this case, to find discrepancies between logs showing the same or dependent events.

Unfortunately, multiple log analysis is very tedious, especially with large logs. To perform multiple log analysis, we need (no surprise here) multiple logs covering the same time period and showing the same events. There are several potential sources of these logs.

The first source is the victim computer itself. If there were multiple logging programs running — for example, a third-party program that creates separate logs — we would have several (or, at least, more than one) views of the same time period.

The easiest way to use these multiple logs is to create an analysis sheet with a column for each log and the times as the rows. By filling in the columns for the time period involved, you'll have a good view of the perspective of each log on what happened at any particular time.

This approach is only effective if you completely understand the nature of the events being observed. The fact that a thing occurred is meaningless unless you understand what that thing means or implies. It is useful to have the help of someone who has a good understanding of the particular operating system. Don't limit yourself to security logs. Use system and application logs to fill in gaps in security logs.

For example, if you see an access in the lastlog at 3:00 P.M., and can show damage to a database file at 3:01 P.M., you may have a correlation. The correlation would be difficult to establish without the combination of the lastlog and the application's log. An even better correlation would be if you could show, through the lastlog, an access at 3:00 P.M., and, through the database log, an access at 3:00:30 P.M., followed by the damage at 3:01 P.M. On Unix machines, an SU (switch user) log is very useful because intruders often enter the system using one account and switch to another within the system.

When we find gaps in one log, we attempt to fill the gaps by looking at the events in a second log for the same period. At this point, we mentally move into a mode of "two out of three" hits required to win. Just because we find something in one log that fills the gaps in another log, we're not at the answer yet. Now, we have to find something that corroborates one or the other of our findings. It isn't uncommon for an attacker to *add* information to a log to misdirect the investigator. Additionally, changing an ID in a log will also misdirect. This takes us to the next use of multiple log analysis: corroboration.

We should never believe a log at face value. If we can't find something to corroborate a critical log entry, we should assume that something's amiss. Nothing in a complex computer system happens in a vacuum. There is always additional indication that an event — especially a catastrophic one — has occurred. For example, on our computers, we routinely compare the security logs with error logs and urgent logs. These logs are made up of entries derived from different sources. The security logs are a combination of security events logged by syslog and those logged by our third-party security programs. The error logs come from the syslog, as do the urgent logs. We add wrapper logs to the security logs and, for every critical event, we should see more than one view.

It's the views that both fill in gaps and provide corroboration. Unfortunately, not everyone logs with this level of completeness. The result is that we have to create the various views manually by examining logs from multiple machines. The effect is the same, but the time required is considerably greater. If you have the luxury of setting up logging, you'll get the best results by spooling all logging off to a loghost and combining the logs in a single log. If you do this, however, be sure that you identify the source of the original log information so that it can be picked out of the consolidated log.

Parsing large logs is a real challenge. Picking the "fly specs out of the pepper," so to speak, can be a daunting task when logs grow. For this, we need some specialized tools. There are, fortunately, several good ones. For much of our work with ASCII logs, we simply use TEXTSEARCH. We can search on times or text strings indicating events. Some of the utilities we have discussed have good search engines. There are also two utilities that are, essentially, scripting languages that allow you to create custom search engines.

For Unix, ASAX is a freeware package that allows you to create log parsing scripts that can search on various text strings. ACL — the Audit Command Language — runs in a DOS/Windows environment and allows the same thing. ACL is a commercial product. Some logging programs allow you to export logs in comma delimited ASCII (CDL) format. CDL allows you to read the logs into a database program for analysis or into a spreadsheet, such as Excel or Lotus 1-2-3. These programs then allow searches on particular text strings.

SUMMARY

In this chapter, we have attacked the meat of our topic: managing the results of an intrusion or other security incident. We began, logically, by defining security incidents and then began the exploration of various forensic techniques. We have now added the on-site investigation to our earlier discussions of investigative philosophies.

In the next chapter we will backtrack a little and look at how you should begin the physical investigation of a computer incident. We will discuss the beginnings of the overall investigative process. There are three phases of an investigation: launching the investigation, determining if the incident represents a computer crime, and analyzing evidence.

The first phase, the launch, includes securing the crime scene, collecting evidence, developing and acting on an intrusion hypothesis, and investigating alternative explanations. The second phase, analyzing the incident, involves analyzing the evidence collected in the first phase along with alternative explanations to determine if you have a security incident or a natural, though perhaps unpleasant, occurrence.

The third phase, analyzing the evidence, is your preparation for presenting the incident and your findings to law enforcement or your corporation. We will cover these three phases in the next three chapters, beginning with the launch.

REFERENCES

1. "The Enemy Within," AuthenTec International Limited.
2. "The New Processing Methodology," User Manual for FILTER_I, New Technologies, Inc.
3. Spafford, E. H. and Weeber, S. A., *Software Forensics: Can We Track Code to Its Authors?* Purdue Technical Report CSD-TR 92-010.

8 Launching the Investigation

In this chapter, we will discuss the first of three overall phases of an investigation. As we pointed out in the last chapter, broadly speaking, an investigation can be broken down into launch activities, incident analysis, and evidence analysis. In Chapter 2, we discussed a framework for conducting an investigation. There, we laid out a set of seven steps for you to follow. You may recall that those steps were:

1. Eliminate the obvious.
2. Hypothesize the attack.
3. Collect evidence, including, possibly, the computers themselves.
4. Reconstruct the crime.
5. Perform a traceback to the suspected source computer.
6. Analyze the source, target, and intermediate computers.
7. Turn your findings and evidentiary material over to corporate investigators or law enforcement for follow-up.

Let's begin this chapter by fitting those steps into the three basic phases of the investigation.

LAUNCHING THE INVESTIGATION

Begin by eliminating the obvious. There will be a lot of chaos around a crime scene when you arrive and you'll want to be able to focus on meaningful information immediately. Also, many "observers" will have theories which can serve to confuse the important issues, making your job as an investigator much more difficult.

A piece of eliminating the obvious is to ensure that nothing can happen to pollute the crime scene. It is at this point you need to take steps to secure the crime scene so that you can gather evidence and preserve it correctly. You'll also want to begin the process of interviewing witnesses.

Your next step is to begin the process of hypothesizing how the attack took place. Use preliminary information gathered from the first step to develop an early theory of what happened and how it occurred. It's too early, in most cases, to start thinking about a culprit at this point.

Your next step is to begin the process of evidence collection. You'll need to proceed as carefully as possible here. We've discussed this in general terms. In this chapter, we'll get to the details. The evidence you collect should help you refine your intrusion hypothesis. It will also lead you to alternative explanations, which you must analyze as well. Analysis begins in the next phase.

ANALYZING THE INCIDENT

You should begin your incident analysis by attempting to reconstruct the crime. The field of computer incident investigation is one of the few today where we can reconstruct the crime — commit the murder all over again, so to speak.

Incident analysis has three major objectives:

1. Refining your hypothesis
2. Examining alternative explanations
3. Generating additional leads for further investigation

Next, we'll perform any tracebacks that our analysis suggests. Tracebacks, as we learned in the previous chapter, are very difficult and time-consuming. Don't even attempt a traceback unless the intruder is online, or you have preserved your evidence and can proceed safely to trace the intruder without damaging evidence. Remember, when you obtain assistance from intermediate sites (those between the victim and the original source of the attack), you must take steps to ensure that the evidence you collect from them will stand up to scrutiny. Later in this chapter we'll discuss evidence in detail — we already have touched on the subject.

The final step in this phase is performing a detailed analysis of the source (if available), intermediate (if accessible), and victim computers. Don't forget that we must perform our analysis on mirror images of these computers — never on the actual computer itself. Our objective here, of course, is to collect more evidence, this time from the computers themselves.

ANALYZING THE EVIDENCE AND PREPARING YOUR PRESENTATION

Now, it's time for the third phase: evidence analysis and report preparation. This is where you will collect all of your findings and evidence, refine and document your hypothesis, and present the whole package to your management, client, or, perhaps, law enforcement.

This phase is very important because your audience is likely to try to "shoot down" your conclusions. Of course, there is a very good reason for this. Neither your management or law enforcement wants to proceed with an investigation, litigation, and/or prosecution based upon weak conclusions unsupported by strong evidence.

The point is that you will need to develop your hypothesis directly and clearly, and support your conclusions with solid evidence, properly collected and preserved. My usual approach in final reports follows. Here is a sample table of contents for a generic investigation report.

Executive summary
 Description of the event
 Brief methodology of the investigation
 Brief evidence collection and preservation methods
 Conclusion with short, generalized reasons
Methodology details
 Investigation
 Evidence collection and preservation
Finding 1 — Description
 Discussion
 Supporting evidence
Finding 2 — Description
 Discussion
 Supporting evidence
Finding N — Description
 Discussion
 Supporting evidence
Summary and Conclusion
Appendix
 List of interviewees
 Evidence listing
 Software and tools used in the investigation
 Outside experts and consultants
 Contacts at assisting sites (such as intermediate sites)
 Other important listings and information

We'll discuss the second and third phases of an investigation in more detail in the next two chapters. For now, let's get into the details of the first phase: the launch. We'll begin at the beginning, with the crime scene.

SECURING THE VIRTUAL CRIME SCENE

In the last chapter we began our discussion of the crime scene with an assumption: you have just entered the virtual crime scene. You'll recall, perhaps, that we had several things we needed to do. Summarizing, those things were:

- Clear everyone away from the computer under investigation.
- Examine for communications connections (modem and network).
- Examine for other connections and observe the screen display — photograph or sketch the display for future reference.
- Unplug communications connections from the computer — turn nothing off at this point.
- Disconnect the modem from the telephone — do not use the phone.
- Document and label all connections to the computer.
- Pull the plug(s).

- Reboot from an external source (bootable floppy or CD-ROM) and make physical images of hard drives.
- Shut down and collect the computer(s), peripherals, printouts (if any), floppies (if any), and any other potential evidence — bag and tag individually. Never write directly on evidence — always use evidence tags.
- If the telephone has "last number redial" capability, perform the redial and note the number called. Connect the modem to your laptop and read the configuration, including, especially, any phone lists saved to it.

Now we'll go through this list in more detail than we did in the preceding chapter.

CLEAR EVERYONE AWAY FROM THE COMPUTER UNDER INVESTIGATION

There is no doubt that a computer security incident investigation generates chaos. When you arrive at the scene, the adrenaline will be flowing and there is an inverse relationship between adrenaline and clear thinking. Your best bet is to automate the process as best you can so that nothing in these early, critical stages of your investigation gets overlooked or done incorrectly.

Experienced investigators develop, over time, a routine that allows them to process all necessary information at a crime scene without missing anything and without polluting critical evidence. Remember, what you do at this point can never be undone. If you scramble evidence, forget something, conduct an interview improperly, or pollute the crime scene, you may invalidate all of your future efforts on this case. An added measure of care at the beginning could pay big dividends later on.

The second point is that there may be several people in the area of the computer you are investigating. One or more of those people may have been involved and may become suspects. At this point, you probably don't know which ones, so your best bet is to clear the area immediately so that nobody can take an action to cover his or her tracks or damage evidence.

The scene of a computer security incident is among the very few crime scenes that can stretch across the planet. Ignoring for now the philosophical and legal issues of where the crime took place (was it at the victim computer or the source computer?), you may find important evidence at both ends and in between. The beginning of the investigation is not the time to try to figure that out. Just treat every involved computer, peripheral, and communications connection or device as part of the crime scene until you know differently.

Finally, if for no other reason, you should clear the scene to give yourself a place to work. Computer workstations are notoriously cramped, under the best of circumstances. A dozen or so well-meaning "assistants" are of no help in these tight quarters.

EXAMINE FOR COMMUNICATIONS CONNECTIONS, DOCUMENT ALL CONNECTIONS, AND UNPLUG COMMUNICATIONS FROM THE COMPUTER

These are very important steps. There is a better-than-even chance that the perpetrator will have remotely accessed the victim computer. Even if the access was local (from the console, for example), at the beginning of your investigation you probably don't know. However, turning off communications devices can cost you information that may be stored in volatile memory. At this point, just disconnect the cables from the computer.

The first connection is the network connection. On some computers that connection will be to a plug-in card on the back of the computer. On newer machines, the network card is built onto the computer's system board. In either case, the network connection is probably one of three types of connections.

The most common in today's networks is *10BaseT*. This type of local area network (LAN) connection is characterized by a wire and jack that look like a telephone cable. The way you can tell the difference between this type of network connection and a modem connection is that there will be a larger, multi-pin connector next to the telephone-like connector (the phone-like connector is called an *RJ45* connector) on a plug-in card, and an icon that indicates a network connection, if the card is on the system board.

The next most common type of network connection is called *thin net*. It looks like the cable used for CB radios or cable TV wire. It will have a tubular, twist-type connector on it called a BNC connector. Finally, there are connections to token ring networks that use an oval multi-pin connector on a fairly thick cable. All of these will plug into connectors on the wall that, usually, are marked as being network connections. Disconnect at the wall so that you will be able to document the computer end correctly.

Modem connections are also of two types: internal and external. External connections are to a modem which looks like a flat box with lots of lights on the front and two, or, perhaps, three cables connecting to it. One will be a telephone cable connecting to a wall jack. The second will be a thicker cable connecting to the computer. The third, if present, will connect to a telephone.

Also, before you disconnect the modem, observe which lights are lit on its front panel. If there are lights flashing, the modem is in use. Disconnect its communications line at once from the wall. Note whether the *AA* (Auto Answer) light is lit. If it is, the modem is configured to receive incoming calls. Document this information for future reference.

Internal modems will appear on the computer simply as two phone jacks. One jack connects to the wall jack, while the other connects, optionally, to a telephone. Again, disconnect at the wall so that you won't have trouble recalling the connections when you document them.

Once you have disconnected all potential communications from the computer, you'll have protected it from external tampering while you gain control of the crime scene. Now, you can proceed to document, either with a camera or by sketching, all connections to the computer and its peripherals. Finally, tag every connection in such a way that you can reassemble the system exactly as it was when you found it.

PULL THE PLUG

We discussed this in great detail in the previous chapter. However, if you are running Unix, and are concerned about damage to hard drives or files, you may be tempted to do a reboot with a bootable floppy or CD-ROM. This may or may not be a good idea, depending upon how you do it. Let's discuss some of the pitfalls specific to Unix.

In most Unix systems there is a group of configuration files called *rc* files. These files are similar to DOS *autoexec.bat* and *config.sys* files. They set up the functions that the computer will execute as it boots. However, in Unix, unlike DOS, there are also rc files (so-called because the filenames begin with rc.) that control how the computer shuts down. These files are all plain text ASCII files and can be easily edited with any text editor. It is easy to add booby traps to any of these files, including the ones that shut the computer down.

Unix allows orderly shutdowns in a variety of ways. The usual method is to use the *shutdown* command. Shutdown has several arguments, but all of them allow an orderly shutdown using the rc files to ensure that there is no damage to the file systems. One of the arguments is the *r* or *reboot* argument. It causes an orderly shutdown and reboot. The reboot command operates exactly like the shutdown -r command. In other words, it causes an orderly shutdown — exactly what we do *not* want if the rc files are booby trapped.

Shutdown and reboot also execute a *halt*. This writes out any data remaining in memory to the disk, and then begins the shutdown process. Obviously, this causes the disk to be altered, something we want to avoid. There are other ways to shutdown most Unix systems without causing an orderly shutdown. However, the effect is the same as simply pulling the plug. For the specifics of these methods, check the manual for the particular type of Unix in question.

In the last chapter, I mentioned a Unix system that had a built-in backup power supply. Pulling the plug only causes a graceful shutdown using the battery backup. This particular computer does not happen to have a floppy drive or any other alternative boot capability. It cannot be shutdown ungracefully. However, many other similarly protected Unix computers can.

If the computer has the ability to boot externally (floppy or CD-ROM), and has a built-in power protection system as I described earlier, you can shut the system down using a variation of the halt command: halt -q. This is a quick halt and it usually (depending upon the flavor of Unix) does not attempt a graceful shutdown.

On many Unix systems this causes the computer to go into single user mode. You can then place the bootable floppy or CD-ROM in place and type "boot" from the single user command prompt. This will cause the computer to boot from the external device, using the external kernel instead of the local operating system.

This does not always work, however. Some versions of Unix will look at local rc files and profiles, even though booting from an external kernel. With Unix it is always best to have an expert on the particular version of the operating system along to answer these questions. NeXT computers, for example, have several ways to shut down. Some go all the way down, some go to single user mode, some are graceful, while some are not. Unix systems are not consistent and the ability to alter the boot and shutdown processes adds to the confusion.

My preference with Unix is to get to single user mode and have a look at the rc files and other configuration files before I do anything. That means operating the computer, and it is always risky. You may feel more comfortable taking my advice in the last chapter and simply pulling the plug. Be aware, though, that some of the larger, more complex Unix machines you might encounter are, as I said in that chapter, a bit too complex to simply unplug. If you encounter one of those, secure the scene and get your expert before you do anything. Just make sure that there are no communications connections of any kind to the computer while you wait for help to arrive.

COLLECTING AND PRESERVING EVIDENCE

We have touched on evidence in an earlier chapter. I promised more detail, so here it is. I recommend that every corporate investigator read the *U.S. Department of Justice Federal Guidelines for Searching and Seizing Computers*. Remember that this document is a set of guidelines only. It is not the law, and following it does not guarantee that you will have collected evidence in a way that the courts will accept it or your opposition cannot refute it. It's a very good starting point, however, and it has a great deal of information that will help you to make a clean seizure, if that's what you end up needing to do.

The "Preface" to the *Guidelines* says it best:[1]

These Guidelines have not been officially adopted by any of the agencies, and are intended only as assistance, not as authority. They have no regulatory effect, and confer no right or remedy on anyone. Moreover, the facts of any particular case may require you to deviate from the methods we generally recommend, or may even demand that you try a completely new approach. Many of our recommendations must be tentative, because there is often so little law directly on point.

This document is intended primarily for use by members of law enforcement agencies. Therefore, it focuses on legal aspects as they apply to law enforcement officials. However, there is a lot of good information in the document which you, as a corporate investigator, can use. Remember that we are treating everything we do as if it were going to end up in court. Following these guidelines where appropriate can only help us reach that goal.

Within the guidelines, we come upon a couple of interesting definitions. You may recall that, in a very early chapter, we said that the FBI defines a computer crime as one where the computer is the victim. In the *Guidelines* we also learn that a computer may have other roles. It may be an *instrumentality* of a crime. In this case, the computer was the means by which the offense was committed — in other words, the attack machine.

The computer may also be evidence of the crime. An example of this could occur when we perform a traceback of an intrusion and find evidence on an intermediate computer that the attacker stole an account on the computer to obfuscate his or her path from the attack machine to the victim. Finally, the computer can be the victim. For most corporate investigators, this is the role most often seen.

A final role for the computer may be, or the computer may contain, the fruits of the crime. In other words, the computer itself may contain stolen documents or files. Don't forget that there is a legal doctrine of *tainted fruit*. In this doctrine, if you have not legally obtained access to the computer, you cannot use information gained from it.

For example, suppose your company has no policy regarding privacy of electronic mail. Earlier we discussed electronic mail and privacy and said that, in the absence of a policy, most courts will find for the individual, not the organization. Courts do this to protect individual rights of privacy.

In this situation, let us further suppose that a highly confidential file has been stolen. You, as the investigator, suspect that Jane Doe, one of your employees, has stolen the file and e-mailed it to a confederate at a rival company. You impound Ms. Doe's computer and proceed to examine her e-mail. You find that she has, indeed, attached the file to a message and sent the whole shebang to your number one competitor. You lower the boom on Jane, and the court throws out the whole thing. Why?

The reason is simple. You had no right to read her e-mail. Therefore, any evidence growing out of that act is *tainted*. You cannot use it. In fact, in what may be the unkindest cut of all, Ms. Doe, the thief that she is, can probably sue you for invading her privacy and win. The moral? First, have a policy (we said that earlier) and, second, stick to it when you search a computer.

Understanding the role of the computer in the incident will help you decide how the computer should be treated. Should you impound it, examine it on site, or ignore it completely? Interestingly, members of law enforcement often have more leeway in these matters than you do. There are federal guidelines that allow the seizure of computers that are either an instrumentality of or evidence of a crime. Of course, a warrant is required, but that may not be a problem. The tightrope you need to walk sometimes gives you the advantage and, sometimes, the advantage goes to law enforcement. Be sure to discuss your particular situation with your legal counsel before taking action that could hamper future prosecution or litigation.

RULES OF EVIDENCE

Let's go to the authority, as interpreted by the *Guidelines*. In federal courts, as in most others, we have rules of evidence. We discussed what constitutes evidence earlier in the book; now, let's get some detail from the *Guidelines*.[2] For this discussion, we will quote directly from the *Guidelines*, Section 8, "Evidence:"

A. INTRODUCTION

Although the primary concern of these Guidelines is search and seizure, the ultimate goal is to obtain evidence admissible in court. From the moment agents seize electronic evidence, they should understand both the legal and technical issues that this sort of evidence presents under the Federal Rules of Evidence.

It can be especially confusing to think about digital proof because, both in our current discussions and in early cases, legal analysts have tended to treat "computer evidence" as if it were its own separate, overarching evidentiary category. Of course, in some very practical ways electronic evidence is unique: it can be created, altered, stored, copied, and moved with unprecedented ease, which creates both problems and opportunities for advocates. But in many important respects, "computer evidence," like any other, must pass a variety of traditional admissibility tests.

Specifically, some commentary is not very clear whether admitting computer records requires a 'best evidence' analysis, an authentication process, a hearsay examination, or all of the above. Advocates and courts have sometimes mixed, matched, and lumped these ideas together by talking simply about the 'reliability' or 'trustworthiness' of computer evidence in general, sweeping terms, rather than asking critically whether the evidence was 'trustworthy' in all required aspects.

Part of the reason for this is probably that the first computer evidence offered in court was information generated by businesses. Long before most people used computers in their homes, telephone companies and banks were using them to record, process, and report information that their businesses required. Not surprisingly, many of the early decisions link computer evidence with the business records exception to the hearsay rule.

Of course, that exception — which is meant to address a substantive hearsay problem — also includes a sort of internal authentication analysis. [*Fed. R. Evid.* 803(6) requires a showing that a record was made 'at or near the time by, or from information transmitted by, a person with knowledge … .]

But "computer evidence" as we know it today covers the universe of documentary materials, and is certainly not limited to business records. Computer evidence may or may not contain hearsay statements. It will always need to be authenticated in some way. And data that has been produced, processed, and retrieved under circumstances other than the discipline of a business probably will not contain the qualities that make electronic evidence "reliable" as a business record. Even business records, themselves, may require a closer look, depending on what the proponent wants to do with them at trial.

The key for advocates will be in understanding the true nature of each electronic exhibit they offer or oppose: for what purpose and by what process (both human and technological) was it created? And what specific issues of evidence (rules of form? rules of substance?) does that particular electronic item raise?

B. The Best Evidence Rule

One of the issues that investigators and lawyers sometimes cite as troublesome in working with electronic evidence turns out, on examination, to be a largely surmountable hurdle: the "best evidence rule." This rule provides that "[t]o prove the content of a writing, recording, or photograph, the original writing, recording, or photograph is required, except as otherwise provided in these rules or by Act of Congress." *Fed. R. Evid.* 1002.

The impact of this rule is softened considerably by its reference to other rules. Indeed, Fed. R. Evid. 1001 makes clear in two separate provisions that when it comes to electronic documents, the term "original" has an expansive meaning. First of all, Fed. R. Evid. 1001(1) defines "writings and recordings" to explicitly include magnetic, mechanical, or electronic methods of "setting down" letters, words, numbers, or their equivalents. Clearly, then, when someone creates a document on a computer hard drive, for example, the electronic data stored on that drive is an admissible writing.

A proponent could obviously offer it to a court by producing the hard drive in court and displaying it with a monitor. But that somewhat cumbersome process is not the only choice. In telling us what constitutes an "original" writing or recording, Fed. R. Evid. 1001(3) says further that "[i]f data are stored in a computer or similar device, any printout or other output readable by sight, shown to reflect the data accurately, is an 'original.'"

Thus, so long as they are accurate, paper printouts from electronic storage devices qualify as "originals" under the rule, and there is clearly no evidentiary need to haul computer equipment into a courtroom simply to admit a document — although there sometimes may be tactical reasons for doing so.

But even having set up that inclusive definition of "original" writing, the Federal Rules go much further to relax the common law standard. Fed. R. Evid. 1003 provides that "[a] duplicate is admissible to the same extent as an original unless (1) a genuine question is raised as to the authenticity of the original or (2) in the circumstances it would be unfair to admit the duplicate in lieu of the original."

Therefore, unless authenticity or some "unfairness" is at issue, courts may freely admit duplicate electronic documents. "Duplicate" is defined in Fed. R. Evid. 1001(4) as "a counterpart produced by the same impression as the original … by mechanical or electronic re-recording … or by other equivalent techniques which accurately reproduces [sic] the original."

Many investigative agencies analyze data evidence from exact electronic copies (called "bit-stream" copies) made with commercial or custom-made software. So long as the copies have been properly made and maintained, the Federal Rules allow judges to accept these copies (or expert opinions based on them) as readily as the originals. Thus, the Federal Rules have, despite their nod to the best evidence rule, made way for a lively courtroom use of electronic evidence in all its many forms.

Questions of admissibility turn not on whether the data before a court is on a hard drive, a duplicate floppy disk, or a printout of either one. Instead, courts must ask whether the original data is authentic and whether any copies offered are accurate.

C. AUTHENTICATING ELECTRONIC DOCUMENTS

Of course, every time trial lawyers offer any piece of evidence, they must be ready to show that, as the authentication rule, Fed. R. Evid. 901(a), states, "the matter in question is what its proponent claims." Clearly, there are many ways to do this, including the ten illustrations offered by Fed. R. Evid. 901(b).

1. Distinctive Evidence

One of the most common methods for authenticating evidence is to show the item's identity through some distinctive characteristic or quality. Indeed, the authentication requirement of Fed. R. Evid. 901(a) is satisfied if an item is "distinctive" in its "appearance, contents, substance, internal patterns, or other distinctive characteristics, taken in conjunction with circumstances." Fed. R. Evid. 901(b)(4).

In fact, it is standard practice to use this method to authenticate some kinds of evidence which may now be digitally created, stored, and reproduced. For example, attorneys offering photographs into evidence invariably just ask a "witness with knowledge" (under Fed. R. Evid. 901(b)(1)) whether a particular photo is "a fair and accurate representation" of something or someone.

But should the process of authenticating photographs recognize that, with the advent of digital photography, it is now possible to alter an electronic image without leaving a trace? Consider the following example.

Agents and prosecutors were shown a photograph of a body — twisted on the floor, a gaping wound in the chest. Across the room, on the floor, was a large pistol. On the white wall above the victim's body, scrawled in the victim's own blood, were the words, "I'll kill again. You'll never catch me."

Unlike conventional photographs, however, this picture was not created with film, but with a digital camera. The entire picture was made up of binary digits, ones and zeros, which could be altered without detection. So two law enforcement agents, using commercially available software, started rearranging the digits. They "cleaned" the wall, removing the bloody words. They closed the chest wound, choosing instead to have blood trickling from the victim's temple. Last, they moved the gun into the victim's hand.

The case was now solved: the report would claim, and the photograph would "prove," the victim committed suicide. This was, of course, only a demonstration, which took place in the summer of 1991 at a meeting of the Federal Computer Investigations Committee. The Committee had been established by a handful of federal and state law enforcement personnel who were among the first to appreciate how emerging technologies were both providing new opportunities for criminals and creating new challenges for law enforcement officials.

For this group, the point of this demonstration was apparent: not only could ordinary photographs not be trusted in the same old way to be reliable, but an ordinary agent might be duped if he or she were not technologically astute enough to realize the potential for sophisticated digital alteration.

The key, of course, is that there is no negative, and the alteration leaves no tracks. Nor will these authenticity problems be limited to photographs. For example, some package delivery services now allow recipients to sign for their packages on a hand-held device which creates a digital copy of the recipient's signature. Although this makes it easy to transfer the information to a computer, it also enables the computer to recreate the signature.

If the hand-held device measures and records the pressure applied by the signer and if the computer reprints that signature with an ink-based printer, the computer-generated copy will look absolutely authentic — even to the author. Despite these examples, there will be many times when electronic evidence — whether photographs or documents — will indeed be identifiable based on distinctive characteristics alone.

An eyewitness can just as easily identify a digital photograph of a person as he could a conventional photo. The question for both judge and jury will be the witness's ability and veracity in observing and recalling the original person, photo, scene, or document with which he compares the in-court version. The fact that it is possible to alter a photo — for example, to extend the skid marks at an accident scene — is far less significant if the authenticating witness is independently sure from observing the site that the skid marks were, in fact, ten feet long.

Similarly, the recipient of a discarded electronic ransom note may recall the content of the original note well enough to authenticate a printout from the accused's computer. But to the extent that in-court photos or documents support incomplete or fading witness memories — or even substitute for witness memory altogether — lawyers must realize that "distinctive characteristics" in electronic evidence may be easy to alter, and may not, depending on the circumstances, satisfy a court.

What witness can independently verify the distinctive accuracy of long lists of names or numbers? Can he say that a digital photo is "a fair and accurate representation of a crime scene" in all details — no matter how minor they may have seemed at the time? While he will probably be able to remember whether there was a knife sticking out of a body, will he be able to verify the precise location of a shoe across the room?

An eyewitness who picked out the defendant at a line-up should be able to look at a photograph of the array and find the defendant again. But can she say for sure, when testifying at a hearing on defendant's motion to suppress an allegedly suggestive line-up, that all the other people in the picture are exactly as she saw them? Has there been no mustache added in this picture, no height or weight changed in any way? And although the recipient of a ransom note may well be able to recall the exact words of the note, will he recall the type face?

It is important to remember that the traditional process of authenticating an item through its uniqueness often carries an unspoken assumption that the thing — the murder weapon, the photo, or the letter, for example — is a package deal. It either is or is not the thing the witness remembers. Thus, if the witness can identify particular aspects of the item with certainty (such as the content of the ransom note), the other aspects (such as the type face) usually follow along without much debate.

Of course, there are times, even with conventional photography, when an authenticating witness will be asked about internal details:

"When you saw the crime scene at 5:30, were the shoes both on the right side of the room?" In those circumstances, attorneys and judges naturally tend to be more exacting in establishing that the witness can authenticate not only part of the package, but all the parts that matter. But with digital photography, this rather minor problem of authentication takes on a new life.

Depending on the way electronic evidence has been produced, stored, and reproduced, the collection of ones and zeros that constitutes the "package" of the photograph is infinitely and independently variable — not by moving shoes at the crime scene, but by changing any digits at any time before the exhibit photo is printed. Perhaps judges will find themselves admitting digital photographs and documents based on "distinctive characteristics" if a witness with knowledge can identify and authenticate the item in all relevant detail. But that, of course, requires a judge to know in advance which details will be relevant to the case and which are insignificant.

If the characteristic that makes the item distinctive is not the same one that makes it relevant, judges might and should be wary about admitting digital evidence in this way. Even if judges are satisfied, attorneys who cross examine an authenticating witness on minute details of digital photographs may affect the witness's credibility with the jury, especially if the attorney shows how easily the evidence could be altered.

One of the potential solutions to this problem which arises from the nature of electronic evidence may actually be electronic: digital signatures. The Digital Signature Standard, proposed by the National Institute of Standards and Technology (NIST) in the Department of Commerce, would allow authors to encrypt their documents with a key known only to them. Assuming the author has not disclosed his password to others, this identifying key could serve as a sort of electronic evidence seal. In that event, the signature would be just the kind of distinctive characteristic the rules already recognize.

For the time being, however, most computer evidence can still be altered electronically — in dramatic ways or in imperceptible detail — without any sign of erasure. But this does not mean that electronic evidence, having become less distinctive, has become any less admissible. It simply may require us to authenticate it in other ways.

2. Chain of Custody

When prosecutors present evidence to a court, they must be ready to show that the thing they offer is the same thing the agents seized. When that evidence is not distinctive but fungible (whether little bags of cocaine, bullet shell casings, or electronic data), the "process or system" [to use the language of Fed. R. Evid. 901(b)(9)] which authenticates the item is a hand-to-hand chain of accountability.

Although courts generally have allowed any witness with knowledge to authenticate a photograph without requiring the photographer to testify, that may not suffice for digital photos.

Indeed, judges may now demand that the proponent of a digital picture be ready to establish a complete chain of custody — from the photographer to the person who produced the printout for trial. Even so, the printout itself may be a distinctive item when it bears the authenticator's initials, or some other recognizable mark. If the photographer takes a picture, and then immediately prints and initials the image that becomes an exhibit, the chain of custody is just that simple. But if the exhibit was made by another person or at a later time, the proponent should be ready to show where the data has been stored and how it was protected from alteration.

3. Electronic Processing of Evidence

When data goes into computers, there are many methods and forms for getting it out. To the extent that computers simply store information for later retrieval, a data printout may qualify as an original document under Fed. R. Evid. 1001(3). Where the computer has merely acted as a technological file cabinet, advocates must be ready to authenticate the in-court version of the document as genuine, but the evidentiary issues (at least those connected to the computer) do not pertain to the substance or content of the document.

But in many cases, attorneys want to introduce evidence that the computer has not only stored, but has also processed in some fashion. If the computer, its operating system, and its applications software have reorganized the relevant information — by comparing, calculating, evaluating, re-grouping, or selectively retrieving — this processing has altered at least the form of the information, and probably the substance as well. The fact that the computer has changed, selected, or evaluated data naturally does not make the resulting product inadmissible, but it does require another analytical step.

The computer processing itself often creates a new meaning, adds new information — which is really the equivalent of an implicit statement. If an advocate wishes to introduce this processed product, he usually offers it for the truth of the conclusion it asserts. For example, when the telephone company compiles raw data into a phone bill for a subscriber, the bill is literally a statement: "The following long distance calls (and no others) were placed from your phone to these numbers on these days and times."

If the computer has created a hearsay statement by turning raw evidence into processed evidence, its proponent should be ready to show that the process is reliable. Computers process data in many different ways by running programs, which can be commercially or privately written. Any of these programs can contain logical errors, called "bugs," which could significantly affect the accuracy of the computer process.

And even if there is no error in the code, a technician may run the program in a way that creates a false result. For example, a particular computer search program may be "case sensitive," which means that the upper- and lower-case versions of any given letter are not interchangeable. If an author working in WordPerfect (a popular word-processing program), searches a document for the word "Evidence," the computer will not find the word "evidence," because the letter "e" was not capitalized.

What does it mean, then, when the computer reports that the word was "not found"? Under what circumstances should a computer's conclusion be admissible in court? Consider a failure-to-file tax case. If a prosecutor asks the IRS to search its databanks to see whether a taxpayer filed a return in a particular year, the IRS may give her two very different products.

If the taxpayer filed electronically, the IRS can produce either an original document from its computers (a printout of the filing) or an admissible duplicate in the form of an electronic copy. In that case, the IRS computers simply acted as storage cabinets to hold and reproduce the information that was entered by the taxpayer. Tax return in; tax return out.

But if, on the other hand, the IRS searches its databanks and finds nothing, the IRS's negative report is clearly a hearsay statement which results from a computer process — the electronic search for the taxpayer's tax return. The hearsay rule (Fed. R. Evid. 803(10)) allows the absence of a public record to be shown by testimony "that diligent search failed to disclose the record ... ."

But testimony in what form? Will the negative computer report suffice, or should the technician who ran the search testify? Must the technician explain not only what keystrokes he entered to conduct the search, but also establish the error-free logic of the program he used? Must he know not only that the program searches for both lower- and upper-case versions of the taxpayer's name, but also exactly how it accomplishes that task?

While the absence of a record is often admitted in evidence, prosecutors can expect that as attorneys become more computer-literate, defense counsel will raise new challenges in this area. Indeed, the accuracy or inaccuracy of the IRS's negative report rests on many different components, including the reliability (both human and technical) of the computer process.

Certainly, the mathematical validity of any program is a question of fact — a question which the opponent of a piece of processed evidence should have an opportunity at some point to explore and to contest. Similarly, the methods and safeguards involved in executing the program must also be fair ground for analysis and challenge. While it would clearly be both unnecessary and bur-densome to prove every step of a computer process in every case, courts must also be ready to look behind these processes when the facts warrant.

As lawyers and judges learn more about all the variables involved in creating evidence through computer processing, this area may become a new battleground for technical experts.

D. The Hearsay Rule

Most agents and prosecutors are familiar with the business records exception to the hearsay rule. Fed. R. Evid. 803(6). Generally speaking, any "memoran-dum, report, record, or data compilation" (1) made at or near the time of the event, (2) by, or from information transmitted by, a person with knowledge, is admissible if the record was kept in the course of a regularly conducted business activity, and it was the regular practice of that business activity to make the record.

A business computer's processing and rearranging of digital information is often part of a company's overall practice of recording its regularly conducted activity. Information from telephone calls, bank transactions, and employee time sheets is regularly processed, as a fundamental part of the business, into customer phone bills, bank account statements, and payroll checks. Logic argues that if the business relies on the accuracy of the computer process, the court probably can as well.

This is different, however, from using a company's raw data (collected and stored in the course of business, perhaps) and electronically processing it in a new or unusual way to create an exhibit for trial. For example, banks regularly process data to show each account-holder's transactions for the month, and most courts would readily accept that monthly statement as a qualifying business record. But may a court presume a similar regularity when the same bank runs a special data search for all checks paid from the account-holder's account over the past year to an account in Switzerland?

In this case, even though the report was not made at or near the time of the event, the document is probably admissible as a summary under Fed. R. Evid. 1006. That rule allows courts to admit a "chart, summary, or calculation" as a substitute for "voluminous writing, recordings, or photographs." None-theless, other parties still have the right to examine and copy the unabridged original data, and to challenge the accuracy of the summary. Of course, this also opens the way to challenges of any computer process which created the summary.

In most other respects, of course, the hearsay rule operates with computer evidence exactly as it does with any other sort of evidence. For instance, statements for purposes of medical treatment, vital statistics, or statements against interest may all qualify as exceptions to the hearsay rule, whether they are oral, written, or electronic. Clearly, an electronic statement against interest must also be authenticated properly, but it does not fail as hearsay.

Conversely, a correctly authenticated electronic message may contain all sorts of hearsay statements for which there are no exceptions. The key is that computer evidence is no longer limited to business records, and the cases that carry that assumption are distinguishable when advocates work with other kinds of electronic evidence. But even with business records, a trial lawyer well versed in the technological world who knows how to ask the right questions may find that the "method or circumstances of preparation indicate lack of trustworthi-ness," under Fed. R. Evid. 803(6), to such a degree that a court will sustain, or at least consider, a challenge to the admissibility of the evidence.

Computers and their products are not inherently reliable, and it is always wise to ask, in any particular case, what computers do and how they do it.

This discussion is probably the most clear and concise I have seen with regards to evidence. It is also, to some degree, at least, authoritative. For example, while the *Guidelines* themselves are only guidelines — in other words, they don't have the force of law — the cites in this section of the document that refer to the Federal Rules of Evidence are the rules of the court. If you follow these guidelines in collecting and preserving your evidence, you won't go far wrong.

INTERROGATING AND INTERVIEWING WITNESSES

From time to time, thus far in this book, we have alluded to "old-fashioned police work" as a key part of the investigative process. While all of these technical procedures are important and useful, most incidents are performed by people. At the end of the day, it's to the people we must go. People can tell us what happened. People can help us rule out natural occurrences. And, people can point a finger at a possible suspect.

Getting answers from people is both an art and a science. As a starting point, forget everything you've seen on TV crime shows regarding the interview process. For example, it has been well established that the "bad cop/good cop" approach, so popular in films, is a very bad idea. Also, remember that you will interview many different types of people with entirely different approaches to the incident. Some will see it from a technical perspective, while others will see the events from the viewpoint of a user. Still others will take a management approach. Your objective, in interviews, is to collect information. It is not, at this point, to judge it.

There are two phases to the questioning process: interview and interrogation. They are very different in objective, technique, and timing. When we are gathering evidence, we use the *interview* process. When an interviewee becomes a suspect, we switch to *interrogation*. Interrogation is best left to experienced investigators, usually from law enforcement. There are several reasons for this.

First, once an individual becomes a suspect, you will have some decisions to make. Will you turn the suspect over to the police? Will your organization take civil action? Is there organized labor involved? How about protection of the suspect's civil rights and rights to privacy? For the inexperienced investigator, entering into a formal interrogation is entering into a murky and potentially dangerous territory.

However, even within the private sector, there are very experienced interrogators. Professional fraud investigators found in larger corporate audit departments, for example, are usually trained and experienced in interrogation. These individuals know how far they can go without treading on the suspect's rights and endangering their investigation. We'll touch on interrogation techniques in a moment, but let's start with plain, simple interviewing.

The goal of the interview is to obtain information about the incident that can help each of us in our objective of accurate recreation. We want to know when the incident occurred, what happened, and why the interviewee knows his or her facts to be accurate. Remember, most interviewees will have been working at the time of the incident. They will have had other things on their minds. As witnesses, they will be, if history is a good teacher, somewhat unreliable as individuals in their recollections. Never stop at one interview. You will need as much corroborating information as you can get to put together a clear picture of the event.

David Zulawski and Douglas Wicklander, writing in *Practical Aspects of Interview and Interrogation* give us a seven-stage approach to interview and interrogation:[3]

1. Preparation and strategy
2. Interviewing
3. Establishing credibility

4. Reducing resistance
5. Obtaining an admission
6. Developing the admission
7. Professional close

We will discuss each of these briefly, with an emphasis on the private sector. In the private sector, the interviewer is less constrained by many of the rules incumbent upon public sector investigators. For example, the corporate investigator does not have to "read the suspect his or her Miranda rights" when the confrontation moves from interview to interrogation. This does not mean, of course, that the corporate investigator can trample upon the rights of the suspect, violate his or her privacy, or harass the individual to get a confession. In fact, the softer the corporate investigator walks, the easier it will be to pursue the case as a criminal matter, if it ever comes to that.

Another point I should emphasize now is the order of an investigation. The thorough investigator does not begin the process of developing a suspect until he or she has completed enough of the fact-gathering to be fairly certain that the suspect is, indeed, a real suspect. Gather the technical facts, interview witnesses, develop your hypothesis, and test it before you go off half-cocked. Making a false accusation, which results in embarrassment or damage to the suspect, can cost your organization seriously if the wrongly accused individual decides to sue. Now, on to the interview/interrogation process.

PREPARATION AND STRATEGY

The goal of this phase of the interview process is to ensure that you get the most out of your interviews. At this point, you may or may not have a suspect. If you do, you may be starting the process of developing an admission of wrongdoing. If not, you will be gathering facts from witnesses.

Before you start the interview process in earnest, collect as many technical facts as you can. Simply walking up to the employee who discovered the incident and asking "What happened?" is not an interview. It may, however, add considerably to your overall knowledge of the facts. You should get as many of these first impressions as you can, and you should get them as early and informally as possible. When the investigator has just arrived on the scene, the event is fresh in everyone's mind and their guards are down. You'll usually get good, although occasionally emotional, quick first impressions. Note these down for use in later interviews and as guidelines for further technical follow-up.

Once you have collected enough evidence to give you a good picture of what happened, start planning who you'll interview. Never conduct an interview without first preparing for it, and avoid interviewing people who you are certain can't add to your body of information. I like to interview supervisors and other senior people fairly early in the process. This allows me to get a good picture of which "worker bees" may have useful knowledge and information for me. Some of these employees will be technical, such as system administrators, who can help me to understand, quickly, the topology and other technical details surrounding the system I'm investigating. They can also point out possible alternative explanations to the conclusion that a crime took place.

Avoid interviewing more than one individual at a time. Keep the information you collect private so that interviewees and potential suspects can't compare notes and concoct matching stories. Conduct your interviews in pairs. One person conducts the interview while the other acts as an observer. Avoid taking notes in an interview, unless you must write down technical information. Make your notes immediately following the interview, out of view of the interviewee. What you find important enough to write down is nobody's business but yours and your fellow investigators. After the interview, both interviewers should compile their notes and then compare them to ensure that nothing important was left out.

Make sure that you have collected your background information, both on the incident and the interviewee. Zulawski and Wicklander suggest that the interviewers have a copy of the case file at each interview. There are two reasons for this. A folder full of paper suggests to the interviewee that there is already information developed about the incident. Second, any notes the interviewer will require should be available without either interviewer having to leave the room, interrupting the flow of the interview.

There are psychological aspects to the interview as well. For example, interviewees will respond better, especially to sensitive questions, if they feel that they are in a private setting. Some investigators actually move closer to the interviewee and lower their voices when asking sensitive questions. In any event, the location for the interview should be such that there are no interruptions or distractions. The locale should not be threatening to the interviewee. Offices, for example, often are less threatening than conference rooms. Smaller conference rooms are less threatening than larger ones, and so on.

Next, consider the role of the interviewer. Zulawski and Wicklander describe the interviewer as a "confident negotiator." If we consider this definition, we can see that it is quite accurate. The interviewer is negotiating for information. At the extreme, he or she is negotiating for an admission of guilt from a suspect.

The negotiating process is always best carried out by a confident, knowledgeable neutral party. That is the role you, as an interviewer, should take. Your preparation makes you knowledgeable. The fact that you only are after the truth (even if it means that no incident actually occurred — the event was natural) makes you neutral, and your experience and training should help make you confident. However, just to keep the law of averages on your side, you will arrange the interview/interrogation to your advantage. That means you will take whatever steps are required to keep it professional, void of distractions, and conducive to obtaining the information you need to complete the investigation.

The interviewer is also a salesperson. You are selling an opportunity for the interviewee to offer true information. At the extreme, you are selling a suspect on the benefits of confessing to the incident. Like most sales techniques, high pressure usually does not work as well as quiet confident persuasion.

I have participated in many interviews with law enforcement personnel in my role as a technical advisor to my clients. In every case, the competent interviewer has matched my technical style, stuck to a line of questioning that was intended to extract as many technical details as possible, with no hint of what the interviewer thought was important. The investigators have always been polite, never intimidating, and have always worked in pairs. I have always been encouraged to begin by relating the story in my own way, before the investigators started digging for information I may have left out. I have never felt pressured, but I have always recalled details during the interview that I left out of my broad description of the incident. A good interviewer, through preparation and good interview techniques, will usually develop a fuller picture by the end of the interview.

Since the interviewee must always make a decision as to whether or not to tell what they know (similar to a customer's buying decision in a sales situation), it is up to the interviewer to "sell" the benefits of revealing information. In my case, it's usually an easy sale. But, it can depend upon what the client wishes to keep confidential; in that case, I always refer the investigator to someone at my client with the authority to discuss the matter. For some interviewees, however, there may be conflicts due to friendship, loyalty to a supervisor, fear of becoming too deeply involved, or actual guilt. The interviewer must "sell around" these objections.

Finally, another word about note taking. Note taking not only offers the interviewee an insight into what you feel is important, or what you may not have known up to that point, it interferes with the development of rapport between the subject and the investigator. For that reason, most experienced interviewers keep note taking to a minimum. However, you will need to note accurately who was present at the interview, ensuring correct spelling of names and accurate addresses, or work locations and phone numbers. Get this information at the end of the interview to avoid "putting the interviewee off" at the beginning.

As part of your preplanning, you should consider what you expect to get from the interview. Make some notes about areas you want to cover. Set some goals. One of the best fraud investigators I know never goes into an interview, no matter how brief, without the whole flow of the interview mapped out. He knows why he is interviewing the subject, what he hopes to learn, what he already knows, what he wishes to confirm, and all of the previously learned details that could impact the interview. He even has a list of suggested questions.

It is important, as you plan your line of questioning, to disguise key questions. Making them obvious may cause a suspect, or an individual with knowledge he or she wishes to hide, to avoid giving truthful or complete answers. I generally insert this type of question into the flow of the interview surrounded by similar, but meaningless, questions. I also ask, a second time, these important questions in different ways to ensure I got the same answer the first time.

THE INTERVIEW

Once the interview has started, our biggest task is to help the interviewee cooperate with us. There are a couple of things we can do to help this along. First, we can minimize the impact of an answer by offering face-saving explanations or support. For example, we might have discovered that a system administrator did not have adequate logging turned on at the time of the incident. There are two or more possible reasons for this. First, it may have been an oversight, perfectly innocent, but lacking in the competence required of an experienced system administrator. The other possibility, of course, is that the sysadmin was involved in the incident and masked his or her involvement by shutting off the logs.

We might offer the administrator a rationalization when we ask about the logs. We must use care, of course, to avoid offering an excuse. A rationalization may be offered, if we are fairly certain the administrator was in error and is holding out in fear of losing his or her job due to incompetence. We might offer that logs often take up a great many resources. Sometimes limiting logging improves performance. Never give the subject a way to escape the truth — just make it easier to be truthful.

There are many methods the interviewer can use to establish rapport with the interview subject. Rapport is very important and should be established as early in the interview as possible. Most experienced interviewers agree that good rapport between the interviewer and the subject is crucial in getting good results. They also agree that a heavy-handed interviewer, one who imposes his or her authority, will be less successful than one who works with the subject to establish some common ground with which the interviewee is comfortable.

How do you know that you have established a good rapport with your interview subject? One way is *mirroring*. Look at your subject. He or she may be performing similar actions to you. Your subject may be sitting like you are. This is called mirroring. Psychologists who study body language — also called *neurolinguistics* — agree that when mirroring occurs between two people, they have established a good rapport. When you have passed this first phase, the next step should be to allow the interviewee to tell, in his or her own words, what happened. While it is a good idea to encourage this narrative description, by nodding your head or asking what happened next, the interviewer should interrupt as little as possible.

The next step in the interview process is to return to the beginning of the narrative and go through parts that require more detail. This is called *leading the interview*. The interviewer, who now has the general picture from the subject's initial story, goes back to the beginning and, through questioning, develops the details he or she feels are pertinent. Remember, during this part of your interview, you will want to mask important details so the interviewee won't know what is and isn't important to you.

ESTABLISHING CREDIBILITY

This phase occurs when the interview becomes an interrogation. As a corporate investigator, you may or may not be involved at this point. If you are, however, your subject has passed from witness to suspect. At this point you must impress upon the suspect that the investigation is serious business, and that you have established enough evidence to consider the subject a suspect.

It is important that you not attempt this part of the investigation — moving from witness to suspect — until you have firmly established that the facts point to the individual as a suspect. There are two reasons for this. First, you cannot get an admission from the suspect as long as he or she believes you are "fishing." You must clearly communicate to the suspect that the investigation has uncovered incontrovertible facts that establish this individual as the perpetrator.

Second, as you will see later in this book, you may be faced with a cover-up. In this case, your facts must speak for themselves, or you will never establish your case. At its worst, a cover-up will manifest as a stated position that no incident ever occurred — the event was a natural failure of the computer. I have experienced at least one investigation that took that turn and I can say, without equivocation, that it is not a pleasant position to be in.

REDUCING RESISTANCE

It's one thing to know a suspect performed an intrusion, or other computer security incident. It is quite another to induce the suspect to admit that he or she did it. The most satisfactory conclusion to an investigation is an admission. Thus, the interrogator must reduce the suspect's resistance until he or she admits to the incident.

Interestingly, an old Shakespearean statement, "... me thinks she doth protest too much," is appropriate here. Upon making an accusation, the interrogator may be faced with an emphatic denial, followed by an explanation. The emphatic denial may take the form of "You must be crazy; I didn't mail-bomb that server!" And possibly followed by, "Why would I do that? It's my server — I administrate it. I wouldn't mail-bomb my own server." In this case, it's a pretty good bet that you've found your culprit.

Experienced investigators have found that truly innocent people don't usually respond quite so vehemently. However, when they do, their vehemence remains, becoming more emphatic with time. Following a strong statement of denial, with an explanation of why it couldn't have happened, is, usually, a giveaway that you have the right person. Innocent suspects will become more and more emphatic, offering few explanations beyond the declaration that they "didn't do it."

If you are faced with an emphatic response, as described above, you must reduce the suspect's resistance to admission. One good way is to offer a rationalization that the suspect can use to justify, at least in his or her own mind, the action that resulted in the incident. For example, you might, as in the incident above, offer, "If I'd had to work as hard as you without a promotion, I probably would want to let the company know how I felt. I bet a mail bomb would get across to them that it takes a lot of effort to protect this network."

This offers the suspect a rationalization and minimizes, in his or her mind, the impact of the incident. Any justification, especially one which you appear to support, also has the effect of reducing the threat of consequences. If you begin to see that this approach is bearing fruit, you are entering the next phase.

OBTAINING THE ADMISSION

When a subject is getting ready to confess to an incident, he or she will undergo a noticeable change in behavior and demeanor. Denials will stop and the suspect may become somewhat withdrawn. He or she has decided that the game is over and admission is the only thing left. Now it's up to you to follow through and obtain the admission.

One technique for obtaining the admission, at this point, is to offer a choice of motives. One motive is likely to be unacceptable to society at large, while the other represents an acceptable rationalization. For example, following our mail bombing above, you might ask the suspect, "Did you mail-bomb the server to destroy it and get even with the company, or simply to demonstrate the importance of protecting the system?" I had an incident of e-mail forgery where the suspect, upon hearing of the investigation, telephoned me with a confession. His rationalization, which I encouraged, was that he wanted to demonstrate that the company was vulnerable to forged e-mail.

DEVELOPING THE ADMISSION

Once you have obtained the admission, you need to pursue the details. You will want to establish the true details of the incident — how it was accomplished, the vulnerabilities exploited, tools used, etc. — so that you can appropriately adjust your technical understanding. Occasionally, you may find that the pieces, as previously thought to be understood, don't fit the admission at all. This may mean you have a lot more investigating to do. You may also use this opportunity to develop leads involving other incidents or other people involved in the particular one under investigation.

To develop the admission, you need to stick as close to the facts as possible. Avoid being judgmental and, above all, avoid reminding the suspect of the consequences of his or her actions. Your only goal at this point is to develop all of the details so your conclusion will be as accurate as possible, and that, should you wish to take either criminal or civil action, you have a sufficient level of detail to win your case.

You may experience a reversal on the part of the suspect. He or she may decide that you really don't have enough to prove involvement in the incident. Now is the time to trot out your evidence. You should avoid revealing any evidence earlier because the subject will expend his or her efforts refuting it. If the suspect reaches a point where he or she is willing to admit only a portion of what you know was done, your evidence can be persuasive. In sales terms, you are providing proof to counter an objection. Still, don't, as a master salesman once told me, "put all your cookies on the table at once." A small tidbit of evidence can show you have the proof and can get the admission back on track. When this happens, go back, briefly, over the admission and, reinforcing it as necessary, continue to the professional close.

THE PROFESSIONAL CLOSE

In a criminal proceeding, a written statement by the suspect is part of the normal process. If you, as a corporate investigator, obtain an admission, it may make sense to get it in writing in the form of a statement. There are two basic types of statements: formal and informal. Informal statements, acceptable in most cases, are narratives in the suspect's own words and handwriting. However, if you are anticipating a major civil or criminal proceeding, you may want to call in a stenographer to take down the statement and witness the suspect's signature. Often, the interrogator will take down the statement during the development of the admission and simply have the suspect sign it. Be sure you have the signature witnessed by a third party. Also — and this is very important — never allow anything to occur that could point to coercion. Make sure that the suspect includes a statement that clearly indicates the confession was not coerced and was of his or her free will. Otherwise, the statement and, likely, the whole investigation will be thrown out of court.

Statements can also be audio or video recordings. Make sure, if you use electronic methods to capture the statement, the subject knows he or she is being recorded and agrees to it. If you record the entire interview, an additional, signed statement is probably not necessary, as long as the recording contains the subject's acknowledgment of and acquiescence to the recording. Statements can be important, not just to a criminal or civil proceeding, but to insurance companies investigating payment for a loss, or during termination or disciplinary actions.

Another important warning: although the interrogator must continue to maintain control over the process, he or she must never dictate the statement. Thus, in addition to a statement that the confession was not coerced, it is important that it's in the subject's own words. There are, generally, five parts in a written statement: introduction, total admission, substantiation of the admission, voluntariness of the admission, and signature and error corrections.

The introduction identifies who is making the statement; the total admission says that the suspect admits to performing the incident; the substantiation gives the details; and the voluntariness covers the issues of coercion and that the statement is in the subject's own words. The signature and error corrections include any other voluntary statements the subject may wish to make, correction of any erroneous statements, and the signatures of the subject and witnesses. Each page of the statement should be numbered as number X of Y pages, and each page should be initialed by the subject.

If the interview does not result in an admission, or, indeed, even an interrogation (as is the case with most witnesses), the professional close is when the interviewer collects correct names, spellings of names, and methods of contact. He or she should also ask the interviewee if there is anything he or she would like to add. Always thank the subject for his or her cooperation as you terminate the interview/interrogation.

DEVELOPING AND TESTING AN INTRUSION HYPOTHESIS

We have touched on the intrusion hypothesis several times. Now we'll dig a bit deeper into this part of your investigation. Not all investigators use this approach. I have found it very useful, because it not only helps me develop a better picture of how the incident occurred; it helps me to see possible alternative explanations. Later in the investigation, it even offers a test bed for other people's theories.

I once had an investigation that resulted in a cover-up. Every time I posed an explanation as to how the incident occurred, I was told that the incident was not a security incident and what really happened was a natural failure of a Unix host.

Because I had the ability to test each of these proffered explanations (there were several over a period of a few months), I was able to refute each one, simply because, in the test situation, they didn't produce the same results as the incident. We now maintain a test lab for just this purpose.

As you begin to collect evidence, begin to think in terms of how the incident occurred. You should, by this stage in your investigation, have physical or *bit-stream* images of the relevant computers. You can restore those images to your test computer(s) and begin to gather evidence, as discussed in Chapter 7. You have another benefit, however. These test machines are an accurate representation of the computers involved in the incident. You can recreate the incident exactly as it happened and may be able to associate one or more individuals with it, either as suspects or witnesses.

Your next step is to take information collected from witnesses and your test bench version of the affected computers and begin to consider how the event occurred. By piecing together your evidence and witness statements, you should arrive at a hypothesis of what really happened. Now, if possible, make it happen again, this time on your test bed. Observe carefully the results of your tests. Were they the same as in the incident? If not, how did they differ? Why? What can you do to make them the same? Is there a possible alternative explanation? Try it and see if it works.

Because the test computer(s) is/are mirrors of those actually involved, you should be able to recreate the events of the incident exactly. Be complete in documenting your setups, tests, and results. You may have to testify about them in court. Also — and this is some of the best advice I can give you here — make sure that your opposition can repeat your setup and tests and get exactly the same results. This is called *repeatability* and it is crucially important in any legal proceeding.

INVESTIGATING ALTERNATIVE EXPLANATIONS

Did the event represent a security incident? Or did it simply represent a failing machine? We clear almost as many people in our investigations as we catch. We had an investigation of a system administrator who was accused of causing a computer to fail (see "The Case of the CAD/CAM Cad" in Chapter 9) so that his friend, who owned a service shop, could fix it and charge the company extra, above their current contract. The subsequent investigation showed that there was a probable alternative explanation and the administrator was cleared.

Alternative explanations are often offered, especially where there is a cover-up. They also are offered where a key party in the investigation has been negligent and wants to protect him- or herself from actions by the boss. I view alternative expla-nations with mixed emotions. If I have done my homework, and developed and tested a good intrusion hypothesis, my initial reaction is there are no other expla-nations. Thirty-two years in high technology, however, tells me differently. There are always possible alternative explanations, and, as ethical investigators, we are compelled to consider them.

There is really only one reliable way to accept or refute an alternative explana-tion: test it. To do this credibly, you must perform your tests on a mirror of the affected computer. Never try to hypothesize a rebuttal without testing. The result will be a "he says/she says." You will find yourself engaged in a battle of the experts. In these battles, the expert with the most [_____] — experience, degrees, cases, friends, fill in the blank — wins.

The way around this obviously political dilemma is to present facts. Facts have one overriding characteristic: they are reproducible. This means the opposition can perform your tests and get exactly the same results. They also, because you are working on a mirror image, must accept that the conditions are the same as those that existed at the time of the incident.

Interestingly, however, this type of testing occasionally does produce the conclusion that the event was not a security incident. In this case, by determining the facts early in your investigation, you have probably saved your company or client a fist-full of money.

YOU MAY NEVER CATCH THE CULPRIT

It's a sad fact of computer security incident investigation: we often can't bring it to a conclusion. There are many causes for this problem:

- The trail is cold — too much time has passed since the incident and there is no evidence.
- Logging was incomplete or nonexistent.
- The investigation cost more than the loss, and there was no point in continuing.
- The universe of possible perpetrators was too large (such as the Internet) and the event occurred only once, leaving little or no evidence.
- The event was inconclusive — it may or may not have been a security incident.
- You can't conclusively point to a suspect.
- You don't have enough evidence to prove your case beyond a reasonable doubt.
- Political pressure stops the investigation.
- Cover-up.

If you are faced with one of these, or any other reason why your investigation must stop short of success, accept it. Law enforcement often is faced with failed computer crime investigations. The FBI estimates that fewer than 1% of all computer crimes are successfully prosecuted (e.g., the perpetrator goes to jail). Part of the reason for this low figure is that most crimes are never reported. That's corporate political pressure at work. Part of it is that computer crimes are tedious and expensive to investigate, and you may come down to one difficult fact: you can prove that the event emanated from a particular attack computer, but you can't place the suspect at the computer at the time of the crime, beyond a reasonable doubt.

You can do all you can to collect your evidence and prove your case, but there is a fact of corporate life: most organizations do not have the will to expose themselves to the potential consequences of prosecuting someone for a computer-related crime. We'll discuss this in much more detail when we discuss the politics of computer crime in Chapter 11.

Don't be discouraged, however. Investigation techniques are improving daily. The competitive edge that organizations gain through their information management systems is becoming ever more important. And many more companies are developing a "zero tolerance" for computer crimes against them.

DAMAGE CONTROL AND CONTAINMENT

When a computer security incident occurs, there is an important step in your launch that we haven't discussed: dealing with the aftermath. I investigated a case where a disgruntled employee used a corporate computer to attack the file server at a credit union related to his employer. He had been the system administrator of the server and had left the bank under a cloud. Apparently, he decided to get even by attacking the server. After we had completed our investigation, which included forensic examination of the attack computer, we were tasked with ensuring that the event could not be repeated. We performed a full suite of tests against the server and "hardened" it against further security incidents.

This step — I call it the "clean up" — is critical. Every computer security incident is enabled by a vulnerability in the victim system that the attacker is able to exploit. Far from being a case of closing the barn door after the horses have left, the clean up ensures that the incident won't occur again. Of course, it would be best if we could have performed the clean up in advance — and that is what information protection is all about — but, in today's computing environment, there is virtually no chance that you can do so with 100% certainty.

The fact is if you have something worth attacking, and a skilled, determined attacker decides to go after it, they will. And, unfortunately, they will probably succeed. All you can do at that point is to close the hole and go on operating. You will, of course, usually be able to restore damaged files from backups. You may be able to determine what, if any, files were stolen. Or you will be able to attempt to catch the bad guy (or girl, as the case may be). But what is most important — more important than catching the perpetrator — is preventing a recurrence.

Thus, part of your business continuity plan must be a process for recovering from all potential consequences of an attack on your information systems. These processes should include everything from virus attacks, to mail bombs, to data theft. You should also periodically rehearse your procedures to ensure that they can be performed. Finally, you should conduct periodic tiger team attacks against your own systems to ensure that you are secure from attack, to the extent practical, and that when an attack succeeds, you have a response mechanism.

SUMMARY

In this chapter we started off the process of investigating a security incident. We discussed the aspects of the investigation launch, including evidence gathering, interviewing, and hypothesis testing. In the next chapter, we'll move on to the second phase: incident analysis. Our first task will be to determine if an incident actually occurred. Then we will use our tools to analyze information gathered as evidence. We'll go deeper into forensics and we'll examine an arcane aspect of Unix analysis: crash dump analysis. We'll show you some of the log analysis tools we discussed in Chapter 7, and discuss how to maintain crime scene integrity. We'll wrap up the chapter with two interesting case studies.

REFERENCES

1. *U.S. Department of Justice Federal Guidelines for Searching and Seizing Computers — Preface.*
2. *U.S. Department of Justice Federal Guidelines for Searching and Seizing Computers — Evidence.*
3. Zulawski, D. E. and Wicklander, D. E., *Practical Aspects of Interview and Interrogation*, CRC Press, Boca Raton, FL, 1994.

9 Determining If a Crime Has Taken Place

In this chapter, we'll tackle the most difficult question you'll have to answer during the course of your investigation: "Is the 'event' really a security *incident*?" As you will see, often a purely benign (though, perhaps, disastrous in its effects) event is mistaken for a security incident. Even if the event really does represent a crime, there is a better-than-even chance that you will be challenged to prove it, because cover-ups are fairly common.

We'll discuss how to determine that a crime has taken place, what you should do as first steps to ensure you lose no evidence, and the technical details of analyzing evidence. You'll notice that we are going over some old territory in this chapter. However, we are going over it in more depth than in earlier chapters. Experience has shown that, because of the evidence issues attached to this type of work, we need to reemphasize basic concepts, and then build on them over the course of the book, rather than dump the whole thing in your lap at once.

We'll also cover a gray area: Internet abuse. Internet abuse is a very important area for corporations because the explosion of Internet connections has unleashed many opportunities for employee abuse. Abuses range from excessive browsing, which wastes productive work time, to use of company resources to visit pornography sites. Easy access to e-mail often tempts employees to use corporate mail as if it were their own. I heard, recently, of an employee running a private business from his employer's corporate e-mail system.

While these abuses don't, usually, constitute a crime, they are likely violations of corporate policy and should be handled accordingly. In this chapter we'll discuss those "non-crime" abuses and show how to deal with them.

STATISTICALLY, YOU PROBABLY DON'T HAVE A CRIME

There is a better-than-even chance that your incident does not represent a crime. Many computer incidents are, actually, little more than normal day-to-day occurrences. For example, many computers, as they are failing, behave as if they are being attacked. Often, it is very difficult to distinguish between a denial of service attack and a failing hard drive.

I have investigated many computer security "incidents," only to find that they represented little more than a failing, aging hard drive. It is critical, if for no other reason than to avoid embarrassment, that you be absolutely certain that a crime has taken place. Unfortunately, there will be people who have a vested interest in representing any incident as a crime. Equally unfortunate, there will also be those who want to cover up every incident, whether it is a crime or not. It will be up to you to make the determination, and then to ensure you can support your position with facts.

Out of the many incidents I have either observed or investigated, I would estimate that as many as 75% are benign in nature. The true incidents are relatively rare. Of the remaining 25%, a significant number, although representing a genuine security incident, are the result of error or poor judgment on the part of a well-meaning worker.

However, the relatively small percentage of genuine attacks tends to be of very high consequence and, often, represents a significantly larger problem than the incident itself. Fraud and abuse have always been with us. Today, computers and high-speed networks make fraud and abuse easier, faster, and less risky for the perpetrator. The bottom line is that you will need to make a determination, and that may not be easy.

In the topics that follow you'll see how to whittle away at the indications surrounding an event and carve out a final picture of what really happened. However, never forget that you, as an investigator, must remain objective and above the politics and emotions that accompany computer incidents.

In mid-1997, I was performing routine firewall testing for a client when he called and said he thought they had been penetrated. He wondered if it was me he was seeing. I told him it wasn't and made a few suggestions to help him determine if he was really under attack. First, I advised him to gather copies of all logs and change the root password to the machine under "attack," just in case the problem was real.

Next, I advised him to query all of the users who had root privileges. This included a contractor who maintained the system. Because the contractor might take some time to contact, I wanted to make sure that the host was not vulnerable while my client waited for a callback, in the event that the contractor was not available.

It turned out that the indications were completely benign and were explained by the contractor as the results of performing a recent upgrade to the operating system. The most the contractor was guilty of, in this case, was not cleaning up completely after the upgrade. By taking the steps I advised, my client was protected from further incidents if the event turned out to be real. And, he had the quickest way to determine if the event was benign in nature.

This approach represents the commonsense way to treat a suspicious event: take fast, reasonable precautions to preserve critical evidence, protect against further damage, and begin to determine if you have anything to investigate. If you can't eliminate the obvious rather quickly, start the investigative process in earnest.

BELIEVE YOUR INDICATIONS

I remember when I was a Navy technician, too many years back to admit to. I had a Chief Petty Officer for a boss who used to drive me crazy telling me to "believe my indications" when I was trouble-shooting a piece of electronic equipment. In subsequent years, I have worked on some very large networks and I can testify that his advice still applies.

In computer systems, as much as we'd like to believe to the contrary, nothing happens without a reason. We may not always understand the reason, or, even, know what it is. But there is always a reason. If we can figure it out, we'll solve the puzzle. The trouble is, equally, nothing in a computer system ever occurs in isolation. If there is one thing going wrong, there are, at least, ten more. Those ten mask each other and the one we think we know, as well.

A good example of this is the events surrounding the installation of an Internet gateway on an ISDN line in one of our offices. We bought a gateway device that consists of an analog modem, a firewall, a connection to an external ISDN modem, a four-port hub, and the software to administrate it. We connected the gateway to an analog line and the ISDN modem, as well as our internal network. It came up in minutes and connected to our service provider. The problem was that it only connected with a single ISDN channel.

Then, in a few days, it started to drop the carrier every three minutes or so. We pursued this through our service provider, his service provider, and the phone company. After the requisite finger-pointing, it was finally determined the phone company had a bad switch. They fixed the switch, which fixed our problem. But wait, as they say on late-night infomercials, there's more.

We no longer went down every three minutes; now we went down precisely every two hours and fifty minutes. More finger-pointing. Suddenly, a few days of trouble-shooting later, we started to drop frequently, but this time randomly. That is almost always a sign of line noise. Rather than believing the indication, the provider immediately assumed the telco was down again. When I switched from ISDN to analog, the problem persisted. I suggested that the problem might be a noise issue at the service provider. After a half hour of argument, he reluctantly agreed to switch me to another terminal server. Immediately the random dropouts stopped. Great! it was a noise problem. But, there's still more. For the next two hours and forty-nine minutes I was glued to the screen of our admin machine waiting for the gateway to drop (I had moved it back to the ISDN line by then).

But, strangely, the drop never happened. So the problem was, clearly, in the terminal server, even though there had also been a problem at the telco switch. Here we have an example of multiple problems that offered conflicting indications. However, if the service provider had performed the simple task of switching terminal servers when the second set of failures (after the telco fixed its switch), he would have avoided a lot of downtime. Because he had no other indications, and because the "telco is always at fault," he assumed it was the telco again.

There is no substitute, it's true, for solid experience. However, too much experience with a single incident can be confusing. Even if you have to draw a picture (I like pictures — they tend to make complicated issues clear) to understand what's happening, do it. Observe where similar indications might overlap and cause confusion. And, remember that the simplest explanation is, often, the correct one. In our example above the explanation was problems (multiple ones, perhaps) in a terminal server. Remember our earlier approach: eliminate the obvious first.

I usually look at each indication and note whether it can be caused by an attack, a benign occurrence, or both. If I have a number of indications that, taken individually, are more likely the result of an attack only, and very few that could be either an attack, or normal (even failures can be normal), or a combination, it's likely that I have a genuine event on my hands. Before I make a final pronouncement, however, I also examine if my attack indications taken together, or in combination with other indicators, might change to benign occurrences. Even then, until I solve the incident, I place percentages of likelihood on the probability of an attack.

I recall an incident where the investigator was absolutely positive that an attack from outside the firewall had caused the incident. He had, as you might imagine, the whole organization stirred up. He investigated for several months without being able to pin down the source. He was, however, unwavering in his assertion that the firewall had been breached. Imagine his embarrassment when he found that the system administrator had set him up by simulating the attack from the inside.

Worse, the investigator had more than enough information in logs to show that the attack came, not from the Internet, but from inside the secure network. Because he couldn't imagine that his "friends" in system administration might be playing a prank on him, he discounted the evidence and opted for the attack scenario.

USING TOOLS TO VERIFY THAT A CRIME HAS OCCURRED

Once you have decided an incident has occurred, and are on your way to deciding if it is benign or the result of an attack, you will need to count on a lot more objective evidence than your intuition (although that's an excellent starting point). The way to gather and analyze information is with a good set of tools. Some of those tools are the forensic utilities we discussed earlier. Some will be new to you.

Remember, we always begin as if a crime has occurred. That's a little like getting a haircut. You can always take some more off if the stylist doesn't cut it short enough. However, you can't put any back if it's too short. You can always lighten up on your investigation if you find it looks as if nothing has really happened. You can't go back to the pristine condition of a hard drive if you trample all over evidence residing on it. So, begin by using the seizure techniques we have already discussed.

Once you have the computer safely under your control and have made a disk image, start examining your evidence. From your intuition, you may have some suspicions. Others may have hypotheses that you can test. There may be multiple, possible explanations for the event's symptoms. Start by using the appropriate tools to test these hypotheses. For example, if you are looking for denial of service, you may want to look for file deletion or corruption. You may want to search for tools on the victim that could be used to cause the disruption. If the computer you are examining is suspected of causing the event, you should look for evidence that the computer connected to the victim. Copies of passwords, password crackers, or other tools may lead you to the evidence you need. You can use one of the NTI utilities to catalog the contents of the disk very quickly.

If you suspect that the attack came into the victim from the Internet, look for signs of a firewall breach. Use a log parser, such as ASAX (freeware) or ACL (Audit Control Language), to examine the firewall logs for anomalies. Use a sniffer to capture activity on your network associated with the victim machine. If you suspect that the user of either the victim or the attack computer has been visiting hacking sites on the Internet, or has downloaded hacking tools or a virus-infected program, use IPFilter, another NTI tool. Collect a list of all e-mail addresses, including FTP sites and URLs, visited from the computer, and the number of times they were visited.

Tools of this type, which help you determine if an incident is real or just a normal occurrence, fall into three categories:

- Tracing tools such as sniffers, TCP port monitors, event loggers, etc.
- Forensic tools, which you can use to examine a hard drive
- Log parsing tools

The purpose of each is to help you gather and examine evidence. At the end of the day, though, it's your analysis that will be the deciding factor. Your experience, common sense, and understanding of how the system you are investigating is supposed to work are what will allow you to focus on the facts and separate attacks from natural, though unpleasant, occurrences. The only tools that can make the determination are between your ears, not on your computer.

UNIX CRASH DUMP ANALYSIS

This is, perhaps, the most arcane topic in this entire book. Of all the causes, both benign and malignant, of incidents in Unix systems, system crashes, panics, and accompanying core dumps rank somewhere at the top of the list. Analyzing these events and determining their cause is a witch's brew of science, art, and sorcery. We'll spend a bit of time with the topic, but if you want a reference with excruciating detail I suggest you get a copy of *Panic! Unix System Crash Dump Analysis* by Chris Drake and Kimberly Brown.[1]

Let's begin with a couple of important points: security and a few definitions. Security first. When a Unix system crashes, it may create a *savecore* file. This file is an image of the system memory at the time of the crash. It is created to help specialists troubleshoot the cause of the crash. It may contain such things as passwords, even if the passwords are shadowed. The file is generated by the panic() function and the savecore command. The information in the file will, generally, center around the program that caused the panic. However, there may be (and often is) other data in memory that you would want to keep secure.

Master hackers have programs which are created for one purpose only: to cause a crash and harvest the resulting crash dump image. Some of these programs attempt to access password files and then crash the system in the process. The result usually is that the password file is captured in the crash dump image and can be processed by a password cracker. SunOS and Solaris systems are vulnerable to this type of attack.

When you investigate a suspicious series of system crashes, look for this type of tool. It will often be in the .tmp directory. Usually, hackers of this skill level will clean up well after themselves, leaving no residue of their tools. But, it never hurts to have a look, just in case the intruder got careless. More important, if your system starts crashing and you know for a fact that there has been an intruder in it, simply change the passwords, especially any superuser ones.

On the definition side of crash dump analysis, we'll begin by understanding what a *panic* is. All Unix computers panic. Panics are nothing more than immediate halts to the system when an event is about to occur that could cause damage. They are the result of the use of the panic() function in the operating system code.

This function cannot be used by an application programmer. So, our master hacker panics the system, not by inserting the panic() function in his or her code, but by exploiting a bug in the operating system that causes it to panic. The trick, from the hacker's perspective, is to cause the panic while the desired information is in memory. If we get very lucky, or if we can use forensic tools to recover the crash dump file (the savecore file), we, too, can see what made the system panic. We might even learn what our hacker did to crash it to the extent that we might be able to recover his or her code from the savecore file. Done properly, this could result in evidence that we can use in a legal proceeding.

As a hint about who was on the system when the panic occurred, have a look at the *lastlog*. Simply type **last | more** to get the top of the log. Have a look at the entry at the time of the crash. You can tell by the word *crash* at the end of a line. At the beginning of the line you'll see the names of people logged in at the time. While a skilled intruder will probably be using a bogus account, you'll be able to get an idea of which account needs to be disabled or have a password change. Because intruders often use the same account names for the back doors they create, you may want to check other machines for the same bogus account.

We have mentioned the savecore file. This is the image created by panic() and placed in a file by the savecore command. It will usually start on whatever swap device you have configured for the machine. Occasionally, it will be somewhere else, especially if the swap device is not big enough to hold a complete image of the memory. The savecore file is then generated by the savecore command and placed in the savecore directory, if the system decides that it is an accurate representation of memory at panic() time. You must have created the savecore directory (it is not necessarily the dump device) prior to its use, because the savecore command will not create it.

From the forensic point of view, we now have two potential sources for the memory image: the dump device and the savecore directory. The image generated by panic() will be at the back end of the dump device, hopefully allowing swapping to continue normally without overwriting the file. On a Sun computer, the savecore file is called vmcore.X where X is a sequence number. Remember that the savecore file we have been discussing is not the same as the *core* file generated when an application crashes. That file is application-specific, does not panic the computer, and is dumped in the directory where the application resides (from which it was executed).

Unix wizards will, often, use the Unix **adb** (absolute debugger) command to analyze a crash dump. In fact, there are a number of adb macros available that can help with crash dump analysis. Analysis to that degree is well beyond our scope.

However, manual analysis offers good insight into the cause of a crash; we will touch on that approach here. This approach to preliminary analysis is the one suggested by Drake and Brown. I recommend it as your first pass at analyzing a reconstructed mirror image of a Unix machine, prior to performing forensic analysis.

Identifying the Unix Release and Hardware Architecture

Drake and Brown recommend beginning by using the Unix **strings** command with the **grep** command to analyze the savecore file for basic release and hardware information. We use the two commands together because the strings command will generate output for every cluster of four or more ASCII characters. As you may imagine, there will be a lot of those! Grep allows us to filter all of those strings to get just the information we need. The command is:

strings vmcore.X | grep <OSName>

X, in this case, is the sequence number attached to the vmcore file. If you are examining a system other than Sun, the name of the savecore file will be different. OSName, in our example, would be SunOS. However, if you are looking at another computer, you'll grep the applicable OSName. We can use a similar command to get the machine type:

strings vmcore.X | grep machine

This will yield a response such as "Using default machine type ...," the result depending upon the computer you are analyzing. You might want to substitute the manufacturer name for "machine" to get similar information, depending upon what type of system you are analyzing. Experiment a bit until you get what you're looking for. Also, be sure not to perform these tests on the live computer. Always take your image to a different machine and keep a chain of custody copy, which you do not analyze as evidence.

The Message Buffer

When something occurs that will go into the messages log, it appears first in the message buffer in memory. Of course, when the machine panics, this information is stuck in memory, not written out to a message file. We can get it out of the image, however, just about the same way we got the machine and OS types. The message buffer is, fortunately, in a part of memory that puts it toward the front of the crash dump file. That means we can use the strings command to page though the savecore file until we find what we are looking for. The command is simple:

strings <savecorefile> | more

In our earlier example, of course, the savecorefile was vmcore.X.

The message buffer may contain a wealth of information. It usually begins within the first few lines of the savecore file and will contain not only the message file data, about to be saved at the time of the crash, but it may also contain such information as syslog entries. Syslog entries show things such as su (switch user) attempts and other items that might have been waiting to be logged. For the investigator, this part of the savecore file may hold evidence of things that were happening at the moment of the crash and before ... items that never made it to the logs. Even though the intruder may have deleted the savecore file, you may still be able to recover it using forensic techniques.

If your system under investigation is an Intel-based system (such as FreeBSD or Linux), you can boot from a DOS floppy, and use your NTI forensic utilities, just as you would on a DOS PC. Remember, you are concerned with the physics of the disk, not the operating system. You may also, if you can transfer the savecore file to a DOS PC, use all of the NTI tools that could be appropriate to analyze the file in detail. They will be far more convenient to use than the Unix commands discussed here.

Using the strings command, and if you have the patience, scan through as much of the savecore file as contains what appears to be useful information. You may find message-of-the-day banners, password files, images of tools used by the intruder, or other useful evidence. Whatever was in the computer's memory at the time of the crash will be in the savecore file. It is like the two "black boxes" on every commercial airplane. When a plane crashes, the investigators start with the black boxes to see what was occurring at the moment of the crash, and the moments leading up to it. The savecore file is your Unix "black box."

Other Unix Utilities

There are several utilities we use routinely in the administration of Unix systems that also can be used against savecore files on most flavors of Unix. These utilities will provide much of the same information about the machine's moment of demise as they would on a properly operating computer. Generally, you'll need both the image of the kernel (in the case of a Solaris 1 machine, that would be the vmunix.X file) and the savecore file. The following are typical Unix status commands:

ps -[options]k <kernel image> <savecorefile>

This command gives you the status of processes running at the time of the crash. This can be useful for finding any tools the intruder was running, which may have caused the computer to panic. Often, an inexperienced intruder will inadvertently cause a panic by using a badly written hacking tool. In that case, he or she may not even know his or her efforts were immortalized in the savecore file. The ps command may provide valuable clues to the identity of the intruder and what he or she was doing.

netstat -[options] <kernel image> <savecorefile>

This gives network status information. You may be able to see connections that are helpful in understanding how the intruder entered your system. Netstat, and many of the other commands we are discussing here, may or may not work. Sometimes they will appear to be working, but are, actually, reporting the information they find on the test machine, not the information in the crash dump files. Be sure to run each command separately on the test machine to ensure you are getting crash dump information when you run it against the files.

nfsstat -[options] <kernel image> <savecorefile>

This gives the status of network file system (NFS), if it was running at the time.

arp -[options] <kernel image> <savecorefile>

This gives the status of the address resolution protocol. It can be very valuable because it may show that your intruder came from a machine on the internal network. Additionally, in many cases, it can show you the ethernet address of the machine.

Any other status commands that are peculiar to a particular type of Unix system might also work on your crash dump files. Remember that the overriding topic of this chapter is deciding whether or not you have a real security incident. Using these crash dump analysis techniques can help tell you. It isn't the crash dump file(s) itself. It's the information you find in it that clearly doesn't belong there. That's why you need to make sure you're getting the right results — results from the files, not the test host — when you run these commands.

Also, be sure that you run the commands and perform your analysis (except for the strings exams) on the same system that you are analyzing. This means your test machine should be the same model running the same OS and OS version as the machine whose crash dump files you are examining.

The rest of the crash dump analysis process is, as I said earlier, arcane. It also is not, necessarily, of great use to you except for one thing: responding to the belief that no incident occurred. A clean crash dump, with clear indications of a benign occurrence, can point to a "normal" crash — one not attributable to an attack. But, if you see indications of actions that are not normal, with the resulting crash, you may have an intruder.

RECOVERING DATA FROM DAMAGED DISKS

Returning to the world of DOS, let's spend a short time looking at what happens when a disk is damaged or badly fragmented. There are techniques for recovering data from badly damaged disks. These techniques are both beyond our scope and outside of our purpose. However, a very badly fragmented disk, from the perspective of the investigator, offers challenges not unlike those presented by a damaged disk. If your disk is badly damaged, I recommend you send it to a recognized data recovery service with forensic training.

Simply recovering the data is not good enough, in most cases, if you can't establish how it was done and don't end up with a physical image. Remember the best evidence rule: your evidence must be the best available representation of the original information. If the original is available, a copy won't do. If the original is not available, you must establish how the data was collected onto the copy. Only data recovery organizations with legal experience know how to do that.

Recovering data from a badly fragmented disk, using a technique known as *chaining*, would, I can say with confidence, try the patience of a saint. To perform chaining you will need three tools: an old copy of the Norton Utilities (or similar), the NTI text search tool, and SafeBack. Use SafeBack to make a physical mirror of the machine under analysis and restore the backup to your test machine. Now, use the NTI tool to search for text that represents the information you are looking for. When you find the text, try to get a unique string. In this manner, you won't have to perform the tedious task that comes next too many times. Finally, use Norton to reconstruct the file containing the text you are searching for. I'll expand on that in a moment. First, let's review disk structure a bit so we'll understand why we need to use Norton.

Recall that DOS stores files in the clusters on the disk. If the file is bigger than a single cluster, DOS looks for another cluster to take more of the file. Ideally, DOS would like the next physical cluster, because the physical movement of the read/write heads will be shorter. However, on a seasoned (old, and/or heavily used) disk, the next physical cluster may not be available. DOS then selects the next available cluster, taking into account head travel time. DOS repeats this process as often as necessary to store the whole file. The result may be that the file is scattered all over the disk. We then say that the disk is badly fragmented.

Our challenge then is to follow the DOS decisions until we can reconstruct the file. When we are able to read the file in normal use, DOS performs this magic for us. But, if the file has been deleted, it may only exist in unallocated space, invisible to the normal workings of DOS. It is then that we must extract the file, a cluster at a time, using our forensic techniques. While this does not relate directly to establishing that an event did or did not occur, it does give us a tool for collecting indirect evidence. If we can reconstruct files that clearly indicate the person who put them there was not supposed to be on the computer, we can establish the probability of an intrusion.

If the file is completely intact, though erased, Norton will tell us that it is recoverable. Depending upon the condition of the disk, this might be all you need. However, if Norton tells you that the file is not recoverable, it's time to bring out the "big guns." Start by trying to find the first cluster of the file. That won't be easy if your text search gave you something in the middle of the file. If that happened, you'll use the same technique I'm about to describe. But, you'll have to move in two directions: forward, from the entry point to the end of the file, and backward, from the entry point to the beginning of the file. Fortunately, Norton gives us what we need to do both.

Once you have your entry point, you'll note that Norton tells you what the previous and next clusters are. Save the cluster you've just located and move to the next cluster. Save that and continue until you have saved each and every cluster in the file. Save each cluster to a file and be sure to name the files such that you can reassemble them into a single file, with all of the pieces in the proper order.

Some of the pieces may not fit into the file. This is because they have been overwritten (that's why Norton thinks that the file is unrecoverable). That's all right unless, of course, Murphy joins the picture and causes the stuff you need to be overwritten. For the most part, though, just reconstruct the original file as well as you can and move on. It is a good idea to keep the individual pieces and to do an MD5 hash on them to ensure you can establish the source of your reconstructed file.

RECOVERING PASSWORDS

Valuable information may reside in password-protected documents or on passworded computers. You may be able to recover those passwords and perform further analysis to establish whether or not you've been attacked. Before we get rolling on this topic, however, I have a very, very important warning for you.

Privacy laws are extremely strict about presumption of privacy when the owner of the computer or information has gone to the trouble to password it. Unless your company has an explicit, acknowledged policy to the contrary, don't perform any password recovery unless the employee has left the company and you need to recover corporate information. In that case, be sure to destroy any information that is not explicitly for company-use only. When in doubt, wipe it out! Don't expose yourself to a lawsuit over invasion of privacy. If you can get the employee's written permission, of course, go ahead and do whatever you need to. That's what this topic is about.

There are three basic ways to recover passwords, none of which is guaranteed to work. The first is physical, the second is by cracking them, and the third is through inference. We'll take each in turn.

Physical Password Recovery

Physical password recovery relates to passwords that are embedded in CMOS and can't be recovered in any other manner. CMOS passwords are used during the bootup of the PC and, often, can be recovered by using password cracking programs. If the PC is passworded, however, you probably won't be able to boot it, even from your DOS floppy boot disk.

Different computers have different ways to defeat the boot password. For example, Dell notebooks often have a small sliding door that, once removed, reveals two prongs extending from the circuit board. Shorting those prongs will clear the password. Other PCs may need to have their CMOS cleared. This can be a pretty touchy process because clearing the CMOS also clears such things as the hard drive type recognition. The process is, simply, to open the case and remove the CMOS battery. Leave it out for about five minutes, replace it, and boot the PC from your floppy.

If the PC won't configure its memory and drive types, go into the setup program — it's different for most PCs, so try several combinations, such as [F2], [Ctrl][Alt][Esc], etc. On most PCs, you'll be told what to do as soon as the PC discovers that it's misconfigured. Watch the screen during bootup and act quickly. You should observe whatever information about the hard drive you can find on the drive's cover when you open the PC. You'll need it at this point.

Password Cracking

To crack passwords, you'll need password cracking programs and, usually, a good cracking dictionary. There are several types of passwords you'll need to crack. Some are for the PC, some are for documents created by programs, like Word or Excel, and some are for compressed files that have been passworded.

For Windows95 passwords, Glide is indispensable. ZipCrack will crack files encrypted and compressed with PKZip. PCUPC and Cracker Jack are for Unix password files you are cracking on a DOS PC. Decrypt will break WordPerfect documents, as will WPCrack, and WordCrack will do the same for MSWord documents.

For network operating systems, try NetCrack on Novell and lOphtCrack for NT. Both of these require second programs to extract the passwords in a Unix-like password file format and superuser privileges. If you plan to use them to get superuser passwords, you're probably out of luck. If you need to extract the password from a PC using AMI Bios, try AMI Decode. The trick, of course, is that you need to be on the PC to use it. That means you will need to catch the PC while it is still turned on. Always run it from the floppy, never the hard drive. I recommend that you add a complete set of password crackers to your tool kit. A skilled intruder will always encrypt and password.

By Inference

Here's the tough one. You won't be able to crack files encrypted with strong encryption, such as PGP or DES. You will need to find the password some other way. For this, we'll take a page from the hackers who use sniffers to capture IDs and passwords. However, we won't actually use sniffers. We'll "sniff" the hard disk using our forensic utilities. This doesn't always work, of course, but I have found passwords stuffed in out-of-the-way places on PCs that work on networks, encrypted files, and all sorts of other computers and systems. In fact, finding a password for a stolen account on a suspect's PC is a pretty good way to establish that they accessed the victim containing that account.

If you have a physical image of your PC, try this. Use any word processor that can search for text and have it search for your password(s). You'll be surprised how many instances of passwords it will find — those you thought you'd never saved. The problem, of course, is that you *know* your password, so you know what to search for. You haven't any idea what you're looking for when you search for someone else's password. Here's how I go about it.

First, I get a good image of the computer I'm going to investigate. Next, I need to get a file without any binary "junk" in it, so I use the NTI FILTER_I program. It will give me a file with only ASCII characters in it. I usually start by building a file with probable English words. Most people do not use strong passwords. However, there is a strong possibility that a skilled intruder will know how to make passwords that are very hard to crack. Those will have characters that don't look like any English word. It's a good idea to try, though. You might get lucky (surprising how often we depend upon luck to get us through a sticky problem, isn't it?) and find a password or two.

Next, I just get rid of the binary characters and scan the rest for probable passwords. The scan is, of course, visual. There is nothing that can do that tedious job for you. If we are sharp-eyed, we'll often find passwords that work this way. They will usually be in slack space or swap files. We can use the NTI GETSLACK and GETFREE programs to cut down on the possible disk space we have to analyze if we use them on the reconstructed test disk. They won't help us on the raw, unrestored image file.

Once we have found a password or two, we should try them everywhere we need to unlock our suspect's secrets. It is amazing how often people use the same passwords for everything. Finding a password that is used for a Windows screen saver (using the Glide utility, perhaps) could cause a PGP-encrypted file to yield immediately. Always try the obvious first. This means to use your crackers and then see if any passwords found work on other things. Resort to forensics only if all else fails. It is tedious, slow, eye-crossing work to infer passwords out of the millions of characters on a multi-gigabyte disk, even with the help of the NTI utilities.

Where does this fit into our discussion of deciding if you have a crime? Many careful, well-trained computer users do all of the things the bad guys (and girls) do, for different reasons. If the owner of the PC is not available (on vacation, sick, temporarily suspended pending completion of your investigation, no longer with your organization, etc.), you may have to resort to breaking into their PC to complete your investigation. Remember the earlier warning, however: privacy laws are strict and the consequences of breaking them can be severe.

EXAMINING LOGS — SPECIAL TOOLS CAN HELP

Log examination is probably the single most productive part of your investigation *if* the logs are kept properly. It is also very tedious, especially when the logs are from multiple machines and are thousands of lines long. We earlier talked a bit about logs; now here are some tools that can help you.

First, I never look at logs on paper. It's too easy to miss something. Also, I use tools that require the logs in "soft" form, usually ASCII. There are many tools that can help, from simple word processors or spreadsheets, to log parsing languages, like ASAX. Generally, I opt for speed in my first pass. For that I use the NTI text search tool. It can help me reduce 100,000 lines of ASCII logs to smaller files that contain only the lines with the keywords I'm searching for.

For example, I might be looking for instances of a user ID — who knows, there might be a password nearby, too. So, I'll run the NTI tool against the log file and search for the ID. I'll pipe all hits into a separate file. The tool saves a single line and the line consists of the characters that surround the target. What I'll see in the new file is my target word, ID, or phrase in the center of the line, with the other characters (the ones that precede and follow) surrounding. That gives me a bit of the context. If I see something that really looks interesting, I can use a standard word processor to search on the whole phrase or set of characters on the line. Because they are unique (or close to it), I'll have very few hits to analyze.

I can do the same thing with dates and times, machine IDs, and other keywords and keyword phrases, such as **su failed for**. This approach is the fastest way I know of to do a quick, one-time (or a couple of times) pass through a huge log, most of which I have no interest in. There are some drawbacks, though. First, the log must be ASCII. Some logs, like the logs that make up the lastlog, are in special formats.

Second, it is still tedious to perform this on multiple logs when we are tracking an event through several computers. The bottom line is that log analysis is a time-consuming task, even with the right tools.

Other tools you might add to your kit are ASAX (a freeware, log parsing language for Unix that works well, but requires a masochist to use); ACL (Audit Control Language — a commercial product that works very well); and chklstlog (check last log), a freeware utility that checks the logs that make up the lastlog for inconsistencies in a Unix environment. This is important since utilities exist (such as MARRY) that allow intruders to remove traces of their presence from the logs that produce output from the **last** command.

The bottom line in log analysis: get rid of the junk before you start your analysis. Then, all you'll be working with are "possibles." Don't forget to look for data that shows no incident occurred in this early stage of your investigation. You could save yourself a lot of grief and work later on.

Investigating Non-Crime Abuses of Corporate Policy

In today's corporate environment there are "crimes that are not crimes." These include abuse of Internet access, use of company e-mail for nonbusiness purposes or for personal use, and acts that are, potentially, violations of law. Most companies do not wish to involve law enforcement, unless it is absolutely necessary. They prefer to investigate these internal incidents and take appropriate action. There are some potential difficulties associated with this approach.

First, if your corporate policies don't allow you to collect the evidence needed to pursue an incident properly, your hands will be tied. Violating an employee's right of privacy, when there is an expectation of privacy, is a very bad thing. At the least, it will get any disciplinary action you take nullified. At the worst, it will subject you and your organization to a lawsuit that your employee will probably win.

Second, investigating these types of abuse and fraud is touchy from a technical standpoint. When you get into a civil court or before an arbitration panel with your evidence, you need to be sure that it is pristine, has been properly collected with proper chains of custody maintained, and that you can establish to the finder of the fact that you did everything correctly. Just because you are in a civil proceeding doesn't mean that your evidence won't be scrutinized as minutely as it would be in a criminal action.

Some of the most common Internet abuses experienced by today's corporations involve pornography and, potentially, child pornography. Child pornography is a federal offense. Companies whose employees visit "kiddy porn" sites on the Internet must act to terminate the practice or be seen to be in complicity with the employee. Companies are expected to make a best faith effort to ensure that such abuse is detected, investigated, and appropriate action is taken.

The problems here are the same, however, as those we've just discussed. If there is no policy allowing search and seizure of the employee's company PC, there really are few ways to pursue a policy of acceptable Internet use. While it's true that companies can monitor access to the Internet and log the sites visited, or limit access to certain known sites, it is easy for the employee to deny guilt based upon the fact that tracking stops at the PC. Placing the employee at the PC, connected to a porn site, can be very tricky.

One solution is to force a second login to the Internet gateway. However, compromised passwords are not uncommon. A dedicated Internet abuser may have the skills to use a sniffer, readily available on the Internet, to capture passwords. Or, he or she (usually he) may be able to social engineer passwords out of colleagues. The best solution to the investigative issues is to have both a policy and the technical skills to establish guilt or innocence. So, for the technical portion of our discussion, let's assume that you have your policies in place and can investigate with full freedom.

To establish that a computer has been used to visit inappropriate sites, you'll need SafeBack, a disk/drive such as a Jaz drive to hold the image, a PC on which to reconstruct the image, copies of the NTI GETSLACK, GETFREE, IPFilter (with DM), FILTER_I, and the text search tool. Begin by impounding the PC, as we discussed in an earlier chapter. Booting from a DOS bootable floppy, run SafeBack and collect your image. Take the image to your test PC and restore it. You now have a mirror of the suspected abuser's PC.

Using your DOS floppy, boot the mirror machine and make sure that the mirror can see the Jaz (or similar) drive. You'll need a new disk in the Jaz drive because you are going to collect evidence from the mirror. Experience has shown me that the evidence from a serious pornography abuser is likely to be substantial. So, you'll need plenty of space to put it. I suggest that you work on a clean Jaz disk and make no subdirectories. Place copies of all tools you will use on the disk. That includes the three NTI tools mentioned above, plus the NTI tool for cataloging the contents of a disk and the NTI CRCMD5 MD5 hashing tool. If you are encrypting, put your encryption program there also.

The purpose of collecting copies of all tools you will use onto a single disk is that you will always be able to demonstrate exactly what you did to analyze the evidence. All release levels will be correct, you'll have everything you need in one place, and you'll avoid the embarrassment of not being able to reproduce your activities because you didn't have the same tools or releases you originally used.

Now, use GETSLACK and GETFREE to make copies of the slack and unallocated space on the mirror. Save the files onto your test disk (the Jaz disk). Use the disk cataloging tool to make a complete catalog, with MD5 values, of every file on the mirror. MD5 hash the resulting file itself (you'll now have a hashed directory file containing a listing of every file on the mirror with its hash). Encrypt the listing and the file with the hash number into a single file, and put it aside in case you need to prove chain of custody.

Next perform hashes on the files resulting from GETSLACK and GETFREE and encrypt the resulting hash file. Use the **dir** command to see if there is a Windows swap file on the mirror. If there is, copy it off onto your Jaz disk, hash it, encrypt the hash file, and get ready to perform your analysis.

We are going to use IPFilter from NTI to analyze the mirror and the files we have collected. IPFilter, used with a freeware program called DM, will tell us every e-mail or URL address appearing on the hard drive, whether in the active area, slack, unallocated, or swap space. Using DM, we can also see the frequency with which the addresses were visited. These two programs will do the same for all graphics file names as well. IPFilter was developed by NTI for law enforcement in support of investigating child pornography. It is an awesome utility!

Start by running IPFilter against the mirror and saving the resulting database on your Jaz disk. You probably won't get much, but you can always try. If you get some addresses, use DM to analyze their frequency. DM is very straightforward to use, as is IPFilter — we'll leave the mechanics of operation to the manuals, help, and readme files. After you have run the utility, be sure to hash the resulting file, encrypt, and save the hash. Run IPFilter and DM on each of the remaining files (the ones you got from GETSLACK, GETFREE, and the Windows swap file, if there is one). This should prove much more productive.

At this point, you will need to examine the output of DM to decide if your suspect actually did what you thought he or she did. If you find no evidence of repeated abuse (the frequency is important because it limits the argument that the site was visited in error), you don't have the right person. If, on the other hand, you harvested multiple addresses and visits to inappropriate addresses, as well as evidence of inappropriate graphics files on the computer, you probably have caught your suspect red-handed. But, there may be one more test you should perform.

Many suspects will complain that they were "framed" by someone else using their IP address. This is a plausible defense in some cases. On systems that use Windows95 or some TCP/IP third-party programs, changing the IP address of the PC is very easy. There are some limits, of course. There can't be two instances of the same IP address active on a subnet at the same time in Windows95. So, if the real user is online, the masquerader can't use that address. Also, systems that assign addresses dynamically are nearly impossible to spoof. However, they're also very hard to perform traces on.

The way to get around this defense (or to use it to establish true innocence) is to locate evidence on the suspect's PC that points to the suspect and nobody else. Some of the things you can look for are IDs, passwords, and credit card numbers that are unique to the suspect. That requires a text search of the mirror, including its slack, unallocated, and swap spaces. You can use the NTI text search tool and FILTER_I for this task. Try to associate these unique identifiers with the inappropriate addresses you harvested earlier. Package everything up on the single Jaz disk, make a backup copy of all of your hash files (a single floppy should be fine for that), and put the evidence into safe keeping until you need it.

CLUES FROM WITNESS INTERVIEWS

Witness interviews can provide a rich source of information about a suspected intrusion. They also can cause real confusion. Different types of witnesses view events differently. For example, operators view the event from the perspective of something that caused their terminal or PC to behave differently. What "differently" means will need to be explored before the term will have any meaning to you.

Technical people, power users, and system administrators can get tangled in technical details, which may or may not point to a real incident. Separating useful information from the chaff of technical detail, without losing access to the detail if you need it in the future, can be a challenge. Supervisors and managers may have hidden agendas that cause them to take one position or another. I have a rule when it comes to witness interviews: get the information in as much detail as possible and sort it out later.

To do that, you will probably need to conduct multiple interviews with some people. I use a "pyramid" approach to planning my interviews. However, everyone has his or her own style. I encourage you to use what works for you. Experienced interviewers, such as retired law enforcement officers, will have, over many years, developed techniques that can be slightly adjusted to incorporate technical validation. I don't recommend that these people change what works for them.

When I plan my interviews, I want to talk to everyone who may be even remotely involved or who can tell me about the system under attack. My first pass is at the base of the pyramid. The base is very large — many potential interview subjects — but I'm not after detail or analysis at this point. I just want to get a few things early in the game:

- What happened?
- Who else observed it or was involved in any way?
- Who is involved with the system (admins, operators, etc.)?
- Who are the responsible managers?
- What gossip has been around regarding the incident? This is a reach, but sometimes gossip can point out other avenues of inquiry — be careful, though... it's often a dead end.
- Was there any loss or damage? What?
- Is this the first time? What other times has this occurred?
- Who does the interview subject suspect? Why?

Those few things should help get us started. They also have the advantage of exploiting the current recollections of interviewees, if you talk to them as soon after the incident as possible. Carefully take measures to document the details (in notes taken after the interview, as we discussed earlier) so that you can return to verify them in later interviews, higher on the pyramid.

After I get the big picture, I select the next group of interviewees — the next step up the pyramid. This is a smaller group. It may include repeats of my first round or witnesses who, I hope, can supply more detail. This group may include a suspect, who can say something to trip up him or herself. It will usually include the technical people, such as administrators. Here I'm looking for a rapid understanding of how the system works, its quirks, past attacks or suspected attacks, and the skill with which the system is being administered.

I also talk with management at this point. My management interviews are concerned with picking up suspicions and identifying any political agendas that could help or hinder my investigation. By the time I finish with this layer of the pyramid, I've been through 95% of potential witnesses at least once. From here on, the process is mostly fine-tuning information I already have and digging for new, though obscure, details and inconsistencies in what I know. It is about at this level that I begin to form a theory about what happened, how it happened, and who did it. Also, if this is not a real incident, I probably know by now. Finally, I know what politics are at work and I can begin to prepare for them.

MAINTAINING CRIME SCENE INTEGRITY UNTIL YOU CAN MAKE A DETERMINATION

Maintaining crime scene integrity is either very difficult or very easy, depending upon the type of computer involved. Simple PCs can be impounded, imaged, and put into a chain of custody. Mainframes can't. With systems that must stay online (such as mainframes and large, mission-critical Unix hosts), your best hope is to collect as much log information as you can, as fast as you can. It will probably be all you have to work with. On smaller computers, impound them, as we have discussed earlier.

The key to examining the scene of cyber crime is to isolate it. The problem, of course, is that the crime scene may stretch half way around the world. Just because you have impounded a PC in New York, doesn't mean that a "hacking buddy" on the other side of the planet doesn't have important evidence. This means you need to analyze your local scene quickly and efficiently. Law enforcement has the advantage of being able to coordinate efforts with other law enforcement agencies, so that a raid in New York coincides with one in London. In the corporate world, unless multiple branches of the same company are involved, or you can get cooperation with another organization that may be involved, you may be out of luck on the "other end."

Another problem is that you will probably be called in to respond to an incident without the benefit of preplanning. Law enforcement can collect information on suspected incidents over a period of time and develop a strategy for responding. In the corporate world, you are expected to "do something" when the incident occurs (or, when someone finally decides to report it).

If you can't impound your end of the crime scene (including floppies, printouts, etc.), move as much of the crime scene off the affected computer and onto as safe a haven as possible. I generally move critical files, such as configuration files, immediately, off of the machine to an isolated site if I can't perform a proper seizure. This requires extensive logging so that I may testify later as to what I did.

Once I get the critical data out of the environment, I perform my hashing and encryption to ensure that nothing gets altered without my knowledge. I always perform these tasks with as many witnesses as possible, detailed logging, and a narrative of what I did and why. It is always a last resort. Finally, always make second copies of everything as work copies. The hashed and encrypted versions immediately go into chain of custody.

CASE STUDY: THE CASE OF THE CAD/CAM CAD

This is the first of two case histories which illustrate the difficulty of establishing that an incident actually occurred. In this case study, we dealt with a situation that looked very much like computer fraud. Remember that the FBI defines a computer crime as one where the computer is the victim. In every sense of the word, that was the case here.

The computer was a heavily used Unix machine, which had been in service for several years, running a multi-user CAD (computer-aided design)/CAM (computer-aided manufacturing) application. The application had been installed by a small contractor and was administered by an employee of my client. The system had begun to fail fairly regularly, with problems that always required the intervention of a contractor who had a maintenance contract with my client. An operator had reported to a supervisor that she believed the administrator was causing the failures.

The informant said that she "knew" the administrator was friendly with the contractor, was disgruntled, and was definitely capable of causing the failures. She believed the administrator and the contractor were conspiring to charge my client significantly more than expected for repairs. As evidence, she pointed to the fact that more had been spent to repair the system than it cost in the first place and, certainly, more than it would cost to replace. It seemed like an open-and-shut case. Motive: money and a disgruntled employee. Means: the administrator knew the system well and had even been part of its installation. Opportunity: the administrator had root access to the system and could work remotely on it through a dial-in.

We began our investigation with the usual interviews; one of my colleagues examined the system's drives while logged in as root. I also requested background and financial checks on the contractor and the administrator. I found that the administrator was probably leaving the company because he had not been promoted for a while. It was true that he was disgruntled. I also found that there was a strong personal relationship between the contractor and the administrator.

The contractor had recently been acquired by another company, and there were no financial records beyond gross revenues. They turned out to be approximately double the amount of money my client paid the contractor, indicating that the contractor did most of its business with my client. The number of failures had been increasing steadily for over a year. In the current year, they had been so frequent and expensive that my client was considering a new system — one that the current contractor could not supply. The contractor was looking at losing 50% of its revenues. Motive enough to keep the system working, not to make it frequently crash. The "incident" was looking less and less malevolent.

Next, we found that the administrator had been offered a job by the contractor, if he should decide to leave my client. Cozy, to be sure, but not an indication of wrongdoing. Finally, the report on the analysis of the victim computer came back from my colleague. He had examined the system thoroughly, including running tests such as FSCK (file system check), which clearly indicated that the drive was failing due to age and heavy use. Frequent panics, analysis of crash dump files, and other indications made it apparent that no crime was taking place.

The combination of straight investigation techniques and technical analysis exonerated the administrator and contractor of any culpability. The client eventually replaced the system and the two suspects never even knew they had been the target of an investigation.

CASE STUDY: THE CASE OF THE CLIENT/SERVER TICKLE

This case is even simpler. However, it clearly shows that even technical-minded individuals can jump to conclusions. The environment surrounding this incident greatly contributed to it. It occurred during a series of investigations into serious vandalism occurrences, during a corporate downsizing, at one of my larger clients. There had been four verifiable incidents on the heels of another very serious incident.

The client had a very large client/server system that included over 60 computers and several thousand users on a core financial application. The system was fairly well secured, and there was no record of a security breach since it had been installed. Then, one day in the midst of the paranoia surrounding the other incidents, an auditor, responsible for verifying system security, presented me with logs that indicated strange activity on the system.

The activity closely resembled the probing an intruder does prior to an attack. It also appeared to be automated, because it occurred regularly at particular times. The times were always at shift change that, again, looked like an intruder. Further analysis pointed to a user ID, and examination of the ID showed it had superuser rights — a potentially bad situation, indeed.

In this case, we did the obvious thing and went straight to the owner of the ID. He readily admitted that the indications were of work he was doing. It turned out that he was installing a new security program on the system and had been having difficulty getting it to work properly. He could only test during slack periods, such as at shift change, to avoid the possibility of causing damage if something went wrong. Third-party interviews verified the individual's story.

Although many of the classic signs of an attack were present, and the system was extremely sensitive due to its ability to dispense money, there was no attack and no security incident of any kind. This is typical of a large percentage of suspected incidents in the corporate environment. The moral to these two stories is that you can't usually tell whether you have a real incident until you begin your investigation. Additionally, you can depend upon the appearance of multiple "incidents" when an atmosphere of paranoia exists. You may be the only level-headed, technically competent person around to sort out these incidents. Be sure that you approach them methodically and calmly.

SUMMARY

In this chapter, we continued our discussion of the facets of a computer security incident investigation by examining the possibility that we don't really have an incident at all. We looked at the techniques you can use to separate real incidents from normal occurrences.

We began by asserting that real computer security breaches are comparatively rare, taken against a backdrop of misinterpretations, failing systems, and general paranoia and overreaction. Then, we discussed some of the tools and techniques you can use to sort out fact from fiction. We discussed the use of password retrieval tools, ways to circumvent encryption, crash dump analysis as a Unix investigation technique, and ended with a couple of case studies to illustrate our points.

In the next chapter, we'll cover the crime in progress. We'll discuss what to do when the intruder is actually online. We will explore the legal and technical issues of trap-and-trace, and pen registers. We'll also look a little closer at traceback issues. Finally, we'll discuss goat files and honey pots, or the techniques to keep an intruder online while you backtrace the connection.

REFERENCE

1. Drake, C. and Brown, K., *Panic! Unix System Crash Dump Analysis*, Prentice-Hall.

10 Handling the Crime in Progress

In this chapter we'll introduce some of the techniques and issues involved with handling an intrusion in process. The issues, both technical and legal, are complex. Additionally, there are ethical issues involved with hacking intrusions. We'll explore some of the attitudes surrounding various types of hacker intrusions, and how they affect your situation when an attack is in progress. Finally, we'll look at various types of back doors that intruders may leave in your system. These may enable them to return at a later time to continue their efforts.

We'll begin by looking at how to handle an online intrusion in progress. Then, we'll explore some things you can and can't do to trap an intruder who is entering your system repeatedly without authorization. We'll conclude by examining legal issues.

INTRUSIONS — THE INTRUDER IS STILL ONLINE

I was doing an intrusion test for one of my larger clients. I had run the ISS SafeSuite scanner against the site of a service provider being considered as a vendor for space to place one of their World Wide Web sites. All of the arrangements had been made in advance with the service provider, and the first round of tests had produced some interesting results. It was time to verify those results with a little manual "hacking" at the site.

When I perform this type of test, my objective is twofold. First, I want to run a structured attack simulator to get an idea of the types of general vulnerabilities present on the target site. Then, I want to attack the system as an intruder might, part of which includes observing the system from the hacker's perspective. Normally, a good site is not particularly visible over the Internet. Of course, a site that makes its business by providing Web services will need to be somewhat visible. It never ceases to amaze me, though, just how visible these sites are.

For example, it is not uncommon to use the external network as the internal one. In other words, there is a single network for the provider's employees and for the customer Web sites. That means the internal information and computers are easily visible from the outside. This turned out to be the case here.

I had nosed around several of the trusted hosts that the ISS scanner discovered. I had found a couple of strange indications and decided to look for a way into the private areas of the system to confirm my suspicions. Often, a system will look far different to the public than it does to an insider. This can be good or bad news. It's good if there is no way an intruder can break into the inside of the system. It's very bad if the intruder can.

Entering a system that is weakly configured to present its best face to the outside means that the system really is far more vulnerable than it seems. On the outside, it looks like it has a hard protective shell. In reality, there is a soft, vulnerable underbelly. Obviously, that type of system would not be in my client's best interests. Therefore, I ran a tool that reveals all of the hosts in the target domain.

Normally, a secure site will have a firewall protecting it from the Internet. This type of site will have a split DNS (domain name server), with very limited information on the outside. Its purpose is to avoid an intruder finding hosts that are inside the firewall and attempting to probe them for back doors, which would allow a successful attack on the firewall. However, the host names are present in the other part of the split DNS. All you have to know is how to find them.

Of course, an open site with no firewall, such as the one I was looking at, is potentially simple to access. The tool readily provided me with a complete list of every host and PC on the network, internal to the company or external, for public use.

Armed with the list, I began to snoop around, looking for a weak computer from which to take a password file. If I could crack a password or two, I might be able to get a closer look at the public server's configuration, an open invitation for an attack. If not, I could go back to my client and tell them that the site was safe for them to use.

I focused on computers that looked as if they might be "inside," instead of part of the public portion of the network. The idea was that such a computer might be less robustly protected than one intended for public use. Perhaps the site administrator thought the "internal" computers, because they didn't advertise their presence, would be missed by an intruder. This is known in some security circles as a form of "security through obscurity." The idea is that if nobody knows about a computer it's presumed safe. Nobody seems to stop and think that it's quite easy to locate any computer on a subnet, and not much harder to find those in the rest of the domain.

I was lucky. I very quickly found a Windows95 PC logged on to the network using a telnet server program, which would allow me to connect to it if I could guess a password. My first try, **guest,** was successful. I was just about to harvest the PC's .pwl (password) file when on my screen appeared, in slow, jerky typing, "who are you?" I was caught.

What happened next was a good example of one way to handle an intrusion in progress. It is not the only or, perhaps, even the best way, but it is one approach. In this case it was the logical approach because the user on the other end had been told I would be snooping around in their system. However, I could just as easily have been a real intruder, responding by social engineering to the person on the other end to let me continue.

I responded that I was a consultant hired by a potential customer to verify the security of the site. I explained that I was poking around trying to see if there were any open vulnerabilities that might compromise my client's information. The person on the other end seemed to understand, and invited me to continue. Obviously, I was through on this computer for the moment. However, I had a vulnerable PC identified. I could come back another time, look to see if it was logged on, and, if there was a lot of idle time since last access. I could then go back in and harvest the password, under the assumption the user was away from the PC doing something else.

This, obviously, represented a vulnerability for my client: generic accounts with generic passwords. A second vulnerability was that the operator of the computer made no effort to verify that I was who I said I was, even though I gave him my cell phone number to call if he wished. This illustrates a very important rule: when you encounter an intruder online, no matter who it appears to be, you should take immediate action.

The intruder online represents a special type of threat. He or she has discovered a way into the computer on which you discover him or her. The intruder knows that they have been discovered. They also know that there is a vulnerability in the computer that allowed access. The big question in the hacker's mind is, do you know. At this point, you are faced with some decisions about what to do next. We'll get to those in a moment. There is no question that you have some quick work to do at this point.

You need to know how the intruder entered. If you are like the user in our example above, it should be pretty obvious. That operator should know that there are very limited ways into the PC as it was being used. The obvious one was straight in, using an account with a guessed password. If the operator created the account, he would know that there was a guest account, probably with the default password. If, however, you have a bit more complex situation, such as a Unix host, you need to take a few immediate steps to find out what's going on. We'll discuss those in the section on trap-and-trace later in this chapter.

Attacks that come in from a dial-in connection may or may not be easy to discover. There are two basic types of phone-based attacks: directly into the computer or into a dial-up system, such as a dial-in gateway or terminal server. Let's look at these separately.

Direct Dial-In

I am constantly amazed by the limited amount of security that system administrators put on direct-connect "maintenance modems" on critical hosts. While nobody can argue that it's reasonable not to expect an admin to live at his or her site, just in case it goes down, there are precautions that should be taken on remote admin dial-ins. There are many good references for that, so we'll skip the countermeasures here and concentrate on catching intruders.

A direct dial-in, unprotected, can be any of several types. Most Unix machines allow you to set up a com port with an auto-answer modem. Windows95 has that capability as well. For PCs and NT computers, there is a wealth of remote access programs, such as PCAnywhere, LapLink, ReachOut, and, arguably, the granddaddy of them all, CarbonCopy. All of these have limited protection. The protection comes from passwords and, in some cases, some form of unique serializing. Remember, if a single use password system, such as a token, isn't used, gaining access usually means doing little more than social engineering a password or stealing a laptop PC.

Once the attacker has dialed in and is online, you don't have any options for tracing that don't involve the phone company. And that means involving law enforcement. Many organizations simply prefer to strengthen their defenses and forget about catching the intruder. If you decide to trace the intruder, however, we'll discuss your options shortly. At the moment, your top priority will be to follow the intruder's activities on your network. A favorite trick of intruders is to plant a sniffer and harvest passwords. You need to determine what account the attacker has stolen to get into the dial-up in the first place. Then you need to track the intruder through the network and find out what he or she is doing. This can be a tedious process of checking logins on multiple servers. On a maintenance modem, however, the intruder may have stayed with the victim computer. Start there.

Some types of remote access software require that the host PC be logged onto the LAN in order to allow LAN access to the legitimate caller. If this is the case on your network, there is a real problem because the intruder, having gained access to a PC, now can wander the LAN as the PC user. Logging may be of little use here since the legitimate accesses by the legitimate user are mixed with purloined accesses by the masquerading intruder.

If you were lucky enough to find that the accessed computer had logging turned on, you may, with the help of the PC owner, determine when the unauthorized access occurred and use it as a starting point to track the intruder's actions. You are faced with another challenge here, however: in a large network, you're likely to be looking for a needle in a haystack if you expect to pick the intruder's next target. Fortunately, our forensic utilities offer us a possible solution.

You may recall we said that there are areas of a DOS disk that collect information the user doesn't know about. Those areas are, typically, slack, unallocated, and swap space. When a user accesses a dial-in program, that program acts as a proxy for the remote user. It echoes his or her keystrokes, and those echoes might be present somewhere in the normally inaccessible spaces we have discussed. Thus, it may be that the address or name of the next computer on the intruder's list may be hidden where you, with your forensic utilities, can find it.

More important, it is possible that the intruder's entire excursion through your network may appear on the remote access computer, which the intruder dialed up first. Thus, if you can impound the computer, image it, and analyze the image, you may have what you need to trace your intrusion. Of course, the intruder won't still be online, but you can, if you wish, lay some traps once you know what the targets are. We'll discuss this later in the chapter. Now, let's discuss what are your options for action when you find an intruder online.

SHOULD YOU TRAP, SHUT DOWN, OR SCARE OFF THE INTRUDER?

You have, basically, three options when you find an intruder online. You can keep him or her on long enough to trap-and-trace. You can terminate the connection, in which case you can probably expect the intruder to return. Or, you can do something in an attempt to scare the intruder into leaving and not coming back. I suspect that the intent of the operator in our opening anecdote was (or would have been) to scare me off. By identifying myself properly, it turned out to be an inappropriate option. Let's begin this topic by analyzing your three options.

TRAP-AND-TRACE

If you decide to trap-and-trace the intruder, how you do it will depend upon how the intruder is connected. If the intruder is coming in over the Internet or an external network, you'll need the cooperation of the administrators downstream, in the intruder's path to your site. If you have an intruder coming in over phone lines, you'll need telephone company cooperation. We'll concentrate on network access, because trap-and-trace over phone lines requires a court order and the help of the phone company.

Suffice it to say, there are two functions involved in phone line trap-and-trace. The first is called a pen register. Like a full trap-and-trace, a pen register requires a court order and the phone company's help. The pen register logs the source of all calls coming into a number. You compare the times in your computer logs with the pen register logs to get a picture of the intruder's actions and the source of the dial-in. A full trap-and-trace gathers the information passing over the phone lines, as well as the source of the call.

We have discussed network backtracing in some detail earlier. However, a little more detail is in order here. We can only guess where an intruder originated, in most cases, when the intruder comes in over the Internet. As we have seen, most intruders jump from system to system when they invade a target. The purpose, of course, is to avoid detection. However, you can, with some help from intermediate system administrators, perform a reasonable trace. The problem is, of course, that you have to move very fast without tipping your hand to the intruder.

Careful intruders will check constantly to see if the admin is online. To do that, they will look for your name (if they know you are the system administrator) or for the root login. This can be done easily using the **w** or **who** commands, or it can be accomplished by looking at the lastlog by typing **last | more**.

One way to avoid calling attention to yourself is to ensure there are no references to you as the system administrator. Another is to use the same tricks the hackers do to obscure their identities and hide their logins. For example, a skilled intruder will usually enter the system through a stolen account. When the administrator lists users online, he or she sees only familiar logins. However, if you **su** to root, you will only be shown as the original user, not as root, if the intruder lists users. This can be very useful.

My preference is to create a second account for myself that does not point to my real identity, but does have the ability to **su** to root. I ensure that this alias follows corporate naming conventions; that way it does not draw attention to itself. If I log onto a Unix machine, do a **w** or **who** (both of which show me who is on line), and see an intruder, I'll immediately **su** to my fake ID. The **w** command gives me information about what those online are doing, while **who** just tells who they are and from where they're logged in. That will eliminate my real ID as being online.

However, if the intruder does **last | more**, he or she will see my **su**. An alternative is to log off and come back in with the bogus ID.

Always avoid the temptation to log in at the console as root. You should not be able, if the computer is configured properly, to log in as root remotely. Once you are in as your normal or fake ID, simply **su** to root. The intruder should not notice you online. Again, you run the risk of being seen in the lastlog. If you are on a Sun machine, you can use one of the utilities from rootkit to edit the files that make up the lastlog. Otherwise, you can use a utility called MARRY, available on the Internet at hacker sites.

If you immediately perform that task, you'll be hidden reasonably well. Now you can observe the intruder without raising an alarm. Remember, however, this does not work on any platform except Unix, and you *will* be altering the log. Be sure you document that action somewhere else so the log won't be excluded as evidence. One trick is to make quick copies of the utmp, wtmp, and lastlog (if there is one) files before you alter the active ones. That way you can compare the two copies and show what your alterations were.

Network Trap-and-Trace Techniques

Your next task, in a trap-and-trace over the Internet (or other large network), is to do some tracing to see where your intruder seems to have come from. On a Unix machine, start by looking at who is online. Simply type **who** and you'll get a list. **w** will get you the same list with a bit different information. I use both. In most cases you'll also get the source of the attack — in other words, the IP address or fully qualified domain name of the location. Don't get too excited yet, though. It's probably not the real source of the attack — just a location where the intruder has stolen an account. But, write it down anyway and take note of the system time on your computer.

Next, you can finger your own computer for a bit more information. Just type **finger**. This will give you a little more information about the intruder than you got from **who**. Remember, there is a very good possibility that the intruder is using a stolen account. Make note of that also so you can close that door if necessary (or desirable, we'll get to that presently).

Now, you need to see what your intruder is doing. To do that you'll want a look at the current processes. Type **ps -ax** (on most Unix computers) and look for processes that you can't explain. You also can get the process that the intruder is currently running using **w**. Note them for future reference.

Be especially observant for sniffers because sniffing passwords is a favorite hacker pastime. A typical sniffer, distributed with rootkit, is **es** (ethernet sniffer). Others are **ensniff**, **sniffit**, and **sunsniff** (on Sun computers). Skilled hackers will usually rename a sniffer, though, to mask its identity, so be especially aware of processes with a single character for a name, or multiple instances of a system daemon or service. Also, there is usually a command line parameter pointing to a log file (often announced with **-f <filename>**). That, of course, is a dead giveaway.

More information about where the intruder is coming from can be had using **netstat**. Try **netstat -A** for a full display of connections. Of course, you can always

man netstat for the manual page and full information on the options for your flavor of Unix. Finally, you can try fingering the originating site with **finger intruder@address,** where intruder is the name of your intruder, and address is the location of the site you see in **who.** It is likely that, if the intruder is using a hijacked account on your system, he or she won't be using the same account name on the site you're fingering. If that is the case (you'll get an indication that no such user exists or is logged on), try **finger@address** to see who is logged on. At that point, you'll have to do some educated guessing based upon what you see. Move fast so you don't call attention to yourself. Tracking a hacker is a bit like *being* a hacker — sort of a game of *Spy vs. Spy.*

Next, you can try to learn a little about the originating site and the user you think is your hacker (it probably won't be, but you can get an idea of whose account is being hijacked on the originating site). Try using **whois** to learn about the originating site. That should give you a site administrator name and phone number. You can get on the horn and let the remote administrator know what's happening. You might also learn a bit about the stolen account there. Don't be surprised if it belongs to the site administrator! With this information, you can start a traceback, if the administrator is cooperative and available at the moment you need him or her.

If possible, perform any tasks that don't require you to be online at the victim computer from another computer, to avoid calling attention to your activities. Remember, you want to try to backtrace the intruder. You can't do that if your quarry turns tail and logs out because you spooked him or her.

This whole process should take you just a couple of minutes to perform. Write everything down and note times, addresses, usernames, and any other information you see that could be useful. I have concentrated on Unix here because it is the most vulnerable to an online attack. However, there is a whole special set of circumstances reserved for online attacks that come in over phone lines, instead of over the Internet (as this example did).

LEGAL ISSUES IN TRAP-AND-TRACE

Trap-and-trace activities may be frowned upon by some courts. Certainly, you can't trap-and-trace over phone lines without a court order. The issue is that of privacy. In our crazy legal system, we hear from time to time about the thief who is shot by the homeowner as a robbery is occurring. The injured thief sues the homeowner and wins. Worse, I've heard of similar situations where the thief is bitten by a watchdog and sues and wins. Courts can be unpredictable and any perceived violation of personal rights tends to be broadly interpreted. However, there are some precautions you can take that will help you avoid legal pitfalls.

First, never trace an intruder back to his or her lair, and attempt to gather files controlled by the intruder, as "evidence" without proper authorization. Here's what that means. If the home system of the intruder has a clear, published, acknowledged policy that allows management to search the computer, let them do it. If not, either forget it or leave it to law enforcement. Stick to tracing the intruder's path and forget the other evidence. If it is important enough to seize, you should probably involve law enforcement.

Second, make no attempt to sniff e-mail or passwords from the intruder. If you are going to backtrace him or her, stick to the path and stop at his or her door. The exception is that you can usually sniff on your machine if it is part of your normal course of business. You should avoid sniffing just to catch the intruder. It is likely that evidence captured just to catch the intruder will be thrown out at any legal proceeding. Also, be aware that sniffing may reveal the passwords of other users, leading to a possible compromise of their privacy as well.

Finally, any type of trap-and-trace may violate wiretap laws. For example, e-mail, while on an intermediate e-mail server, is considered to be "in transit." That means it is "on the wire" and subject to wiretap laws. Once it lands in the recipient's mail box, it is the private property of the recipient and the Communications Privacy Act takes over. Generally, you are allowed to follow a path as long as you don't intercept information.

Also, remember that a test that many courts have imposed is the test of normal business activity. If you implement safeguards that gather continuous information about users, in general, and intruders, in particular, you'll have a far better chance of being able to use the information gathered than if you invoke the same system specifically and solely to catch a particular intruder.

Another important issue is the one we started with: should you trap-and-trace, ignore, or scare off the intruder? We've covered trap-and-trace. Let's spend a moment with your other alternatives.

Ignoring the intruder, or enticing him or her to hang around while you trace the intrusion, has some potential consequences. One is damage to the system. Another is that you may allow the intruder to move on to other systems, either on your network or someone else's. Knowingly allowing your network to be a springboard for an attack on another system could have serious liability ramifications for your company. Finally, you may put your own system at greater risk.

Most courts apply the doctrine of evenhandedness. If you don't prosecute all infractions of a particular type and severity, you may not be successful in prosecuting any. The argument is that you have singled out a particular situation to prosecute, while other attackers have been allowed to get away with the same thing. Allowing a particular intruder to remain in your system and roam at will, for whatever reason, may be seen as permissiveness and may be used against you in other, similar cases.

Scaring off an intruder usually won't work with any but the rankest of amateurs. A skilled intruder may leave, it's true, if confronted by the administrator, but you can bet he or she will be back. I usually advise against striking up a conversation with an intruder. It's a waste of time. You'll probably tip your investigative hand and, most likely, won't succeed in getting the intruder to leave and stay away.

BACK DOORS — HOW INTRUDERS GET BACK IN

Earlier we briefly discussed the subject of back doors. A back door is a mechanism an intruder leaves on the victim to allow him or her to return at a later time, without repeating the compromise. The idea behind a back door is to place an entry point on the victim such that it won't be discovered and removed by an administrator. If the administrator discovers the method of the original intrusion, he or she may close the hole, leaving the intruder out in the cold. However, a well-hidden back door is the attacker's solution. Back doors fit especially well into this chapter because they are one mechanism that allows the intruder to beat a hasty retreat, if discovered online, without worrying about how he or she can get back in to complete the attack.

The section that follows is an edited version of a technical paper on back doors written by Christopher Klaus. Christopher is the inventor of the Internet Security Scanner — now called SafeSuite — and a leading expert on hacking techniques and Internet-based attacks.[1]

Back Doors in the Unix and NT Operating Systems

Since the early days of computer break-ins, intruders have tried to develop techniques or back doors that allow them to get back into the compromised system. In this paper, we will focus on many common back doors and some ways to check for them. Most of the focus will be on Unix back doors, with some discussion on future Windows NT back doors. We will describe the complexity of the issues involved in determining the methods that intruders use. We will establish a basis for administrators to understand how they might be able to stop intruders from successfully establishing return paths into compromised systems.

When an administrator understands how difficult it can be to stop an intruder once the system has been penetrated, the need to be proactive in blocking the intruder from ever getting in in the first place becomes clearer. We will cover many of the popular commonly used back doors by beginner and advanced intruders. We do not intend to cover every possible way to create a back door simply because the possibilities are, essentially, limitless.

The back door for most intruders provides three main functions:

1. Be able to get back into a machine even if the administrator tries to secure it, for example, by changing all the passwords.
2. Be able to get back into the machine with the least amount of visibility. Most back doors provide a way to avoid being logged and many times the machine can appear to have no one online, even while an intruder is using it.
3. Be able to get back into the machine with the least amount of time. Most intruders want to get back into the machine easily without having to do all the work of exploiting a hole to gain repeat access.

In some cases, if the intruder thinks the administrator may detect any installed back door, he or she will resort to using a vulnerability repeatedly as the only back door, thus avoiding any action that may tip off the administrator. Therefore, in some cases, the vulnerabilities on a machine may remain the only unnoticed back door.

Password Cracking Back Door

One of the oldest methods intruders use, not only to gain access to a Unix machine, but to establish back doors, is to run a password cracker. This technique uncovers weak passworded accounts. All these weak accounts become possible back doors into a machine, even if the system administrator locks out the intruder's current account. Many times, the intruder will look for unused accounts with easy passwords and change the password to something difficult. When the administrator looks for all the weakly passworded accounts, the accounts with modified passwords will not appear. Thus, the administrator will not be able to determine easily which accounts to lock out.

Rhosts++ Back Door

On networked Unix machines, services like Rsh and Rlogin use a simple authentication method based on hostnames that appear in the .rhosts files. A user could, therefore, easily configure which machines will not require a password to log into. An intruder who gains access to a user's .rhosts file could put a "+ +" in the file. That entry allows anyone from anywhere to log into that account without a password. Many intruders use this method, especially when NFS exports home directories to the world.

These accounts become back doors for intruders to get back into the system. Many intruders prefer using Rsh over Rlogin because it often lacks any logging capability. Many administrators check for "+ +." Therefore, an experienced intruder may actually put in a hostname and username from another compromised account on the network, making it less obvious to spot.

Checksum and Timestamp Back Doors

Since the early days of Unix, intruders have replaced binaries with their own Trojan versions. System administrators relied on timestamping and the system checksum programs (e.g., the Unix sum program) to try to determine when a binary file has been modified. Intruders have developed technology that will recreate the same timestamp for the Trojan file as for the original file. This is accomplished by setting the system clock time back to the original file's time, and then adjusting the Trojan file's time to the system clock. Once the binary Trojan file has the exact same time as the original, the system clock is reset to the current time.

The Unix sum program relies on a CRC checksum and is easily spoofed. Intruders have developed programs that would modify the Trojan binary to have the necessary original checksum, thus fooling the administrators. The MD5 message digest is the currently recommended choice for most vendors. MD5 is based on an algorithm that no one has yet proven vulnerable to spoofing.

Login Back Door

On Unix, the login program is the software that usually does the password authentication when someone telnets to the machine. Intruders took the source code to login.c and modified it such that, when login compared the user's password with the stored password, it would first check for a back door password. If the user typed in the back door password, login would allow the logon, regardless of what the administrator set the passwords to. This allows the intruder to log into any account, even root.

The password backdoor spawns access before the user actually logs in and appears in the utmp and wtmp logs. Therefore, an intruder can be logged in and have shell access without it appearing anyone is logged into the machine as that account. Administrators started noticing these back doors, especially if they did a "strings" command to find what text was in the login program. Many times the back door password would show up. The intruders then better encrypted, or hid, the back door password so it would not appear simply by using the strings command. Using MD5, many administrators detect this type of back door.

Telnetd Back Door

When a user telnets to a Unix machine, the inetd service listens on the port, receives the connection, and then passes it to in.telnetd, which then runs login. Some intruders know the administrator checks the login program for tampering, so they modify in.telnetd. Within in.telnetd, there are several checks of the user's profile for items such as the kind of terminal being used. For example, the terminal setting might be Xterm or VT100. An intruder can back-door in.telnetd so that, when the terminal type is set to "letmein," in.telnetd will spawn a shell without requiring any authentication. Intruders have back-doored some services so that any connection from a specific source port can spawn a shell.

Services Back Door

Almost every network service has at one time or another been back-doored by an intruder. Back-doored versions of rsh, rexec, rlogin, ftp, inetd, etc. have been available for some time. There are programs that are nothing more than a shell connected to a TCP port, with possibly a back door password to gain access. These programs sometimes replace a service, like uucp, that never gets used, or they get added to the inetd.conf file as a new service. Administrators should be very wary of what services are running and analyze the original services with MD5.

Cronjob Back Door

Cron on Unix schedules when certain programs should be run. An intruder could add a back door shell program to run, for example, between 1 A.M. and 2 A.M. So, for one hour every night, the intruder could gain access. Intruders have also looked at legitimate programs that typically run as cronjobs and built back doors into those programs as well.

Library Back Doors

Almost every Unix system uses shared libraries. The shared libraries are intended to reuse many of the same routines, thus cutting down on the size of programs. Some intruders have back-doored some of the routines, such as crypt.c and crypt.c. Programs such as login.c use the crypt() routine, and, if a back door password was installed, it would spawn a shell when used. Therefore, even if the administrator was checking the MD5 hash of the login program, no error would be found, because many administrators do not check the libraries as a possible source of back doors. The login process would still spawn a back door routine.

One problem for many intruders is that some administrators perform MD5 message digests of almost everything. One method intruders used to get around that is to back-door the open() and file access routines. The back door routines are configured to read the original files, but execute the Trojan back doors. Therefore, when the MD5 program reads these files, the checksums always look good. However, when the system runs the program, it executes the Trojan version. Even the Trojan library, itself, could be hidden from MD5. One way an administrator could get around this back door is to statically link the MD5 checker and run it on the system. The statically linked program does not use the Trojan shared libraries.

Kernel Back Doors

The Unix kernel is the core of how Unix works. The same method used on libraries for bypassing MD5 could be used at the kernel level. Under this condition, even a statically linked message digest program could not tell the difference between a good kernel and a Trojaned one. A competently back-doored kernel is probably one of the hardest back doors to find. Fortunately, kernel back door scripts have not yet become widely available, but no one knows how widespread they really are.

File System Back Doors

An intruder may want to store data on a server somewhere without the administrator finding the files. The intruder's files typically contain a toolbox of exploit scripts, back doors, sniffer logs, copied data, such as e-mail messages, source code, etc. To hide these sometimes large files from an administrator, an intruder may patch the file system commands like "ls," "du," and "fsck" to hide the existence of certain directories or files. At a very low level, one intruder's back door modified a section on the hard drive to have a proprietary format that was designated as "bad" sectors on the hard drive. Thus, the intruder could access those hidden files only with special tools. However, to the regular administrator, it would be very difficult to determine that the marked "bad" sectors were indeed a storage area for the hidden file system.

Bootblock Back Doors

In the PC world, many viruses hide themselves within the bootblock section, and most anti-virus software will check to see if the bootblock has been altered. On Unix, most administrators do not have any software that checks the bootblock; therefore, some intruders have hidden back doors in the bootblock area.

Process Hiding Back Doors

Many times intruders want to hide the programs they are running. The programs they want to hide are commonly a password cracker or a sniffer. There are quite a few methods, but here are some of the more common:

- An intruder may write the program to modify its own argv[ ] to make it look like another process name.
- An intruder could rename the sniffer program to a legitimate service like in.syslog and run it. Thus, when an administrator does a "ps," or looks at what is running, the standard service names appear.
- An intruder could modify the library routines so that "ps" does not show all the processes.
- An intruder could patch a back door or program into an interrupt-driven routine so it does not appear in the process table.
- An intruder could modify the kernel to hide certain processes, as well.

Rootkit

One of the most popular packages used by attackers to install back doors is rootkit. It can be easily located using Web search engines. From the Rootkit README, the following are the typical files that are installed:

- z2 — removes entries from utmp, wtmp, and lastlog.
- Es — rokstar's ethernet sniffer for sun4-based kernels.
- Fix — tries to fake checksums, install with same dates/perms/u/g.
- Sl — becomes root via a magic password sent to login.
- Ic — modifies ifconfig to remove PROMISC flag from output.
- ps: — hides the processes.
- Ns — modifies netstat to hide connections to certain machines.
- Ls — hides certain directories and files from being listed.
- du5 — hides how much space is being used on your hard drive.
- ls5 — hides certain files and directories from being listed.

Network Traffic Back Doors

Not only do intruders want to hide their tracks on the machine, they also want to hide their network traffic as much as possible. These network traffic back doors sometimes allow an intruder to gain access through a firewall. There are many network back door programs that allow an intruder to set up on a certain port number on a machine, allowing access without ever going through the normal services. Because the traffic is going to a nonstandard network port, the administrator may overlook the intruder's traffic. These network traffic backdoors typically use TCP, UDP, and ICMP, but they could use many other kinds of packets.

TCP Shell Back Doors

The intruder can set up TCP Shell back doors on some high port number, possibly where the firewall is not blocking that TCP port. Many times, the back door will be protected with a password so that when an administrator connects to it, shell access will not be immediately seen. An administrator can look for these connections with netstat to know what ports are listening and where current connections are going to and from. Many times, this type of back door will allow an intruder to get past TCP Wrapper technology. These back doors could be run on the SMTP port, through which many firewalls allow traffic for e-mail.

UDP Shell Back Doors

Administrators often can spot a TCP connection and notice associated odd behavior. However, UDP shell back doors lack any connection; therefore, utilities such as netstat will not show an intruder accessing the Unix machine. Many firewalls have been configured to allow through UDP packets for services like DNS. Many times, intruders will place the UDP Shell back door on that port and it will allow packets to bypass the firewall.

ICMP Shell Back Doors

PING is one of the most common ways to learn if a machine is alive. It works by sending and receiving ICMP packets. Firewalls may allow outsiders to PING internal machines. An intruder can put data in the PING ICMP packets and tunnel a shell between the pinging machines. An administrator may notice a flurry of PING packets, but unless the administrator looks at the data in the packets, the intruder can go unnoticed.

Encrypted Link

An administrator can set up a sniffer trying to see if data appears as someone accessing a shell, but an intruder can add encryption to the network traffic back doors. It then becomes almost impossible to determine what is actually being trans-mitted between two machines.

Windows NT

Because Windows NT does not easily allow multiple users on a single machine with remote access, in a similar manner to Unix, it becomes harder for the intruder to break into Windows NT, install a back door, and launch an attack from it. Thus, you will more frequently find network attacks that are springboarded from a Unix host than from a Windows NT server. As Windows NT advances in multi-user technol-ogies, this may encourage more intruders to attempt to use Windows NT to their advantage. If this does happen, many of the functions of Unix back doors can be ported to Windows NT, and administrators can expect more intruders. Today, there are already telnet daemons available for Windows NT. Equipped with Network Traffic back doors, they are very feasible mechanisms for intruders to use to back-door Windows NT.

STINGING — GOAT FILES AND HONEY POTS

There may, for all of the above, be times you want to entice the intruder to stay around a bit. If you decide to entice the attacker to remain in your system so you can trace his or her path, you will need to take some precautions and you'll need some good bait. We call the bait *goat files* or *honey pots*. Here's the general technique.

First, you need to know what account your intruder uses to gain access to your system. If the account is a stolen one, reassign the real owner to a new account and keep the stolen account active. Change the rights of the stolen account to limit its abilities and rights and create a directory that contains very large and tempting files. This is the tricky part.

If your intruder has been wandering your system for very long, he or she will notice the reconfiguration and be suspicious. Also, you probably don't know what kind of information will tempt the intruder into a download. Clearly, this is not the type of action to take against the casual hacker. We reserve this for serious, professional intruders who we suspect of something as dangerous as industrial espionage.

Our objective is to confine the intruder to a harmless area of our system (hard to do, if the intruder has gained root) and entice him or her into a very large download. During a large download, we have a good chance of tracking the intruder to his or her source. There are several things that can go wrong here, however. Even though a large download takes time and is obvious enough to provide time for backtracing and logging, there is no guarantee the intruder will haul his or her bounty all the way home. Your attacker may simply stash it on another computer he or she has compromised and read it there. When the intruder finds that the file is bogus, you'll lose all track of him or her because the virtual cat will be out of the logical bag.

Another problem is that the intruder may become alarmed at the system's reconfiguration and run. Legal issues may include entrapment. I generally advise that honey pots are a last resort. If it's important to catch the intruder — and you intend to prosecute — get law enforcement involved. That, at least, protects you from legal issues because the police will act under warrants.

SUMMARY

In this short chapter we have discussed the issues surrounding catching an intruder "in the act." We discussed trap-and-trace over a network and the techniques you can use to backtrace an intruder. We raised issues of legal liability and addressed the use of honey pots. We also explored back doors and the ways that intruders get back into systems after an initial intrusion.

In the next chapter, we'll talk about politics. Throughout this book we have alluded to some of the things that can stall or stop an investigation. In the next chapter, we'll introduce you to some of them in detail. We'll discuss a case where the intruder was protected by her supervisor. Then, we'll talk about documenting your evidence, and we'll revisit chain of custody with more "how to" details. We'll see what corporate politics can do when it's in someone's best interests to cover up an event and protect the perpetrator. Finally, we'll try to answer the question of why organizations choose not to prosecute a perpetrator, even though he or she is caught red-handed.

REFERENCE

1. Klaus, C., "Backdoors," Bugtraq Internet mail list, 8/16/97, no copyright attached, edited by Peter Stephenson, 8/28/97.

11 "It Never Happened" — Cover-Ups Are Common

In this chapter, we'll begin our discussion of the political aspects of computer incident investigation. Within any organization, there will be people who want an investigation to proceed, those who don't, and those who have personal agendas relating to an investigation.

Whenever I describe a particular investigation which is interrupted or terminated for political reasons, my listeners always stare in disbelief. Why, they wonder, would any organization go to the expense and trouble of an investigation only to quash the results when it's finished? In this chapter we'll try to answer that question and show you how to deal with the consequences of an investigation that ends up, as they say in Hollywood, "on the cutting room floor." We'll begin with a true story of such an investigation.

CASE STUDY: THE CASE OF THE INNOCENT INTRUDER

The scene is a very large corporation with numerous mission-critical applications running on a variety of platforms. As with most large companies whose systems have evolved over the years, this organization has Unix, LANs, stand-alone PCs, and mainframes. Some of these systems are, not surprisingly, somewhat fragile in that they are old, as are the platforms on which they run. It is in this critical and sensitive, albeit fragile, environment that our case study begins.

As with most large organizations, our victim company is run, at least in part, by politics. That's a reality managers at all levels in big business have learned to live with. However, it can be a mixed blessing. On one level, politics is the corporate version of Darwin's survival of the fittest. On another level, it may promote deceit, back room dealing, and emphasis on survival of the individual instead of the good of the organization. Companies flourish that have their politics under control. Those that don't either stagnate or perish. A study by a major management consulting firm reported, in *Fortune* magazine, that managers estimated they spend more than half their time politicking. Those in organizations reorganizing or downsizing spend as much as 80% of their time at protecting their backs.

In the case of our example, the company had undergone and would undergo several reorganizations. Dissatisfaction within the labor force was running high. Management was focused on protecting itself, and the executive suites were working overtime to keep the company competitive and profitable. A relatively obscure system administrator decided to take steps to protect her job. Her steps nearly resulted in serious damage to a system that was among the company's most critical.

Another system administrator returned, after a weekend, to work to find his system in need of clean-up. Over the weekend the Unix computer for which he was responsible had complained it was running out of disk space. This was nothing new — the administrator had seen it many times before and had developed a process for dealing with it. He simply went into the system logs, which routinely grew to epic size, and archived them. Next, he pruned them down to size and proceeded to reboot the computer. To his horror, the computer would not reboot.

The administrator got out the system disk, a CD, and booted the computer. He than examined the critical files and found several missing. Well, they were not exactly missing — they had been reduced to zero length. It was clear they had been deleted and "touched," a technique which creates a zero-length file. He restored the damaged files from a backup and reported the incident.

Upon investigation, we were satisfied there was no reasonable explanation for the damage, except that someone had attacked the computer. At the client's request, we began an investigation. We discovered there was some question that what few logs were in existence may have been altered. We performed numerous tests and concluded that there was little doubt that the damage to the files was intentional. We reported that fact to the client and were encouraged to find the culprit.

After several interviews and days of analyzing logs from every computer that might possibly have participated in the incident, we were able to recreate a minute-by-minute chronology of what probably occurred and what was the probable source of the damage. We reported our findings to the client, only to be met with disbelief and support for the administrator who we believed had caused the damage. It was only a matter of hours before a full-scale cover-up was in progress.

Meanwhile, our suspect proceeded to shut down a system under her control ungracefully, resulting in the destruction of the file system. Over a period of several weeks, we reconstructed the events surrounding the incident several times, only to be met by resistance from all quarters, including corporate security, who denied that an incident had ever occurred. The party line, it appeared, would be that there was never an incident and that the lost files were due to an aging computer that often failed. Why? In the course of our investigation we learned the following:

- The system was unique — a one-of-a-kind application built by a contractor who had a good relationship with the department for which it was built. It was so good, in fact, that the company was considering standardizing on the application and porting it to a more robust platform, certainly a boon for a consultant in individual practice.
- The suspect was known to her management to be a bit of a "loose cannon." However, her supervisor had never taken any action to bring her in line with best practices and the professional expectations of her position. This, of course, placed her supervisor in a bit of a bad light at a politically inopportune time.
- The group using the application was known to be very "independent."
- Reorganization was a pending threat to all involved.

- The suspect had believed for a long time that the administrator of the victim machine was not competent to administer the system.
- The suspect had a history of "tinkering" with online production systems.
- The suspect had accessed all involved systems at about the time the damage occurred; the victim administrator was out of the state at the time.
- User IDs, with superuser rights not legitimately assigned to the victim machine, were present in the victim's password file. These turned out, by her own admission, to have been created by the suspect, both on the victim computer and on several others.

In the face of this seemingly damning evidence, the client passed the whole incident off as a failing computer, quashed our findings, and terminated the investigation. Why? What could have been done to carry the investigation to its proper conclusion? Could we have ever achieved positive results in this environment? The answer to the last question is, sadly, "no."

When this type of cover-up occurs, is there anything you can do to make "lemonade out of a lemon"? There is, and in this case we did. We were able to get the client to admit that, whether or not the incident had occurred, for a great many technical and administrative reasons, it could have. Thus, there was good reason to shore up the system's somewhat weak security so that such an incident could not occur in the future. We were able to turn the whole fiasco into a good example of "lessons learned." While our egos may have been bruised, the client, in the long run, benefited. Today, that system has been rebuilt on a more robust platform and is a model for applications of its type.

Let's follow this incident and examine our own set of "lessons learned."

THE IMPORTANCE OF WELL-DOCUMENTED EVIDENCE

The first and most important lesson is that evidence must be thoroughly documented. While we documented everything completely, it still wasn't enough to carry the day. However, without it the company might not even have redesigned the aging system and brought it up to today's computing standards. The rebuild was expensive and, while it was under strong consideration at the time, it might have languished or been superseded by other, more urgent, requirements for limited budget constraints. With the strong evidence and thorough documentation, the rebuild got top priority.

If the incident had ever resulted in legal action, whether civil or criminal, our evidence would have been crucial to a successful outcome. At the time we were conducting our investigation, we had no idea how our findings would be used.

How do you document your evidence? There are several answers to that question. First, remember our rules of evidence. Key points are that the evidence must be the best possible representation of the actual occurrence; we must be able to support our evidence collection methodology; we must be able to show that it could not have been tampered with; and it must be clear, unambiguous, and relevant to the issues involved.

Second, take notes on everything you do.

Third, make MD5 message digests of every file you work on so you can show that the file you examined was not altered by you or anyone else. When you backtrace an intrusion, log all of your actions and protect the log with an MD5 hash and encryption with your private key. When you use forensics, protect your forensic files with MD5 hashes and encryption.

Fourth, and perhaps most important, develop a personal style of evidence collection that meets all of the requirements of good forensic practice and that you adhere to, almost without thinking about it. The more automatic your actions are — the closer they come to being a habit — the less likely you are to forget some critical step or make an error in collection.

We probably all recall the O.J. Simpson trial where the defense made much out of sloppy evidence collection. Whether the results of the trial turned on that point will be a subject for debate for years to come, I'm sure. However, we can all agree that it didn't help the prosecution at all. Such loose collection techniques not only are potential instruments of legal defeat, they are fodder for internal cover-ups. If a supervisor with a personal political agenda that could be damaged by a security incident can discredit your investigation, you can be sure that you will suffer for it.

MAINTAINING A CHAIN OF CUSTODY

Another important point is the chain of custody. Lack of control over evidence can lead to it being discredited completely. This is absolutely true in a criminal investigation. It can be true in civil litigation. It may be of assistance as well for those who want to discredit your investigation. The point is, you don't know which set of circumstances is going to be the one with which you will have to deal. Under extreme circumstances, it may be all three. How do you maintain chain of custody? The simple answer is to never let the evidence out of your sight. That, unfortunately, is not very practical.

Chain of custody depends upon being able to verify that your evidence never could have been tampered with. You have to be able to verify this of your own personal, firsthand, knowledge. There are several ways to ensure you can, in fact, offer this assurance. All of the methods have to do with locks — both physical and virtual.

If you impound a computer, common sense dictates that you lock it up. You will probably label it as evidence and place it in a closet with a lock on the door. I usually perform a couple of additional tasks. First, I put a piece of tape over the connector on the computer for the power plug. That way, if someone wants to use the computer, they'll have to go to the trouble of removing the tape first. Hopefully they'll see my "Do Not Use — Evidence" note in the process.

Just in case they don't, however, I also put a bootable floppy disk in the A: drive. If all else fails, the computer won't boot from the hard drive and destroy evidence. I also include a standard text file in the autoexec.bat file on the floppy (this only works for PCs, of course). That file paints a large "Leave This Computer Alone" message on the screen. People still do stupid things, it's true, but these measures usually get the point across and protect the evidence on the hard drive along the way.

Floppy disks, spare or removable hard drives, backup tapes, etc. all go into sealed evidence bags labeled clearly with appropriate details. I usually include my name, a way to contact me, the date I took custody, and a few details about the case and the items in the bag. I always include serial numbers, if available. In the case of floppies, I also put labels on them with my initials and date on it. Never write directly on evidence. Everything in a seizure gets cared for in this manner. That includes innocuous things like cables, power cords, stacks of blank paper, and so on.

So much for physical locks. Logical locks include encryption and MD5 message digests. The idea behind these two methods is that, in order to protect something, you have to lock it up, be able to prove that it was you who locked it up, be able to prove that it's locked, and be able to prove that it hasn't been unlocked and altered. For something as nebulous as a computer file, that's a pretty big order.

With a physical object, all you need to do is put it in a room, lock the room, and keep the only key. We do the same thing, logically, with computer files. The first thing we want to do is ensure that, when we examine a file in the future, we can prove that it is either the same file or a perfect, unaltered copy. For that, we use the MD5 message digest. It is not, using today's technology, possible to alter an MD5 digested file such that the alteration doesn't also alter the MD5 hash. If we "hash" a file using MD5, a file that produces the same hash number must be the same file. So, my first step with a critical file is to hash it.

Second, I may need a copy of the file as a work copy. I make the copy and hash it, too. I perform the hash such that the results are in a file which I can seal. It wouldn't do to have someone able to alter the file, run a new hash, and substitute their results for mine. Finally, I take any files that I want to preserve and encrypt them using my own public key. That allows me to add a digital signature to the encrypted file.

I have now provided a means of verifying the integrity of the file (MD5), I have sealed the file in a locked container, for which I have the only key (encryption), and I have signed the evidence label (digital signature). I then take the disks containing the evidence I want to preserve, bag them, and treat them like any other physical evidence. If I have to open those files in court to prove that they are what I represent them to be, I'll be able to reverse the process and show that nothing could have been changed. If I have to, I can do this as a live demonstration in front of a jury. I use strong encryption, usually PGP because it allows digital signatures. Also, if I have an assistant helping me, I can let that person use my public key to encrypt, knowing that I'll always be able to extract the file using my secret key at a later time.

POLITICALLY INCORRECT — UNDERSTANDING WHY PEOPLE COVER UP FOR A CYBER CROOK

Understanding why people cover up for a cyber crook may help us to prevent it from happening. Returning to our original example, we can identify several possible motivations. For example, the company was in a time of turmoil. The administrator's supervisor may have thought that she would be at a political disadvantage if her system administrator was found to be deliberately causing damage to the system for which she was responsible.

Additionally, the supervisor might have had a friendly personal relationship with this system administrator. Although we know that it is sometimes a bad practice for supervisors and those they supervise to become overly friendly, we also know that such friendships are common, and even beneficial under some circumstances.

Another very common cause of cover-ups is the fear that an important staff position will become vacant. At a time when the organization was downsizing through staff cuts, there may have been the real possibility that loss of the administrator would be permanent. Finally, there are times when the supervisory personnel simply do not believe that the individual accused could or would have performed the act.

What can we do to prevent a cover-up? The short answer is that sometimes we can't. However, there are some things that we can do before an investigation, during our inquiries, and after the fact.

Before the Investigation

Before we began an investigation, we can take some simple precautions to help avoid the potential for a cover-up. If we are employed by the organization we are investigating, we can greatly benefit by continuously being aware of the political atmosphere that surrounds us. Knowing where pockets of political power exist can help us avoid an open clash.

Whether or not we should notify supervisors and managers that we are investigating one of their employees is a topic of much controversy. On one hand, it is considered the professional thing to do to keep supervisory personnel "in the loop." This especially applies to the suspect's immediate supervisor. On the other hand, if there exists an especially friendly relationship between the subject of our investigation and his or her supervisor, it is likely that the supervisor will compromise our efforts.

I have seen instances where an investigator could not discuss his intentions to interrogate a suspect until immediately preceding the actual interrogation. The suspect's immediate supervisor, his supervisor, and his manager all believed that the incident under investigation was trivial and not worthy of scrutiny. Coupled with close personal relationships, the investigator would surely have been compromised had he approached these supervisory personnel early in the investigation.

I have also seen instances where a supervisor or manager stonewalls the investigator if he or she thinks that the investigation is bypassing his or her authority. This is a particularly sensitive situation. There are times when supervisory personnel may be implicated in the incident itself. Obviously, they must be kept in the dark regarding the progress of, or even the existence of, the investigation. In my experience, however, it is usually best to involve the suspect's immediate supervisor at the earliest possible point in the investigation. Of course, that point cannot come until involvement by the supervisor will not compromise the results of the investigation.

During the Investigation

Paying attention to the political atmosphere before an investigation commences is not enough. We must also manage the political environment during the course of the investigation to avoid developing situations that result in cover-ups. The easiest way to ensure cooperation during an investigation is, as we pointed out in the last topic, involving the suspect's supervisor when possible. However, there are other situations that can impede our progress.

For example, there is, often, the requirement for corporate security personnel to work closely with internal auditing or information protection investigators. These situations can result in turf wars. Therefore, it is important to establish appropriate working relationships among members of these various groups. One of the best ways to establish these relationships, as we will see in a later chapter, is to implement a computer security incident response team. If such a team does not exist at the time of the incident, you may need to develop appropriate relationships "on the fly."

During the course of your investigation, you should identify, as early as possible, any potential impediments to your success. Dealing with those impediments, as they are uncovered, is critically important. Allowing negative attitudes to develop without addressing them head on may result in your investigation going nowhere. The best advice I can give in this regard is keep your eyes open, your political senses alert, and address any negative issue that confronts your investigation as early as you can. Finally, do everything in your power to avoid development of rumors. For a very few, extremely politically astute investigators, the rumor mill can be quite helpful. For the rest, it can spell disaster. Your best bet is to avoid it altogether.

AFTER THE INVESTIGATION

If all your best efforts fail, and you reach the end of the investigation with both results and resistance, there may still be ways to salvage your work. Begin by identifying the source of resistance to your results. Of course, it is critical that you do everything we discussed earlier to ensure that your results are accurate and that your investigation supports your conclusions. Assuming that to be the case, your next step is, possibly, going to require that you build a consensus.

If you have been able to involve the suspect's supervisor and, perhaps, supervisors and managers up the corporate ladder, you may have a good start on building a consensus. Do everything you can to understand the source of your antagonist's objections. Professional salespeople make the distinction between objections and sales resistance. These sales professionals tell us that objections usually are based upon some negative perception. Often, that perception is accurate. When that is the case, sales professionals tell us to meet the objection head on. Determine the nature of the objection and minimize it. You minimize an objection by emphasizing other, positive, points.

If the objection is based upon a misconception, sales professionals tell us to correct the misconception. Most important, however, is understanding the objection. Often we hear an objection and wrongly interpret it in our own way. The result, of course, is that we can't understand why the person we are selling to thinks that there is a problem. Sales professionals tell us that the best way to ensure that we understand the objection is to feed back our understanding to the objector. Once we thoroughly understand what the that person is objecting to, we can address it.

Professional salespeople also tell us that there is a thing called sales resistance. Sales resistance is not as well defined as an objection. Very often, the objector doesn't understand what it is that he or she is objecting to. Often, the resistance is purely emotional. Sales professionals say that overcoming sales resistance is much more difficult than overcoming a genuine objection.

The point, of course, is that if your antagonist has a valid objection, you can address the objection in exactly the same manner we learn from the sales folks. If, on the other hand, you are dealing with sales resistance, your job may be much more difficult. There is, obviously, one more possible reason for resistance to your results. That reason is the well-known "hidden agenda." When this happens, your only hope is to find out where the issues lie and address them as honestly and directly as you can.

WHEN COVER-UPS APPEAR LEGITIMATE

Under certain circumstances, organizations may attempt to cover up a computer security incident for what they believe are good reasons. We frequently see this type of cover-up in the banking industry. I know of at least one bank which routinely reports teller pilferage as mathematical error. The reason is, they claim, that it costs more to pursue this petty crime than the crime is worth. The truth, probably, is that bank regulators don't like to see tellers stealing from the bank. My personal opinion is that this type of cover-up sends a message that it's okay to steal from the bank, as long as you don't steal too much.

A similar type of cover-up occurs when the value of the incident is less than the cost of pursuing it. Unfortunately, organizations often don't know that this is the case until they spend the money to investigate. At that point, with a solution in hand, money spent to investigate, and a decision as to next steps pending, the organization may simply drop the whole thing. I had a similar experience.

Our investigation clearly led to a solution and a suspect. All of the facts suggested that the suspect, likely, was guilty. There was a brief meeting to assess my results. At the meeting, the responsible manager asked how much damage had been done. He then asked what the cost of my investigation had been. Finally, he asked what the cost of legal action against the suspect would be. When he compared the cost of the investigation and the cost of the damage with the cost of legal action (and no likelihood of restitution), he concluded that the investigation was over. He thanked me, paid my bill, and promptly forgot the whole thing.

Why did the manager drop the investigation? There was, it turned out, no dispute with my findings. It was simply a matter of the cost of doing business. The manager believed that no benefit to the organization could be served by "throwing good money after bad." Again, in my opinion, this sends the message that it's okay to commit a crime as long as it costs more to pursue action against the perpetrator than the crime is worth. Is this approach, in the context of the corporate environment, legitimate? As competitive as business is today, can managers justify the cost of pursuing criminal acts within their organizations? My personal opinion is that they cannot afford not to.

Sadly, in today's corporate world there is very little loyalty between employers and the employees. To tolerate illegal acts by employees or contractors, simply because it is expensive to pursue them, is bad business. Large corporations subject themselves to the possibility of shareholder lawsuits and, in some cases, regulatory action by not pursuing illegal acts within their organizations. For example, software piracy is against the law. It is also very common in large organizations. It is usually common because employees often are unaware that they are stealing software.

The obvious solution is a good awareness program. However, there are cases of out-and-out software theft within such organizations. The law can be extremely tough on the thief, the organization, and any individual deemed responsible for ensuring that software piracy does not occur. Therefore, it only makes sense to pursue incidents involving software piracy as fully as possible. Strangely, such aggressive pursuit rarely occurs. Managers believe, in many cases, that the cost of pursuing a software thief exceeds the value of the software. Unfortunately, they don't consider the very high price that they will pay, both corporately and personally.

You, as a corporate investigator, have the task of bringing computer security incidents to a satisfactory conclusion. In most cases, that means fully pursuing the perpetrator. While you may find that criminal action will not be taken against the suspect (due to cost, availability of law enforcement resources, etc.), you should be prepared to pursue appropriate civil action. When you begin an investigation, begin it with the idea in mind that you will pursue it to its end. Encourage your management to do the same.

SUMMARY

In this chapter we have discussed the various issues surrounding cover-ups. Essentially, this has been a "people" chapter. Our objective has been to present some examples of how and why people cover up the actions of a cyber crook. We began with a case study of a significant cover-up. Then we discussed ways in which you can arm yourself against internal politics that may generate resistance to your investigation or its outcome.

We showed you how to document your evidence and maintain a chain of custody. Then, we finished with a brief discussion of why people cover up and what you can do about it. In the next chapter, we'll address the subject of law enforcement involvement. Will discuss when law enforcement can be called, when it must be called, and who has jurisdiction in your case. We'll also tell you a bit about what to expect when you involve a law enforcement agency.

12 Involving the Authorities

In this chapter, we will address one of the most difficult decisions organizations face when confronted with a computer security incident. This is an extension of our last chapter: cover-ups. Actually, the question of involving law enforcement may be moot for some organizations because their governing regulations require it. Even so, as we saw in the last chapter, some managers try to cover up the incident so that law enforcement won't get involved. I've been told by more than one banker that he or she didn't like to see anything about an investigation or incident written down anywhere so that the bank examiners wouldn't see it.

While these are iffy reasons to avoid pursuing a security incident, there are some very good reasons not to call the police. Here are just a few:

- The incident is neither serious enough for local authorities, nor does it involve a federal interest computer.
- There is little likelihood that the crime will be prosecuted and public knowledge would only needlessly serve to hurt the victim's reputation.
- The incident cannot be solved.
- Pursuing the perpetrator would cost more than the loss.
- Pursuing the perpetrator would damage the victim in some way (loss of business, loss of shareholder confidence, shareholder lawsuit, etc.).

We will discuss these issues in more detail, when we address reasons to stop an investigation, in the next chapter. Nonetheless, if you do plan on calling the police, you will have questions about who to call, how to present your case, and what will happen when you turn over the investigation to the authorities. That's what this chapter is about.

WHEN TO INVOLVE LAW ENFORCEMENT

Involving the police, either local, state, or federal, is not altogether your decision. There are certain situations that call for police involvement and some that don't. In any event, you'll need to sell law enforcement on coming to your aid.

A computer security breach is not like a murder. There are few, if any, laws that require investigation and prosecution of computer crime. In fact, most law enforcement agencies are so overburdened, underfunded, and understaffed that they usually avoid all but the most major computer crimes. Remember, a computer crime is defined as one where the computer is the victim. Far more commonly, the computer simply holds the key to some other crime, often (for the purposes of "corporate America") involving fraud. Most law enforcement agencies have their hands full investigating that type of crime, whether or not computers are involved.

Computers may also be the instrument of a crime. This occurs with, for example, illegal gambling and child pornography. I have investigated incidents where the computer was a corporate machine used in the commission of an intrusion against another system, downloading of pornographic materials, and transfer of stolen (pirated) software to and from warez (pirate) Internet sites. All of these incidents put my clients at substantial risk of being accessories both before and after the fact. They all required that the client take (or, at least, be seen to take) positive action.

In virtually all of the above examples, the computer was a PC or small Unix workstation. These computers are far easier to manage than a large Unix host or mainframe. There are, however, a few types of incidents where the computer is so critical that, even though it may not be a federal interest computer, anything you can do to sell the authorities on helping you is important.

Recall our example in the last chapter of the cover-up of a significant incident where the perpetrator was defended by her supervisor, even though there was no doubt she committed the incident. That particular incident involved, potentially, public safety. However, the organization involved chose to cover it up. This is an example of a situation where, although the computer was not, technically, a federal interest computer, the incident should have involved the FBI. The client chose to cover it up.

What, then, is a federal interest computer? The answer is, actually, fairly simple. Federal interest computers fit into a very few and narrow classifications. Computers involved in crimes that cross state lines are always federal interest. Computers materially involved in any crime that is a federal crime are federal interest computers. However, *materially* is the operative word here. You may have no idea just *how* materially the computer is involved. Your best bet is to let the authorities answer the question for you. Withholding evidence (e.g., covering up a computer incident) in a federal crime has serious consequences.

Computers involved in any way in a crime involving a bank may be federal interest computers. Let the FBI answer that for you. The same is true of computers involved in gambling, kidnapping, and a number of other possible federal crimes. When in doubt, get competent legal advice.

WHO HAS JURISDICTION?

The question of who has jurisdiction may be much easier to answer than our previous dilemma: when to call the police. There are some types of incidents that clearly are the province of a law enforcement agency. Any federal interest computer, for example, suggests that the FBI may be interested.

However, there are several agencies that may be interested in your problem. For example, we worked on a case where the computer involved contained possible evidence in a case of fraud and conspiracy to commit fraud against HUD. HUD is responsible for the administration of policies that involve government funding or underwriting of home and property mortgages. On the face of it, that area of responsibility has nothing to do with computers or computer crime.

However, in our case, there was evidence on one or more computers that could determine guilt or innocence. Although the computer was not the victim, there was a clear issue. More important, HUD would have been the first government agency called after discovery of the incident, even though the primary actor in the incident was not a computer.

What is important to understand in this case is that the agency contacted is the one which has jurisdiction over the *crime* — not the computer. If the computer is a primary actor in the crime, that may or may not complicate matters. For example, if, in the HUD example, the fraud was alleged to have been committed using the computer as an *instrument* of committing the crime, would a different agency have been called?

The answer here is probably not. However, there are some interesting implications. The FBI and the Secret Service both have jurisdiction over computer crimes involving federal interest computers. Certainly, a crime against a federal agency (HUD) is a crime which, if a computer is involved, is a federal interest crime. However, in this case, neither the FBI nor the Secret Service was called. Why? For two reasons: first, the primary crime was against HUD — alleged fraud and conspiracy. That is clearly a HUD matter. Second, the computer possibly contained evidence. It was not the means of committing the crime (the "actor").

Thus, when we examine the incident in that light, the jurisdictional answer is clear. Or is it? Government agencies are no different from the corporations for whom we all work. There are political battles and turf wars. There are also some interesting legal issues that may be raised. Was the proper agency involved? Does another agency have a "claim" in the case (e.g., would another agency also like to file a complaint)? Is the action being brought in the proper court? This reflects the differences between local agencies, state or county agencies, and federal agencies. A local police force may, for example, bring the case before the local district attorney, who would not try the case in a federal court. If it is, actually, a federal case, however, it could languish for an extended period, be dropped, be lost in one court, or could not be brought to trial in another court ("double jeopardy"). What, as an investigator, should you do? You are probably the best advisor your organization has in matters of computer security incidents.

First, you need to seek the advice of an attorney specialized in computer security incidents *and* the particular area of law involved in the incident. In our HUD example, we would need a computer law expert and a HUD expert. Determining jurisdiction may materially affect the outcome of your case. It could cause you to lose based upon incorrect jurisdiction, or it could force you into a criminal case in which you do not wish to participate.

My law enforcement friends will, most likely, object to this section. However, it is reality, and, sometimes, reality is not what we'd like to see. There are times where an organization, for reasons of its own, does not wish to participate in a criminal proceeding. For example, if a teller in a bank steals money from the bank, there is no question that a federal crime has been committed. Yet most banks, depending upon the amount stolen, will not report the incident. Technically, they probably are breaking the law by not reporting the incident.

But what would happen if the "word" got out that the bank had been defrauded by a teller? Would customer confidence be affected? Would bank regulators or law enforcement officers take action that would jeopardize customer deposits? What would happen? These are the questions that banks ask themselves as they formulate their policies. The result is that most such incidents go unreported. Thus, we have a situation where, if the incident were reported, the bank would lose control over the investigation (as you'll soon see). The decision of bank officials is to hush up the incident and handle it (if at all) internally. Not the "right thing" in most people's minds, but reality nonetheless.

The easy answer to the jurisdictional question is go for the obvious. If there is any question as to what that means in your case, don't hesitate for a moment to get good legal advice. In general, of course, legal advice should *always* be an integral part of your investigation. However, there are, sadly, a couple of problems with that.

First, many corporate lawyers are ill-equipped to deal with this sort of issue. Most corporate lawyers are hired to do what the corporation does. If the corporation sells real estate, the lawyers are real estate specialists. If the corporation is an environmental firm, the corporate lawyers are environmentalists, and so on.

Second, corporations need to understand the consequences either of not involving the authorities or of not involving the *correct* ones. Instigating a jurisdictional dispute in a criminal action could tie up the corporation for years as the involved agencies resolve their disagreements and bring the case to a conclusion. It could also result in the case never being successfully prosecuted. Getting the right opinion usually means getting an outside opinion. Remember that when you bring your recommendation to senior management.

WHAT HAPPENS WHEN YOU INVOLVE LAW ENFORCEMENT AGENCIES?

There is a simple answer to this question: you lose control over the investigation. Period. It is law enforcement's investigation, and it may or may not progress in your best interests. It is not law enforcement's job to protect the private interests of a single individual or organization. They are tasked with protecting our society as a whole. Sometimes the good of the many, as *Star Trek*'s Mr. Spock would say, outweighs the good of the few.

With this in mind, you should weigh your options very carefully. However, where your options are limited, or none, don't simply back away from involving the authorities. You may have little choice as we have previously discussed. Let's look at the law enforcement process in these matters.

The agency you approach will need to be convinced of several things before they will take on your case. First, they will need to be certain that the case is within their jurisdiction. That's not always obvious, as we discussed in the preceding section. Second, they will have to be satisfied that a crime has taken place. Not all computer security incidents, or incidents involving computers, are crimes. Some are simply unethical and some are civil matters.

Next, there has to be enough at stake (a large enough loss, a significant issue, such as a federal agency or large bank) to warrant the use of very limited law enforcement resources. It is not uncommon for a federal agency to refuse to pursue a case where the loss has been small, even though the crime was obvious and within their jurisdiction. The reason is simple: there are limited personnel and financial resources for investigating computer-related crimes, and the crimes are very expensive and time-consuming to investigate and prosecute.

Finally, there has to be a reasonable hope of solving the case and successful prosecution. Law enforcement does not prosecute crime — it simply investigates it. If the appropriate legal organization (district attorney, U.S. attorney, etc.) doesn't want to prosecute, for whatever reason, law enforcement can't waste their precious time and financial resources to continue the investigation.

Unfortunately, district attorneys are elected officials, while FBI agents are not. Getting reelected depends, in part, on the degree of success the D.A. had in his or her previous term. That, sadly, sometimes gets in the way of investigations. More commonly, however, there simply are not enough people and dollars to continue a small investigation with little at stake. It is up to you to convince the criminal justice community, if it comes to that, to pursue your case.

If the "system" takes your case, however, here's what you can expect. First, law enforcement can do things you can't. They can issue subpoenas to look at things that would be invasions of privacy if you did it. They can seize computers without warning and without regard for what the user may have on it. They can impound computers and disks indefinitely. If the FBI impounds one of your computers, you'll likely never see it again. They are bound by law to hold all evidence until the case has passed through the appeals process. That can take years.

Law enforcement can tap phone lines. They can institute surveillance. They can place undercover officers in your organization. They can question your employees. They can detain suspects. They can examine company records. In short, once an investigation begins, law enforcement can do just about anything necessary to bring the case to a conclusion. That's good and bad.

It's good because law enforcement agencies have the power to go where you can't go and do what you can't do, if it means solving the case. They are protected by law as long as they don't break the law themselves. Their rules are different from yours, and that can help get the case solved and prosecuted.

It's bad because most law enforcement agencies, especially local ones, don't have the training or budgets to investigate sophisticated computer-related crimes. That, unfortunately, often won't stop them from trying. The results can be catastrophic (or comedic, depending upon your perspective).

The first thing that will happen when you call the law enforcement agency you believe has jurisdiction is that an appropriate representative will visit you for an interview. Usually that will mean an investigator and a computer specialist. They will want to hear your story in as much detail as you can muster. It is very helpful to have conducted your own internal investigation by this point, but **only** if you have conducted it properly (as we have discussed). Corrupted evidence, incomplete results, bias, etc., will all serve to hurt your case. Of course, it's fair to say that you could not (because it is beyond your skills and resources) conduct an appropriate investigation internally. In that case, however, it is best if you have at least preserved the crime scene.

If you have performed any forensic work, be sure that you have correctly preserved chain of evidence. Present your case, internal investigation, and conclusions in as much detail as possible. The investigators will need that information to present the case to the appropriate prosecutor. If this sounds a bit like a sales job to you, you're getting the idea!

You can expect to be questioned in detail about everything and everybody surrounding the case. Regardless of what you might have seen on TV, nothing is "off the record." I heard a very sarcastic response to the suggestion that a line of questioning was off the record: "What do you think I am," asked the officer, "a newspaper reporter? We're investigating a federal crime. Nothing is 'off the record'!" Good point! In a formal investigation conducted by law enforcement, you can assume that everything you say is, potentially, part of the public record. While it's true that most seasoned investigators are discreet to the extent they can be, if you tell it to the investigator, it can appear in court (or sooner, unfortunately) and, then, in the news.

In order for the investigator to be effective, he or she will expect your full cooperation. If you can't cooperate fully, don't call them. An investigator can't create a case out of thin air. If you want (or, must have) the involvement of the criminal justice system, be prepared to bare your soul at their request. It's a good idea to make sure that your management understands this *before* calling in the big guns. When we perform an investigation that leads to calling law enforcement, we make sure that everyone understands what will happen at that point. Executive management hates surprises, and the police treat everyone equally in an investigation. That has been known to get more than one executive's nose out of joint.

Finally, it's often hard to know in advance what may become evidence. Legally, the FBI can come in and truck out your mainframe, if they can satisfy a judge that it contains critical (and perishable) evidence in the investigation of a serious crime. From a practical standpoint, of course, that doesn't happen very often.

When there is the threat (implied or otherwise) of such a catastrophic occurrence (you'd probably never see the mainframe again), you can almost always negotiate. Experienced computer crime investigators know what the consequences are to your organization of doing something as extreme as impounding a mainframe. They will almost always work with you to get what they need without putting you out of business. Be polite and deal honestly and completely with the investigators.

Remember, however, the law is on their side. Even though you initiate the investigation, it becomes a state matter (or federal, or whatever) once the criminal justice system kicks in. Unlike a civil matter, it's not you against the bad guy — it's the government and the perpetrator. That can put you and your company at a disadvantage.

Now, a couple of positive comments: first, law enforcement will almost always work hard to do what is in your organization's best interests, as long as it doesn't conflict with their official duties and objectives. Second, the number of trained investigators is growing. The level of sophistication is improving almost daily. And, you have an increasing number of private resources at your disposal. There can be a partnership between your organization and the criminal justice system. It just requires an effort on your part and an understanding of the process and its limitations.

MAKING THE DECISION

Your perspective as a security or audit professional will, often, differ from the perspective of executive management. We have discussed the political issues that surround a computer security incident. They also have a place at this stage of the process. As you have seen above, involving law enforcement takes the control out of your organization's hands. Sometimes that can be a good thing. The availability of search warrants, subpoenas, and judges who get up in the middle of the night to authorize a search-and-seizure are a far cry from the way a civil case pokes along at a snail's pace.

In my experience you need to do two things when making the decision to bring in law enforcement. First, you need to evaluate your objectives in pursuing the incident. Second, you need to examine the potential consequences of giving up control over the investigation. Let's begin with your objectives.

At the beginning of almost every incident I investigate, at least one senior executive will want to string up the perpetrator and hang him or her publicly. By the time the investigation is over, that same executive may want to cover the whole thing up. Why? Being the victim of a crime of any kind is very emotional. If we get our home broken into it feels, by some accounts, like a personal violation.

Recently my wife's car was seriously vandalized as she was celebrating her birthday at our son's apartment. Although the insurance company and the car dealership will make it good as new, she felt a deep sense of personal loss and rage at the people who vandalized the vehicle. I was 2,500 miles away at a client site when I heard about it and I, too, was outraged. Crimes directed at us and ours trigger an emotional response. Most good executives and managers take their jobs personally and an attack against their organization is an attack against them. By the time the investigation is over, the emotion has worn off and cooler heads prevail. That's the time to decide if law enforcement involvement is appropriate.

At this point you should begin to consider why you want to prosecute. Consider what you should do with the evidence. You might think that the time to make these decisions is before the investigation — before a lot of money has been spent. At the beginning, however, you don't know what you know. You haven't evaluated the implications of the incident. You don't know if it was an isolated occurrence, part of a coordinated attack, symptomatic of an employee revolt, or just a benign occurrence that looks like an attack.

Most important, perhaps, you don't have any lessons learned to feed back into Avoidance. You may have security holes, uncovered by the attacker, which you should plug. Even if you do nothing with the perpetrator, you should complete the investigation and take appropriate action with your system and its security. I have yet to work with a client who didn't put as top priority — once the emotion died down — ensuring that the incident could not be repeated. That, at the very least, is the right attitude.

As part of your deliberations, consider possible backlash. I had a client who was accused of trading in child pornography by a co-worker. The client was immediately fired and law enforcement was contacted. I won't tell you the final outcome of this, but consider the position of the employer if the individual was to be found not guilty in a criminal trial. Perhaps the employer should have considered the possible consequences of such dramatic action and moved with a bit more care.

In general, you have three possible courses of action. You can completely handle the incident internally. You can take civil action. Or, you can report the incident to the authorities. I almost always recommend to my clients that they begin by handling the incident internally, until they are comfortable with what really happened. At that time they can decide to continue or to switch course.

I also have clients who want to take legal action to "make a statement" or "send a message." In my experience, that's usually not a good reason for involving law enforcement. Harsh internal action can send as much of a message as turning the culprit over to the local gendarmes. It also has the benefit of keeping your "dirty laundry" private.

Interestingly, even crimes that would trigger a massive investigation by law enforcement — software piracy, for example — can be handled internally without involving law enforcement. The Software Publishers Association (SPA) encourages organizations faced with a piracy problem to do all they can to manage the problem internally. This is the same organization which will, with law enforcement, serve a warrant on an organization requiring a software license audit at the drop of a hat.

The difference in attitudes is the appearance of an effort on the part of the organization. It is as important to be "seen" to be doing something as it is to be doing it. In other words, an organization which is taking positive and visible measures to curb piracy is not seen by the SPA and the criminal justice system as being a problem. Rather, they are seen as adding to the solution. This is the right place to be for most organizations faced with a computer crime. It avoids involving law enforcement while effectively solving the problem.

The point here is that you can have a strict and effective policy regarding computer abuse and usually can enforce it internally. However, you must be prepared to do just that. I had a client that, when faced with Internet abuse by employees, professed not to "have the will" to take action of any kind. Such action was, I was told, "against the company's culture." The abuse continued until a proxy server, requiring explicit login, was installed and users were forced to "apply" for continued Internet access. Of course, that helped solve the abuse problem, but it did not make it go away, and there were many disgruntled employees who lost Internet access.

If your goal, then, is simply solving the problem, you can usually do that with internal action. If, on the other hand, the attack comes from outside your organization, you probably have only two options: forget it or call the cops. The reason, of course, is that you don't have control over external, hostile environments and their denizens. If you choose to forget the incident, your investigation can, at least, lead to hardening your system against further, similar intrusions. If you involve law enforcement, you may or may not solve the crime. I generally advise my clients to save the big guns for repeated attacks, an apparent coordinated effort to damage data or systems, or an attempt to steal sensitive data or money.

I have one big exception to this advice: if it looks like cyber-terrorism, call in law enforcement at once. Financial institutions in the United Kingdom and the United States have been the targets of extortion by cyber-terrorists since approximately 1996. Experts in the field of cyber-terrorism predict ever-increasing instances of and motivation for terrorist attacks on computer systems. The FBI is equipped to deal with this issue, and is becoming increasingly proficient at solving cases and protecting organizations where terrorist activity, aimed at computers, is involved.

I have never seen a case where civil action was of any benefit. Perpetrators usually don't have anything to gain — certainly not enough to recover court costs and damages — and the cost of civil action is very high. If your organization is into revenge, and doesn't care what the cost is, civil action may be for you. There are two other times where this rule doesn't apply: corporate espionage and financial fraud.

Corporate espionage is becoming a way of life. When one company targets another, and uses computers to gain an advantage in the marketplace through guile, civil action is warranted. In fact, it may be the only reasonable remedy, because law enforcement often declines to be involved.

Financial fraud is another matter altogether. Law enforcement often is interested, especially if the amounts are large, financial or other regulated institutions are involved, or state lines have been crossed. Here your decision may be based upon regulatory requirements. My best advice here is to consult, at length, with an appropriate attorney. Remember, financial fraud is fraud, first, and a computer incident, second. In this regard, it is similar to cyber-terrorism. Cyber-terrorism is terrorism, first, and a computer incident, second.

SUMMARY

In this chapter, we explored the issues surrounding involvement of the criminal justice system in your incident. This is a decision not to be taken lightly. Hopefully, I have provided a few guidelines to clarify the issues and possible consequences. However, the most important advice in this chapter appears in its last paragraph: when faced with the decision as to involving law enforcement agencies, consult at length with an appropriate attorney.

In the next chapter we will discuss the issues surrounding the premature termination of an investigation. There are times when continuing an incident investigation either makes no sense or cannot occur. We'll see what are those times, how to handle them, and how to get the most out of an interrupted computer incident investigation.

13 When an Investigation Can't Continue

In this chapter, we will discuss the various issues that can stall or stop an investigation. Not all investigations continue until they are solved. In some cases, the investigation must stop in order to return affected systems to proper operation. In some cases, management may decide that enough money has been spent on an investigation with no results. Finally, and most unfortunately, investigations stop for political reasons. We'll explore these situations in this chapter, before we move on to discuss preparation for investigating computer security incidents.

WHEN AND WHY SHOULD YOU STOP AN INVESTIGATION?

The investigator in you will probably answer "never" and "for no reason." It is our natural inclination to continue an investigation until we are pleased that we have brought it to a satisfactory conclusion. We read, from time to time, about the detective who doggedly pursues a murder for years until he solves it. We respect that kind of dedication and, of course, it makes great press. Sadly, the real world of corporate computer crime doesn't operate the same way.

There are economic realities that drive all businesses. Investigations cost money and personnel. Like everything else in our fast-moving corporate world, costs involved with solving computer incidents have to be controlled. Thus, there are times when, like it or not, investigations must terminate prematurely. We hope that we can "beat the clock," however, and get to some useful conclusion before management pulls the plug.

Basically, there are some issues that can cause an early end to an investigation. These issues include liability of some sort, privacy issues, politics, the duty to return critical systems to production, and excessive cost of continuing. We'll explore those in more detail.

Most organizations have an unspoken rule that, when the cost of an investigation exceeds the expected return, the effort stops. It is a corporate reality in competitive environments that money can't be wasted. Within reasonable limits, that makes some sense. The cost of an investigation can be very high. We have had investigations go on for months and cost tens of thousands of dollars. Forensic work alone can chew through a budget with frightening speed.

When an investigation must stop for lack of resources, you have some choices. You can scrap the whole thing and hope it never happens again. You can turn over what you have to law enforcement and hope they take some action. Or you can, as we will discuss a bit later, try to salvage some benefit from your efforts. As you will see, most organizations can benefit from the lessons learned, regardless of when, in the course of an investigation, you are forced to abandon it.

As a general rule, no investigation should end without deriving some benefit. Thus, when you begin the investigative process, it is a good idea to set some parameters. One of these should be an early warning that termination is eminent. This gives you time to collect your data, create some sort of report (depending upon how far you have gone), and present some solutions to the problem for the future, based upon your findings up to that point. When you do this, of course, you must be sure to set management's expectations appropriately. It won't do to have management expect a full solution when the investigation is only about half complete.

LEGAL LIABILITY AND FIDUCIARY DUTY

One legitimate reason for early termination of an investigation is your duty to the organization. An investigation, if continued, may impose a potential legal liability upon the organization.

For example, a financial organization has a legal responsibility to protect the financial records of its depositors. If, for some reason, your investigation would cause those records to be exposed to the public, you could be subjecting your organization to potential lawsuits. There are legal remedies, of course, such as protective orders. However, during an investigation, it is unlikely that you will be able to control completely the consequences of exposing sensitive information to the investigative process.

It is a good idea, considering that such exposures could cause an investigation to terminate prematurely, to set a procedure in place in advance of your investigation. Procedures should anticipate the potential for exposing sensitive information to compromise. The time to create such a procedure is before you need it, not in the heat of an investigation.

One approach is to set up several "break points" in any investigation. These break points are events which require that you stop and take certain steps, such as reevaluating exposures. An example of a break point is the potential exposure of trade secrets. Suppose, for example, an R & D server has sustained an attack. Imaging the drive of this server will mean that a third party (a consultant, perhaps) will have access to the trade secrets on the disk. It could also mean that, if the investigation is successful, the offender may have access to the information. At this stage, you don't know who the offender is, what the purpose of the attack was, whether the offender was working for your competition, or whether the offender has already accessed your confidential data. It's time to insert a break point.

There are several possibilities that you should consider. You should perform what amounts to a mini risk analysis and consider your possible responses. If you don't continue, what could be the consequences? If you do, how can you protect the sensitive data? And so on.

Another time to insert a break point is when you are dealing with critical resources. Critical resources differ from sensitive resources in that critical resources may or may not contain information that could harm the organization if revealed. They do, however, contain information assets that are required to keep the business going. An example is a file server containing customer account records.

While it is certainly true that customer account records are sensitive, it is also true that those records are necessary to keep the business going. Sales need to be made, customers need to be invoiced, and money needs to be collected. Without the customer account server, none of these things can happen. What if the server has been attacked? Can you take it offline for the period of the investigation? Probably not. So, you need an alternative that preserves critical investigation information and allows the company to stay in business.

This is a perfect place for a break point. It is also a perfect place to have a set of preplanned responses ready so that you won't lose time in your investigation. The probable response to this example is to take the server offline, image the disk, remove the original hard disk from the server, replace it with a new drive, and restore the image to the new drive. That lets you get the server back online in the briefest time, preserve the original evidence "both in its original form and on a bit stream image," and get on with your investigation. While it's always a good idea to impound the entire computer as evidence, that often (and more frequently so, as we become more dependent on computers) is not possible.

Potential downstream liability can also bring an investigation to a halt. Consider the choice between allowing an intruder to continue his or her excursions through our system, so that we can gather more evidence, or complete a backtrace. Now, imagine that the intruder establishes a beachhead on our system and uses it to attack other systems. What is our risk if the owner of the other victim blames us for permitting the attack to continue?

Additionally, what might be the additional risk to our own systems and the data in them? Suppose the intruder compromises sensitive client data, information protected under any of several privacy laws, or critical data that could affect the operation of our other systems.

It is critical that you answer these questions in advance of an incident because during the incident you won't have a great deal of time for discussion. My rule of thumb is that an attack should never be allowed to continue if there is any risk to other systems, sensitive or critical data, or systems outside of our organization's control.

Occasionally, the issue of entrapment rears its head. As a general rule, entrapment does not occur if you have not enticed someone to do something they would not otherwise (without your influence) do. Thus, if you place a "honey pot" on your file server, you are not enticing the intruder to intrude. You are, simply, offering him or her an enticing target, once he or she already has violated your system. The act has already been completed and you did nothing to encourage it. Further actions to control the intruder and prevent damage to your system are not entrapment.

Of all the things that can stop an investigation, legal liability and fiduciary duty are the most likely to have a satisfactory resolution. Our next topic, politics, is the least likely to let us continue unhampered with our inquiry.

POLITICAL ISSUES

Political impediments to continuing an investigation cause more problems for us than all of the intruders we will encounter in our entire careers. Politics, at its simplest, results in cover-ups. At its worst, political intrigue can cause us to be misled, prevent us from collecting and preserving evidence, and corrupt the results of our witness interviews. Politics is a fact of life in large corporations. It usually is a problem in smaller ones as well. However, smaller organizations are less likely to take cover-ups to the extremes common in big companies. Fortunately, there are some things you can do to limit, if not eliminate, the impact of politics on your investigation.

BEFORE THE INVESTIGATION BEGINS

The time to begin managing the political environment is before the investigation begins. It is important to build the credibility of your investigative team from its inception. By credibility we do not, in this case, refer to the team's skills or professional qualifications. In this case, we mean its authority to investigate.

It is crucial that your investigative body, such as a Computer Incident Response Team (CIRT), has its investigative mandate from the most senior executive in the organization. It must have the power to investigate an incident by interviewing any employee of the organization, without regard for seniority, position, or political connections. This power must be granted by policy signed at the highest levels of the company. In fact, the policy should not just *allow* the team to investigate, it should *require* it.

The second task in managing the political atmosphere is to begin the process of seeking out one or more advocates for your efforts. These advocates must be in a position to influence management in your favor. Good advocates are CIOs, audit managers, general counsel, and any other manager who, by virtue of their fiduciary duty to the organization, has the ear of the CEO.

Begin working with your advocates to identify and preplan responses to any interference in an investigation *before* it has a chance to start. In some cases, you can anticipate where incidents could occur and who might pose a political brick wall to your success. Where you can do that, identify ways to address the potential problem(s) in advance. Once the investigation gets going, you won't have a lot of time to play the political game.

DURING THE INVESTIGATION

Your number one objective during the investigation is to collect evidence. Computer incident evidence is very fragile. Any delay in isolating and collecting evidence could mean that you won't be able to solve the crime. Political disruptions in your investigation might make a solution impossible or, at best, difficult. Therefore, it is in your best interests to do everything possible to prevent petty interruptions.

Before you can prevent politics from setting up roadblocks to your success, you must understand the political environment in which you are working. People interfere subtly for a variety of reasons. Rarely will anyone place overt barriers in your way. To interfere obviously with an investigation that is being conducted in accordance with policy, and in the full view of senior management, is to commit a CLM (career limiting move). Most people won't be stupid enough to do that. However, the subtle interference is what you need to avoid.

If you have done your homework in advance of the event, you'll have a pretty good idea of what or who is going to get in your way before it happens. That doesn't mean you've got all the answers. It simply means that you're on your way. However, if you follow a few simple procedures during your investigation, you'll experience a limited amount of frustration.

Start by watching the political environment carefully. If the event points to an insider, for example, you can expect that someone will attempt to cover up. You'll need to know who has the most reason to prevent the investigation from being successful. Does your analysis point to someone in the IT shop as the likely culprit? Expect that other engineers will cover for the suspect. In today's IT shops loss of even a single individual can spell overload for the rest. Potential loss of a good worker is a strong motivator for a cover-up.

When you sense that there is resistance to your inquiries, step back and figure out why. Whenever you can, involve the suspect's supervisor. Occasionally, the supervisor is, of course, part of the problem. In those cases, you have to keep him or her in the dark.

We conducted an investigation where we were certain the culprit was an insider. Why? Because the problem ceased as soon as our investigation started and critical evidence was deleted from the victim computer. Of course, we had copies of the evidence, but considering that only four people knew of the investigation, it seemed obvious that, somehow, one of those four either was involved or had communicated the investigation to the culprit without realizing it. Because evidence was damaged so early in the investigation, and because the events we were looking at stopped abruptly, it is unlikely that we'll ever arrive at a solution.

There is a secondary lesson here: evidence is very fragile. Had we not had a copy of the damning information on the victim computer, we would never have been able to draw any conclusions at all. Further, we would not have any evidence whatever that the events even occurred.

After the Investigation Is Completed

Okay, you've conducted your investigation, collected your evidence, and drawn your conclusions. Will anyone believe you? If you have settled on a suspect within the organization, you can expect comments such as, "Oh, he would never do a thing like that. I've known him for years." When that starts, you need to step back and start the process of consensus building.

If you haven't done your political job well before and during the investigation, this is going to be tough. You need your advocates. You need to work the politics while you're investigating. You need to do a first-rate job of conducting the investigation and managing your evidence. But, sometimes, even when the results are in, you still have resistance.

Your best approach is to build a consensus among the people whose backing you will need. You should start this process early in the game, but, whenever you start it, start it. Pick the individuals whose support you'll need as early in the investigation as possible. Start quietly and informally, including them in your process. If you "bring them along" throughout the investigation, you'll find them easier to convince when the time comes. You'll also find they will be more likely to support you at the end of your efforts. At least, they will be *less* likely to resist your conclusions.

CIVIL VS. CRIMINAL ACTIONS

Many criminal actions evolve from civil actions. Some civil actions are the result of a successful criminal prosecution. There are significant differences between the two. Criminal actions require proof beyond the shadow of a doubt, while civil ones require the preponderance of the evidence. Civil actions allow both sides to hold discoveries. In a criminal action, the investigation takes the place of discoveries. There are other differences, beyond the scope of this book, between the two types of litigation.

However, one thing is clear: within an organization, both can be equally contentious and disruptive. Many organizations and individuals within the organizations resent the disruptions caused by an investigation. The degree of tolerance varies with the organization's culture and personality.

Organizations with a culture of "zero tolerance" for wrongdoing are more likely to support your efforts. However, the threat of criminal action is, by itself, disrupting. Further, as we have seen, when law enforcement becomes involved, you can expect to lose control of the investigation. That is, probably, the biggest difference between civil and criminal investigations.

However, regardless of the eventual disposition of your investigation, you should treat it from the beginning as if it was a major criminal incident. There is a very good reason for this: you want to maintain the highest standards for your evidence management. Conducting an investigation is like getting your hair cut. If you cut it too short, you can never put it back. Unlike a hair cut, though, badly collected evidence never comes back. It just stays in your evidence locker and haunts you.

Probably the best source of guidelines for conducting your investigation, and dealing with computer-related evidence, is the *Federal Guidelines for Search and Seizure of Computers*, developed by the U.S. Department of Justice. While these are just guidelines, they are very comprehensive and give you the information needed to conduct your investigation to the standards that will be expected by law enforcement, if they take over the case.

Another source, which we have discussed in earlier chapters, is the book by Kenneth S. Rosenblatt, *High Technology Crime — Investigating Cases Involving Computers*. Both of these sources focus on the proper approach for law enforcement. Thus, they give the corporate investigator a solid foundation for conducting a professional inquiry, regardless of the venue.

The point of this topic is, actually, quite simple. You need to adhere, in your investigation, to the same high standards whether it will be prosecuted in criminal or civil court. If you cannot, for whatever reason, you may be forced to discontinue your efforts. Many organizations monitor ongoing investigations, affecting their information assets, and will call a halt, if the case is not going anywhere and the quality of evidence is unsatisfactory.

PRIVACY ISSUES

We'll cover privacy and policy issues in detail in Chapter 15. However, at this point, we will introduce you to the basic issues and see how they may force you to discontinue your investigation.

Earlier in this book we briefly alluded to the role of policies. To recap, policies determine what you can and cannot do in an investigation. If you do not have a policy that allows you to view employee e-mail and data on disks, you cannot complete your investigation. If you attempt to do so, there is a strong likelihood that most, if not all, of your evidence will be disallowed by the court. Sadly, not only will the evidence that you collected improperly be thrown out, any conclusions or evidence collected as a result of the tainted evidence will be useless as well.

If you reach a point in your investigation where you recognize that there are restrictions on your efforts because of privacy issues, it's a good point to stop and discuss the problem with your attorney. There are two possible outcomes of continuing. One is that the evidence will not be usable. The other, potentially far more damaging, is that your suspect may sue you for violating his or her privacy and, if they lost their job as the result of the investigation, wrongful termination.

SALVAGING SOME BENEFIT

Even when an investigation must stop prematurely, you can try to salvage some benefit for the organization. We have said that one of the important results of any investigation is lessons learned. In the Intrusion Management model, we feed lessons learned back into Avoidance, enabling us not to be the victim of a similar event in the future.

Regardless of how the event ends, we can evaluate what we know and use that knowledge to the benefit of the organization. A "post-mortem" of the event and the investigation should always be a part of every computer security incident. At the least, you usually can learn what root causes permitted the intrusion, where improvements can be made to systems or security measures, and what damage or loss was incurred.

One important benefit can accrue to other groups in your organization, such as risk management or business resumption. Knowing the nature of the threat, the vulnerability that permitted it to be realized against the information asset, and the countermeasures required to prevent it from recurring, allows these groups to take the risk into account for the future. You should never underestimate the positive benefits of your investigation even if you couldn't, for some reason, complete it.

SUMMARY

In this chapter, we considered the potential for prematurely concluding or interrupting an ongoing investigation. We recognized that there are times when an investigation cannot continue. We examined legal issues, as well as political and policy mechanisms. We also recognized that, regardless of the final disposition of an investigation, there may be benefits to be derived, not only for those groups involved directly, but for other groups within the company.

In the next chapter we will begin Section 3, "Preparing for Cyber Crime." In this short section, we will look at those things you need to do in advance of your first incident. We'll begin by discussing the planning for and implementation of a Computer Incident Response Team (CIRT), sometimes thought of as a "Cyber SWAT Team." We'll conclude Section 3 by exploring, in more detail, policies and the privacy laws that affect your investigation.

Section 3

Preparing for Cyber Crime

14 Building a Corporate Cyber "SWAT Team"

In this chapter, we will examine the requirements for a captive in-house investigative team. These "cyber SWAT teams" are referred to as Computer Incident Response Teams (CIRTs), or Computer Emergency Response Teams (CERTs). Most organizations prefer the "CIRT" over "CERT," to distinguish them from public response teams, such as the "official" CERT at Carnegie–Mellon University.

We will discuss the need for such teams, what the teams do and how they do it, who belongs on the team, and what training the teams require. We will include a sample standard practice for implementing, training, and managing a CIRT.

WHY DO ORGANIZATIONS NEED A CYBER SWAT TEAM?

The simple answer is that all organizations will, at some point, experience an intrusion that is successful enough to bypass their safeguards. That point accepted, it follows that someone needs to be trained to investigate and respond to an incident. The time to prepare for that eventuality is before, not during, the incident.

The more complex answer is that organizations are political animals. When an incident occurs, there will be segments of the organization that, for whatever reasons, do not wish to see a full investigation with full disclosure of lessons learned. It is necessary to ensure that such an investigation can occur and that the investigators are empowered at the highest levels, well-trained, and well-equipped. The only way to ensure this is by implementing a formal CIRT.

CIRTs are implemented by policy and managed under a standard practice or procedure. It is necessary for the authority of the CIRT to investigate, as well as its reporting structure, to be a matter of policy implemented at the highest levels of the organization. The details of the CIRT day-to-day operation are left to a standard practice or procedure. That allows the CIRT to be responsive to the evolution of business drivers, as well as technology drivers. We have included a sample statement, which should be placed in a policy, so that standard practices can operate under policy authority. We have also included a sample standard practice that demonstrates all important details of CIRT implementation and management.

WHAT DOES A CYBER SWAT TEAM DO?

CIRTs investigate computer security incidents. They plan the investigation, manage evidence collection, interview witnesses, perform backtraces, contain damage, and, generally, do everything discussed in this book when a computer security incident occurs.

It is important that the CIRT be well-trained and the members periodically practice their skills. They should have up-do-date tools and be current on typical attacks and vulnerabilities. In some organizations, the CIRT is a full-time entity. In most it is *ad hoc,* assembled from trained individuals who make up the team when an incident happens.

Most CIRTs consist of two teams. The first, or *core* team contains the individuals who will always conduct and manage the investigation. The second team is made up of backup members who are called upon when their specific skills are required. We will explore CIRT membership in more detail later in this chapter.

STANDARD PRACTICE EXAMPLE

What follows is an actual standard practice used to implement an incident response team. We put it here to give you an idea of how the pieces of a CIRT fall together to provide the investigative capabilities required by your organization. As you browse through this standard practice, recognize that it contains each of the elements you will require to define, implement, and manage the investigative process using a team of trained professionals. Also, note that the standard practice is implemented under the authority of a policy, usually the organization's information security policy. When you implement a standard practice under the authority of a policy, the policy should contain the following statement:

> **Authority to Create Standard Practices:** This Policy recognizes that it will be necessary, from time to time, to create standards, standard practices, and procedures relating to the subject matter herein for the purposes of supporting evolving business practices and technologies. Such standards, standard practices, and procedures will, when approved by **[insert appropriate authority here]**, have the same scope and authority as if they were included in this Policy. This Policy will, in such cases, be incorporated in the standard, standard practice, or procedure by reference.
>
> Additionally, it may be appropriate, from time to time, to issue guidelines for actions relating to the contents of this Policy or the standards, standard practices, or procedures created pursuant to it. Such guidelines will be considered to be suggestions for appropriate action and will incorporate this Policy by reference.
>
> When a standard, standard practice, procedure, or guideline is intended to become an extension of this Policy under this section, such document will include the following statement:
>
> "This [standard, standard practice, procedure, guideline] is created pursuant to **[Policy name here]** which is incorporated by reference."

Now, here is a sample standard practice. We are indebted to Nanette Poulios, a principal consultant for the Intrusion Management & Forensics Group, for her work on this document.

IMPLEMENTATION AND MANAGEMENT OF A COMPUTER INCIDENT RESPONSE TEAM (CIRT) — A SAMPLE STANDARD PRACTICE

Overview

Information Security Standard and Procedures defines the establishment of a computer incident response team (CIRT) to respond and manage any intrusion of the company's computer systems, networks, or data resources effectively.

The standards in this chapter are written under the authority and in support of the company's information security policy. The standards apply to any suspected intrusion of the company's computer systems, networks, and data resources.

These standards will be updated annually or prior to a major infrastructure change. Nonetheless, due to ongoing changes in the data processing and network environment, situations may occur where the applicability of these standards may be unclear. It is the user's responsibility to seek a definition or interpretation of the standards through Computer Technology Information Security.

Undefined or unclear standards cannot be construed to imply ignorance of a possible intrusion or reporting obligation.

The standards apply to all persons who have access to the company's computer systems, networks, and data resources.

Authority

This standard practice is issued under the authority of the Chief Information Officer.

Establishment of CIRT

The CIRT (Computer Incident Response Team) is a team of specialists established by the Chief Information Officer to investigate any suspected intrusion into the company's computer systems, networks, or data resources.

Mission

The objective of the CIRT is to investigate apparent intrusion attempts and report their findings, in a timely manner, to executive management. The CIRT provides a centralized approach to managing computer security incidents so that current incidents can be controlled as quickly as possible, to avoid serious damage to the company's systems, and so that future incidents can be prevented. Additionally, the CIRT will provide increased security awareness so that the company's computer systems will be better prepared and protected in the future.

Description

Role of CIRT

The CIRT is an investigative body only, convened strictly for investigating an apparent information security incident. The role of the CIRT is to respond rapidly to any suspected security incident by reporting all findings to management, identifying and controlling the suspected intrusion, and notifying users of proper procedures to preserve evidence and control the intrusion. By being prepared to respond to serious incidents, the CIRT can minimize damage to the company's computer systems, networks, and data.

CIRT Ownership

The CIRT is owned by the Chief Information Officer (CIO). The CIO is responsible for all CIRT activities and will ensure that the CIRT operates according to this standard practice, as well as the appropriate policies.

Duties of CIRT owner. All decisions relating to incident resolution are the responsibility of the CIO, who will make such decisions after conferring with the General Manager and General Counsel. The CIO will institute clean-up and "hardening" implementation when he or she deems it appropriate.

The CIO will alert affected external organizations, which may share compromised or potentially compromised resources with the company. Such public investigative organizations as CERT, FIRST, and law enforcement will be contacted only under direction from the CIO. Should the CIO decide to release details of an incident to a public investigative organization, the form of the information release will be approved by the General Counsel.

Responsibilities of CIRT

- Identify affected critical systems.
- Respond to all referred security incidents or suspected incidents involving the company's computer system, networks, and data resources.
- Establish a 24-hour, 7-day-a-week hotline to report security incidents.
- Convene within 3 hours of notification of a reported computer security incident.
- Establish classifications of security incidents requiring an investigation.
- Investigate and report all evidence to management.
- Assess damage and scope of intrusion.
- Control and contain intrusion.
- Collect and document all evidence relating to a computer security incident, according to established procedures.
- Maintain a chain of custody of all evidence, according to established procedures.
- Notify users of correct procedures to ensure that evidence will be protected.

- Notify users of any precautions to contain a security incident.
- Coordinate reposes to similar incidents or affected technology.
- Select additional support members as necessary for the investigation.
- Follow privacy guidelines as established by the company's policy.
- Provide liaisons to proper criminal and legal authorities.

Availability of CIRT

Security incidents can arise at any time of the day and on any day of the week. Often attacks happen during nonbusiness hours in the hope that the attack will go undiscovered until the damage has been completed. In order to detect possible incidents and react swiftly to minimize damage to the company's computer systems, networks, and data, the CIRT must be available 24 hours a day and 7 days a week. A hotline for reporting computer security incidents will be established by the CIRT.

Each core member must be on call to respond to hotline reports for a week's duration. This on-call responsibility will be rotated on a weekly basis among the core members of the CIRT.

The on-call member's responsibilities include:

- Availability by pager, 24 hours a day, 7 days a week
- Availability to report in person to the affected system immediately after being notified

Responsibilities of all other members of the core team and technical support team include:

- Available to the on-call member by pager

Composition

Members

Two kinds of members will comprise the CIRT team: core members and support members. The Chief Information Officer will select the core members and appoint the team leader.

Core members. The core members will convene when a security incident has occurred. They will be responsible for:

- Determining if the incident warrants further investigation
- Categorizing the security incident
- Adding support members to the investigation, if necessary

IT audit. A senior member of the IT Audit Services will be a core member of the CIRT.

Responsibilities include:

- Ensuring that best practices are followed
- Ensuring the auditability of the investigation process
- Ensuring that chain of custody procedures are followed correctly
- Maintaining accountability for all evidence collected during the investigation
- Documenting investigation

Information security. A member of Information Security will be a core member of the CIRT.
   Responsibilities include:

- Informing all other users affected by the security incident of the necessary actions to control the incident
- Performing appropriate backtracing, forensic analysis, and other technical tasks required by the investigation
- Providing an analysis of the incident, including root causes
- Compiling the final report and recommendations of the CIRT
- Availability as an expert witness

Corporate security. Responsibilities include:

- Providing a liaison with law enforcement
- Ensuring that investigative best practices are followed
- Containing the incident locale, as appropriate
- Managing the interview process for witnesses and suspects

Legal. Counsel from the legal department will be a member of the core group.
   Responsibilities include:

- Briefing other core and support members on privacy, Fourth Amendment, search-and-seizure, and wiretap issues
- Ensuring that suspects' rights are protected appropriately
- Acting as spokesperson with the media
- Reviewing any press releases before they are dispersed to the media
- Reviewing any management reports
- Acting as liaison with outside legal counsel

Support members. Support members will not be full-time members of the CIRT team. These members have valuable expertise in their fields. When the core team determines that the investigation requires the added expertise of a support member, that member will be added to the team for the duration of the investigation.

Platform specialists. A platform specialist for each critical system will be a member of the support team.

Responsibilities include:

- Reviewing audit logs and reporting any unusual or suspect activities
- Reporting any unusual behaviors of the critical systems
- Being prepared to brief the CIRT on operations procedures
- Protecting evidence of incident according to The Company's guidelines and instructions of the core team
- Assessing and reporting damage to system and/or data to CIRT
- Aiding in the determination of the scope of the intrusion
- Aiding in identification of the point of access or the source of the intrusion
- Making recommendations to close the source or point of access of the intrusion

Financial auditors. A member of financial auditing will be a member of the support team.

Responsibilities include:

- Being prepared to brief the team on financial procedures
- Being prepared to conduct a financial audit, if the core team deems it necessary for investigative reasons
- Reporting findings to the CIRT
- Following investigative procedures as determined by the CIRT

Fraud examiners. Often a computer system will be used to commit fraud or will be the target of fraud. When this situation occurs, a member of the fraud examiners group will be added to the investigation by the core team members.

Responsibilities include:

- Aiding the core members of the CIRT in discovery and recognition of fraud
- Following guidelines for lawful search
- Following the company's privacy policies
- Aiding in identifying objects and materials used to commit suspected fraud
- Preserving, using CIRT guidelines, any evidence collected until transported to CIRT
- Transporting evidence to CIRT for safekeeping until resolution of investigation
- Reporting findings to the CIRT

Personnel services. A representative who is well acquainted with personnel and human resource policies will be a support member of the team.

Responsibilities include:

- Advising the core members on personnel policies and procedures

- Making recommendations for handling sensitive employee information
- Managing issues involving labor union or other special contracts

Public information officer. In the event that the intrusion has become public knowledge, the Public Information Officer will be added to the investigative team.

Responsibilities include:

- Acting as a single point of contact for the media
- Obtaining legal advice before any interview or press release is given to the media
- Obtaining approval from the CIRT that any interview or press release will not interfere with the investigation
- Informing all other affected users to refer any media inquires to the Public Information Officer

Team leadership. The Chief Information Officer will appoint one of the members of the core team to act as the Team Leader. This role can be static or it can rotate through the team members at the discretion of the CIO.

Definition. The Team Leader is responsible for convening the CIRT, managing team meetings, and directing the activities of the team. The Team Leader is the CIRT manager for the term of his or her duties.

Role. The Team Leader fills the role of a group manager. As such he or she has management responsibility for the activities of the CIRT and the authority to convene an investigation.

Requirements. The Team Leader must be a member of the core team. He or she must have received the required training and must be appointed by the Chief Information Officer.

Duties. The Team Leader will perform the following duties:

- Convene the CIRT
- Contact the Chief Information Officer
- Conduct meetings of the CIRT
- Periodically report status of investigations to the CIO
- Manage investigations
- Take responsibility for verifying chain of custody of evidence
- Coordinate team activities
- Appoint support members as required for particular investigations
- Present findings to management
- Monitor the investigation
- Conduct a "post-mortem" analysis of lessons learned and report to the CIO

Duties of the CIRT. The CIRT is an investigative body only. It does not make policy or take action following an investigation, except at the express instruction of the Chief Information Officer. The CIRT is a completely independent body. It receives its direction from the Chief Information Officer, but is accountable directly to the General Manager or the General Manager's appointee.

In cases where an incident may have originated from an employee or employees reporting, either directly or indirectly, to the Chief Information Officer, the team will report a conflict of interest to the CIO. A temporary alternative reporting structure will then be implemented by the General Manager. In the event that a similar conflict of interest involves a core team member, that conflict must be immediately reported to the team and to the Chief Information Officer. The CIO will determine the appropriate course of action, based upon the circumstances surrounding the incident and the nature of the conflict of interest. In general, the CIRT duties include:

- Determining if an event constitutes an investigatable security incident
- Conducting an appropriate investigation to determine the root cause, source, nature, extent of damage, and recommended response to a computer security incident
- Preserving evidence of the incident
- Interviewing witnesses and suspects
- Providing appropriate liaison with law enforcement and outside legal counsel
- Managing the release of information to the media
- Managing interaction between Human Resources and witnesses, suspects, organized labor, and other appropriate interested parties
- Preparing a report of findings, root causes, lessons learned, and recommended actions for management review
- Carrying out the directions of management, communicated through the Chief Information Officer
- Containing the incident scene to prevent contamination of evidence

Training requirements
Core member training. Core members are required to obtain training in the following areas:

- Legal, Fourth Amendment, privacy, and lawful search issues
- The company's policies and procedures
- Investigative process
- Storing and transporting evidence according to legal guidelines
- Vendor training on all current detection and investigative tools
- Collecting, preserving, and analyzing evidence of a computer security incident
- Procedures for coordinating with outside organizations, such as CERT, FIRST, and law enforcement

Support member training. Support members are required to obtain training in the following areas:

- Legal, Fourth Amendment, privacy, and lawful search issues
- The company's policies and procedures
- Investigative process
- Storing and transporting evidence according to legal guidelines
- Technical training on all platforms, operating systems, and applications that a member is responsible for. These platforms include, but are not limited to, all computer operating systems and platforms currently used in the company, telephone PBX, and voice mail systems.

Ongoing training. Core team members will obtain periodic training to account for:

- Updates in tools used in their investigations
- Updates in investigative and forensic techniques
- Updates in appropriate technologies
- Updates and changes in laws, regulations, and the company's policies that affect investigations

Periodic computer incident simulation drills. The CIRT will conduct incident simulation drills twice per year. These drills will be monitored by the Chief Information Officer and the Manager of Internal Auditing. The objective of these drills is to simulate computer security incidents for the purpose of maintaining the appropriate skills of team members. All core members will be required to participate, and support team members will be selected to fulfill appropriate roles. The drills will strive for realism, thoroughness, and appropriateness. A post-mortem will be held at the completion of the drill to identify weaknesses in member performance and the appropriate remedial training.

Computer Security Incident Classifications

Identifying computer security incidents. A security incident is any event resulting in the company's computer systems, networks, or data being viewed, manipulated, damaged, destroyed, or made inaccessible by an unauthorized person.

CIRT notification process. All computer security incidents will be reported immediately to the company's help desk. The help desk operator will notify the CIRT member-on-call, using the CIRT pager. The CIRT member-on-call will analyze available information immediately and make a determination as to whether the core team should be convened. If the on-call member determines that the CIRT should convene, the core team will meet within three hours of initial notification.

If it is, in the judgment of the on-call member, appropriate to isolate the incident scene, he or she will notify corporate security through the team representative. That member will immediately arrange to contain the site following appropriate processes. If a technical platform specialist is required, the on-call member will identify and contact that individual immediately.

Classification of severity of incidents. There will be three classes of incidents: Class 1, Class 2, and Special. Class 1 incidents are those which are localized, minor, and do not require CIRT involvement. They are investigated by the appropriate department manager. Examples of Class 1 incidents are:

- Localized virus attacks
- Internet abuse
- Incidents traceable to user error or system failure
- Minor attempts at intrusion, scanning, or pinging

Class 2 incidents require CIRT involvement. These incidents are major incidents that put the company's information assets at risk. Examples of Class 2 incidents are:

- Attacks against a firewall
- Coordinated, distributed attacks
- Systemwide virus attack
- Financial fraud involving computers
- Attacks against a file server or host
- Theft of proprietary information
- Attacks against any sensitive system (human resources, legal, financial, etc.)

It is the responsibility of the CIRT to classify suspected security incidents. However, the CIRT or corporate management can escalate a Class 1 incident into a Class 2, if appropriate.

Special incidents are those which are referred to the CIRT as a result of a request by a department manager. Such requests must be approved by the Chief Information Officer. Disposition of Special incidents will be determined by the Chief Information Officer, in consultation with the requester and the CIRT Team Leader.

Escalation process. An incident may be escalated from a Class 1 to a Class 2 incident in any of the following ways:

- Decision of the CIRT Team Leader
- Decision of the Chief Information Officer
- Additional related events (i.e., emergence of a distributed, coordinated attack, as an example)
- Request by executive management

Class 1 incidents. Escalation from symptoms of an equipment failure or user error to a Class 1 incident may be initiated by the responsible manager. Once the escalation occurs, however, the incident must be reported to the CIRT team leader or the team member-on-call.

Class 2 incidents. Escalation from a Class 1 to a Class 2 incident may be initiated by the CIRT, the Chief Information Officer, or corporate management. The escalation and the reason for the escalation must be documented as part of the investigation.

Investigative Process
In all CIRT investigations, a formal investigative process will be used. That process will be appropriate to the incident, consistent with investigative best practices, and thoroughly documented. All members of the investigating team are expected to document their actions thoroughly, retain a copy of their notes for future personal use (i.e., as an expert witness in resulting litigation or criminal proceeding), and submit a copy to the team for use in preparing the final report. The member of the team from IT auditing will retain all records, notes, and reports for a period of 3 years after the incident.

Methodologies. The investigative team will use current best practices in their investigations. These practices are intended to ensure the following:

- Suspect's rights are preserved to the extent dictated by current company policies
- Evidence is properly collected, preserved, and documented
- Conclusions are supported fully by facts in evidence
- A full and complete investigation is conducted, free from contamination by outside influence
- Appropriate confidentiality is maintained
- The incident is contained appropriately to protect the company's information assets from further exposure

Investigative tool kit. Appropriate investigative tools will be assembled and maintained in a single location to support rapid response to an incident. These tools will be appropriate to the current state of the art, both from the perspective of the tools themselves and the systems against which they are directed. Physical security regarding these tools will be maintained at all times. In addition to on-site tools, such as backup devices, cameras, and forensic software, a forensic laboratory, consisting of a PC, backup/restore device, and forensic software, will be maintained and will be physically secure. The team leader will review available investigative tools from time to time to ensure that the tool kit contains state-of-the-art hardware and software.

Evidence collection
Evidence collection responsibilities matrix. The team leader will establish an Evidence Collection Responsibilities Matrix. This matrix will assign evidence collection duties to various team members consistent with their profession and personal skills, as well as with their functions on the CIRT.

Interviews. Interviews will be conducted in a professional manner using standard investigative interviewing techniques. Interviews will be documented, usually immediately after the interview. All confessions either will be recorded, using video or audio, or will be handwritten and signed by the suspect. Written confessions must be witnessed. The company's investigation procedures, as used by corporate security personnel, will be followed in all interviews and interrogations. Where interviews are governed under labor contracts, a member of Human Resources, as well as the team member from the Legal Department, must be consulted to ensure compliance with contract provisions.

Physical evidence. Physical evidence must be collected and preserved using an appropriate chain of custody. A lockable room, cabinet, or locker will be provided for securing evidence. Custody of all keys, lock combinations, or electronic key cards will be accounted for. Only one person, the custodian of the evidence, should have access to the room, cabinet, or locker. All transfers of evidence must be thoroughly documented and signed for. At no time should the custodian of the evidence be unaware of its location or physical security. See "Storage" below.

Preserving evidence. Evidence must be protected and preserved once it has been seized. Improper handling, labeling, and storage could destroy valuable evidence or make it unusable as evidence. All persons involved in the chain of custody of evidence must follow these guidelines to protect and preserve evidence:

Labeling. The requirements for labeling collected evidence are:

- Each piece of evidence should be placed in a sealed envelope or evidence bag.
- A label containing your signature, date, complete description of contents, and identification number should be placed over the envelope seal to ensure that no one has tampered with the contents.
- Anyone who takes possession of the evidence must sign and date the evidence label.
- Envelopes should be placed into a binder, if possible.
- Label, with tags, all equipment and cables. Make sure that all cables and connections are labeled to ensure they can be reconnected in the proper order.

Transporting. Evidence being transported must continue to conform to chain of custody requirements. At no time should evidence be out of the direct control of the custodian. When evidence, such as computers, must be transported in such a manner that it is outside of the custodian's direct control, it must be sealed in packaging that will reveal any attempt at tampering, and transported by an agency that can attest to its specific location and handling. Examples would be UPS, Federal Express, or airlines counter-to-counter. Signed acceptance (i.e., via signed airbill) must be obtained by the custodian, and the receiver (when delivered by the shipper) must take immediate, personal custody, and obtain a delivery signature from the delivery agent. U.S. mail is not an acceptable method of transport, in most cases.

Storage. The storage facility for computer evidence must be a friendly environment for electronic equipment and media, as well as a secured area.

The constraints for the storage facility include:

- Must be locked at all times
- All persons entering or leaving the locked area must be logged according to time, date, and identification by a core member of the CIRT
- All evidence entered or checked out of the storage facility must be documented
- All temperature, light, and humidity requirements of all electronic media must be met

Retention period. Civil litigation can take years to complete. Therefore, the retention period of evidence is tied to the ultimate resolution of the incident. Litigation and criminal prosecution may be subject to appeal, extending the time that evidence must be preserved. Therefore, some judgment must be exercised regarding the length of time evidence must be retained.

In no case should case evidence be disposed of before it is concluded, including the appeal process. Such evidence should then be retained for at least a year past the supposed conclusion of the entire case, including appeals. Where it is not apparent whether the incident will ultimately result in civil litigation or criminal prosecution, evidence should be retained for a minimum of three years or, in the case of possible criminal action, until the statute of limitations expires for the particular crime involved.

Report Process

The CIRT is responsible for reporting their findings to management at the conclusion of the investigation. This report should include the following:

- Executive summary — include a description of the incident, methods of investigation, and general conclusions.
- Detailed conclusions — include one section for each conclusion drawn by the CIRT. This section describes how the CIRT arrived at the conclusion, lists exculpatory evidence that may prove contradictory, and evidence that supports the conclusion. Log entries can show a chain of events that support the CIRT conclusion.
- Recommendations — the report should conclude with the CIRT recommendations for avoidance of future or repeat incidents.

Investigation Resolution

Ideally, an investigation concludes when an appropriate explanation of the incident is found, a final report is delivered, and management declares the case "closed." From a practical perspective, however, there are events and circumstances which can terminate an investigation prematurely or extend its final resolution beyond report production. Generally, the acceptance of a final report by management concludes the investigation. However, the investigation may extend beyond that point when:

- Litigation or criminal prosecution results
- There are technical challenges to the conclusions of the CIRT
- Management is dissatisfied with the conclusion
- Assistance from the CIRT is required to implement preventive measures

The investigation may terminate prematurely when:

- The Chief Information Officer terminates the investigation
- In the considered opinion of the CIRT, the incident cannot be solved
- Management declares that the incident investigation should be terminated
- The investigation passes to law enforcement
- Legal action to terminate is brought by a party involved in the investigation
- The investigation, key evidence, or critical information becomes contaminated, rendering a reliable conclusion impossible

Relationship with Law Enforcement Agencies

The CIRT will initiate and maintain a close relationship with appropriate law enforcement agencies in advance of any information security incident. The intent of this relationship is to foster an atmosphere of cooperation and encourage rapid response, should law enforcement involvement be required.

Additionally, the CIRT should become aware, through direct law enforcement contact, of the standards and requirements for law enforcement involvement in the CIRT local community. The CIRT relationship with law enforcement, and the standards dictating a request by the company for involvement by law enforcement in a particular investigation, are set forth both in the law and in the company's policy. The CIRT member from the Legal Department will become thoroughly familiar with all aspects of law enforcement involvement and will ensure that the team is briefed fully on those aspects. It will be the responsibility of the member from Corporate Security to maintain official liaison with the appropriate law enforcement agencies, including federal, state, county, local, and any computer crime task forces in the immediate area.

The member of the team from the Legal Department will become thoroughly familiar with the various laws and statutes involving computer-related crime. They will ensure that the law enforcement agencies with appropriate jurisdiction are contacted when required.

The Chief Information Officer will determine when and if law enforcement agencies should be called during the course of the investigation. He or she will confer with the CIRT, the General Manager, and the General Counsel before contacting a law enforcement agency. Executive management will determine, after the investigation is complete and the CIRT has reached a resolution to the incident as declared by the CIO, what resultant action is to be taken.

WHO BELONGS ON A CYBER SWAT TEAM?

The CIRT is composed, as we said earlier (and as is demonstrated in the sample standard practice) of two teams. The core team generally contains those groups that will always participate in an investigation. I suggest that a good starting point for the core team includes representatives from:

- Information security
- IT auditing
- Corporate security
- Corporate legal

To that group, we can add secondary team members from the following:

- Human resources (or personnel)
- Corporate communications (or public relations/public information)
- IT department (platform specialists)
- Financial auditing
- Fraud examination
- Other groups as required by the circumstances

While the actual membership may rotate, these groups should identify those people who are appropriate for CIRT participation and ensure that they are trained properly.

TRAINING INVESTIGATIVE TEAMS

Investigative team members need training when they join and over time to keep their skills sharp. Training programs are outlined previously in the standard practice, and to reiterate here would be a waste of time. However, this is a good place to make a couple of important points.

First, training takes more than one form. When a new member joins the team, he or she should receive the core training, as described in the standard practice. Since tools, technologies, laws, and policies constantly change, it is also necessary to provide refresher training on an ongoing basis.

As it happens, there are several good conferences that can facilitate this training. Some examples are:

- Various SANS conferences — very technical, aimed at IT professionals with security duties. Information at http://www.sans.org
- Various Computer Security Institute events and conferences — mid-range technical, a great of general policy information, as well as more technical platform-related security information. Information at http://www.gocsi.com
- MIS Training Institute events and conferences — focused primarily on IT audit issues. Information at http://www.misti.com
- HTCIA (High Technology Crime Investigation Association) annual forensics conference — the premier computer forensics event of the year. Information at http://www.htcia.org

Additionally, there are several very specialized conferences and events sponsored by such organizations as ISSA (Information Systems Security Association), ACFE (Association of Certified Fraud Examiners), ISACA (Information Systems Audit and Control Association), and IIA (Institute of Internal Auditing). Most of these organizations offer CEU (continuing education units) or CPE (continuing professional education) credits.

I recommend that the CIRT establish a requirement for annually attaining a certain number of these credits, mixed between the individual's specialty and the other core specialties. Thus, the technical members will also receive training in IT audit techniques, legal issues, and so forth. The secondary training need not be exhaustive, but some cross-training is necessary.

SUMMARY

In this chapter, we have examined the role of the CIRT. We learned who is on the response team, what they do, and how to train them. We presented a sample standard practice that you can use as a basis for your own formal procedure for forming and managing the team.

In the next chapter, we will wrap up our discussions of investigative procedures and all of the other issues surrounding them. This chapter deals with the privacy issues, with which you must be familiar, and the policy issues, that must be in place if you are to be able to investigate successfully. Upon completion of that chapter, we will introduce an excellent forensic tool set and demonstrate the use of the individual tools for collecting, preserving, and analyzing evidence.

15 Privacy and Computer Crime

Don't let the fact that this chapter comes toward the end of the book denigrate its importance to the investigative process. One of the leading impediments to a successful investigation is the lack of enabling policies. In this chapter, we will discuss policies and their impact on your investigation.

An appropriate policy, dictating what you can and can't do in an investigation, can either allow your efforts to go forward or can stop you dead in your investigative tracks. In terms of personal privacy and the expectation of privacy, the lack of a policy can ensure that the law protects the guilty.

We will explore policy issues, and I will introduce you to the laws that govern what you can and can't do in areas of monitoring, intercepting, and using a suspect's data in an investigation and subsequent legal action.

As is often the case, however, I have a couple of caveats at this point. The intent of this chapter is to get you started in your understanding of applicable laws and how they can affect your inquiry. For a more thorough understanding of legal issues, how to draft subpoenas and warrants, I recommend Kenneth Rosenblatt's book cited elsewhere in this work. It contains a wealth of detail and is written from the perspective of a lawyer and prosecutor.

Finally, never conduct an investigation without consulting your corporate legal department for local guidance. The information in this chapter applies specifically to the United States. However, many other countries have similar laws. In all events, the policies we discuss here, with a bit of adjustment for other country's laws (or lack thereof), are good starting points anywhere in the world.

THE IMPORTANCE OF FORMAL POLICIES

There are two kinds of laws: statutory and case. Statutory laws are those passed by legislators, either in the state or national government. Case law is how the finders of fact (judges and juries) have interpreted statutory law in actual court actions. Local interpretation of laws, both at the state and federal levels, varies widely from region to region.

In many cases, there is so little background that the same law may be interpreted differently in various parts of the country, favoring, in one geographic area, the individual, and, in another, the organization. Cyber law is such a new area of legal interpretation that there has not been sufficient time or examples to more than just begin the process of sorting out consistent interpretations of many issues. One such issue lies in the area of the individual's expectation of privacy. Expectation of personal privacy is often at odds with the best interests of the organization.

Certain laws, which we will discuss in more detail later, provide solutions to this difficulty. However, the solutions have safeguards built in and do not, *de facto,* support the interests of the organization. Understanding what you can and can't do in privacy matters dictates the policies you will need to protect the organization's rights and property. While these policies do not, by intent and design, favor the individual, we must remember that the welfare of the organization enables it to employ people and pay salaries. Thus, as *Star Trek*'s Mr. Spock would say, "The good of the many outweighs the good of the few."

A common error of many organizations is to assume that because they own the computers, the network, and the other corporate information assets, that employees using those assets must do so for business purposes. Failure to use them properly subjects the wrongdoer to disciplinary action. To assume that such automatically is the case is an error.

All individuals, in the absence of a strong policy to the contrary, have an expectation of privacy in their daily lives, even if those lives belong, for an eight-hour workday, to their employers. The extent of that expectation and the extent to which their lives belong to the employer is a source of debate, often in front of a judge and jury. There are ways to stack the deck on the organization's side, however, which is what this chapter is about.

At this point, let's just accept that you need to do something, and that something is to create appropriate policies, standards, practices, and acceptable-use rules that protect your organization's interests. For most employees, this is no imposition at all. For a few, it means the difference between being able to do damage to you and getting caught and doing so with impunity.

Putting things in the simplest possible language, without a policy to the contrary, you cannot monitor or intercept anything that your employees do on your network, except those portions of a message or data packet that provide source and destination information. You may monitor the perimeter of your network, but only to protect your property from attack.

The employee can download pornography, steal software, and hide it on his or her company desktop computer, and send your company secrets to your competitors in e-mail. Without a specific policy, acknowledged in writing by the employee, it is likely that he or she will get away with all of those abuses. That, in a nutshell, is the importance of privacy, ethical behavior, and acceptable-use policies. The details surrounding the nutshell version are a bit more complex, tend to have regional overtones, and should be worked out with your corporate legal department or an attorney experienced in privacy matters.

The keys to good privacy policies are:

- They cannot violate any laws.
- They must be in easy-to-understand language.
- They must be acknowledged in writing by the employee (this constitutes "prior consent" under the law).

We will explore the roots of these requirements a bit more when we discuss some specific privacy laws that can interfere with your investigation.

WHO OWNS THE E-MAIL?

If there is no policy to the contrary, the employee has an expectation of privacy with regard to electronic mail. Thus, any information contained in e-mail is disclosed at the will and pleasure of the employee, not the employer.

This can cause a bit of a problem for the organization because there is no *de facto* assumption that the contents of an e-mail message involves the company. If the employee wishes to reveal the contents of the message, that's his or her business.

However, when the organization specifically, by policy, decrees that all information passing on the company network, residing on company computers, or residing on disks within the company is the explicit property of the organization, the ballgame changes radically. Now, the organization may examine any source, destination, or intermediate repository of information of any kind within its authority. This can include computers, mass storage devices, e-mail servers, voice mail systems, and anything else likely to contain company information or information germane to company function, including that which may be necessary to an investigation.

Additionally, the policy should explicitly state that the employee has no expectation of privacy and that all employee activities are subject to monitoring. However, be careful how you word this. You want to avoid any implication that the monitoring is for anything other than protecting your property. Keystroke monitoring, which can be tied to employee performance, has been widely met with disapproval.

Another area of concern is the evenhandedness with which you investigate and enforce this policy. If you investigate and/or enforce any policy unevenly, that policy may be thrown out of court if challenged. In other words, if you investigate and discipline workers who download pornography some of the time, instead of all of the time, you will find your cases starting to get thrown out of court.

THE DISK BELONGS TO THE ORGANIZATION, BUT WHAT ABOUT THE DATA?

The ownership of data in mass storage is treated similarly to e-mail. If you have no policy to the contrary, you will probably not be allowed to investigate (or use evidence gained in an investigation) information stored on the hard disks of computers in your organization.

This can include information obtained illegally or contrary to your policy, such as pornography, pirated software, corporate secrets, etc. A further risk is that, in cases that violate law, your organization can be found to be equally guilty because they are not seen to be taking aggressive action to curb the abuse.

THE "PRIVACY ACT(S)"

There are several federal statutes that fit into the general classification of "privacy laws." Some of those are:

- Computer Fraud and Abuse Act
- Electronic Communications Privacy Act
- Privacy Protection Act
- Fourth Amendment
- State and local laws

We will discuss these in a bit more detail shortly. First, let's examine which laws might be appropriate in a given situation. When a federal law has been broken, that branch of law enforcement selected to assist you (if you chose to involve law enforcement) will usually be the FBI. Thus, it is useful to know which law (or laws) applies to the particular incident you are investigating. Here is a table that can help you make that decision.[1]

Did Your Intruder:	Then Look At:
• Access a computer across state lines?	• 18 USC 1030 (Computer Fraud and Abuse Act) and state laws
• Access a U.S. government computer?	• 18 USC 1030 (Computer Fraud and Abuse Act) and state laws
• Access another computer?	• State laws
• Add, alter, or destroy data?	• State laws
• Copy information	• 18 USC 1343 (wire fraud); 18 USC 2314 and 2315 (transportation and receipt of stolen property); 17 USC 506(a) and 18 USC 2319 (copyright infringement); state laws punishing intrusion with theft of information and state laws punishing theft of information
• Steal credit or financial information from a financial institution?	• Same as copying information plus 18 USC
• Use or trafficking in unauthorized access devices (passwords, etc.) or possess more than 15 such devices	• 18 USC 1029 plus applicable state laws
• Intercept electronic communications?	• 18 USC 2510 (Electronic Communications Privacy Act)

THE COMPUTER FRAUD AND ABUSE ACT

The Computer Fraud and Abuse Act is actually Title 18 of the U.S. Code, Section 1030. It covers the following:

- Accessing a computer and obtaining classified information
- Accessing a computer and obtaining financial information

- Accessing a government computer
- Accessing a computer across state lines
- Trafficking in passwords

This is a federal law. However, it does not generally punish joy riders and usually requires malicious intent. You violate this act if you:

- Access a computer and obtain classified information
- Access and obtain credit or financial information from a bank, credit issuer, or consumer reporting agency
- Access a U.S. government computer, or a computer partially used by the government, where the offense affects the government's use of the computer
- Intentionally and without authorization transmit a program, command, or information
- With intent to damage a computer system, network, information, data or program, or deny the use of same, or with reckless disregard of a substantial and unjustifiable risk that the transmission may cause such a result; and the transmission causes a loss of more than $1,000 during the course of a year, or actually or potentially interferes with a patient's medical care or treatment; or traffics in passwords, if that trafficking:
  - Affects interstate commerce or involves the password to a computer owned or used by the U.S. government

ELECTRONIC COMMUNICATIONS PRIVACY ACT

This is a federal law. Its major importance to you is that it dictates the extent of the monitoring you may perform. It covers:

- Owner's right to monitor systems
- Right to monitor employee communications

The details are:

- Owner may intercept communications between an intruder and that owner's computer system.
- Owner, providing others with the ability to use that computer to communicate with other computer systems, may:
  - make routine backups and perform other routine monitoring;
  - intercept with prior consent of the user;
  - intercept portions of communications necessary to determine origin and destination;
  - intercept, where necessary, to protect owner's rights or property;
  - disclose to law enforcement any communications inadvertently discovered which reveal criminal activity.

- Business may monitor employee communications using its computer system where:
  - employees have no right to use the computer for any reason;
  - policy states that employer will monitor all employee communications;
  - employer monitors a legitimate investigation of criminal misconduct by an employee using equipment provided by the telephone company.

Notice a couple of important issues here. First, this is the act that, if you create your policy correctly, empowers you to monitor employee use of organizational systems. This is explicit where the act states that the employer may "intercept with prior consent of the user." An acknowledged policy, in plain language, provides this prior consent.

Second, you may monitor where "policy states that employer will monitor all employee communications." Additionally, the act gives you the right, under all conditions, to monitor to protect your property (such as perimeter connections to external networks, e.g., the Internet) and to monitor portions of communications that indicate source and destination. This is, if applied appropriately, a very powerful, enabling law for monitoring and your investigations.

THE PRIVACY PROTECTION ACT

This is another part of Title 18 of the U.S. Code. In most cases, we don't have to be concerned with this one because it applies to materials intended for publication. If you fall under this law, I suggest you look it up and then consult with your attorney.

STATE AND LOCAL LAWS

These laws generally cover such things as:

- Obtaining free telephone service by fraud
- Obtaining and/or using stolen access codes
- Stealing data
- Accessing a computer without permission
- Using a computer without permission
- Disrupting computer services
- Altering, damaging, or deleting computer data
- Copying or using data stored in the computer without permission

As with the remainder of the laws we have described here, it is recommended that you familiarize yourself with these laws and consult your attorney. You will find that most of the incidents you investigate have elements of violations of these acts.

WIRETAP LAWS

Wiretap laws affect your monitoring in general, but they have an additional, specific, impact. Wiretap laws apply directly to the monitoring of electronic mail.

For the purposes of wiretap laws, e-mail is considered to be in transit, or "on the wire," if it is not residing on the user's computer at either end of the circuit. This means that e-mail is in transit, and covered by wiretap laws, when it is actually in transit between servers, or when it is stored on an intermediate server. The safe rule of thumb is, if the mail has been written, but not yet read, it is in transit. There are some nits to be picked with this interpretation, but if you live by it, you probably won't get in trouble.

FOURTH AMENDMENT TO THE U.S. CONSTITUTION

This amendment covers protection against unreasonable search-and-seizure. If you are in the corporate (nongovernment) world, this probably doesn't apply to you. You can always seize your own computer. Of course, what you can do with it after the seizure depends upon your policies. This was written to protect citizens from oppressive police actions.

There is one exception that may, under certain conditions, apply to nongovernment/law enforcement agencies. If you become an agent of law enforcement, you will have to play by the same rules they do, which includes abiding by the Fourth Amendment. The following conditions, all of which must be present, apply and, if they exist, will make you an agent of law enforcement:

- The private party performs a search that the government would need a search warrant to conduct; and
- The private party performs that search to assist the government, as opposed to furthering its own interests (e.g., protecting its rights or property); and
- The government is aware of that party's conduct and does not object to it.

SUMMARY

In this chapter, we have examined a few of the laws that impact your investigation. We have discussed the policies you must have in place if you are to investigate an incident properly, and what the impact of the law is where privacy issues are involved, if you have no such policies.

In the next section we will walk you through the use of a forensic tool kit from New Technologies, Inc. (NTI) in Gresham, OR.

REFERENCE

1. Rosenblatt, K., *High Technology Crime*, KSK Publications, San Jose, CA, 1995.

Section 4

Using the Forensic Utilities

Preface — How the Section Is Organized

This section covers the specific use of the NTI Forensic Utilities. NTI (New Technologies, Inc.) is located in Gresham, OR. In my opinion, they offer the most comprehensive set of tools for collecting, preserving, and analyzing computer evidence available today. Current tool sets are focused on MS-DOS and Microsoft Windows 3.X, 95, and 98 file systems. They have some usefulness on NetWare, NT, and Unix environments as well. However, at this writing, NTI is working on tool sets for Microsoft Windows NT and Novell NetWare.

I have roughly organized this section the way the tools would be used in an actual investigation. In Chapter 7, we discussed the investigative process. In this section, I will apply the tools specifically to that process. I will explain how to use many of the forensic tools and what to expect from them.

I will, however, in the interest of this book's useful shelf-life, keep to a fairly general (nonversion specific) discussion of the individual tools. Thus, if the NTI tools undergo revision and update, as, of course, they must over time, you will still have a good idea of how to use them from this book.

NTI also offers stringent training in the tools, as well as in forensic computer science in general. It is important to note that the general NTI policy is to avoid selling these tools without appropriate training, because they can do significant damage to evidence in the hands of an untrained user. I caution you not to consider this book the only training you need to use the Forensic Tool Kit in a real investigation.

The first chapter in this section addresses the basic concepts we have discussed earlier, this time in specific context of the tools. We will consider evidence collection and preservation issues. We will then, in the next chapter, move on to the specifics of using SafeBack to create a bit stream, or physical, image of a disk. We will use the image to create a mirror on which we can begin our investigation. We will then explain the next step, using FileList to take a disk inventory.

Chapter 18 explains how to use the tools to analyze the evidence you have collected in Chapter 17. We will discuss each of the NTI analysis tools and their roles in processing evidence to uncover leads that the investigator can use to solve the case.

Finally, in the last chapter, we will discuss the evidence collection, preservation, and analysis techniques for floppy disks.

16 Preserving Evidence — Basic Concepts

As you learned in earlier chapters, the techniques we use to collect, preserve, and analyze forensic computer evidence are critical ingredients in our investigative process. In this chapter, we will briefly review issues involving evidence collection, maintaining chain of custody, and marking evidence, so that we can testify to its source, condition, and custody from the time of its collection until it is used in a legal action. Unlike our other discussions of this topic, we will marry the theory to the practice using actual tools.

TIMELY EVIDENCE COLLECTION AND CHAIN OF CUSTODY

Computer evidence is very fragile. As you have learned already, evidence sitting on a hard disk in a computer, being used for normal computing tasks, can be deleted, overwritten, or altered in some other manner, rendering it useless, unrecoverable, or contaminated.

Thus, it is critical to isolate a computer involved in an incident as quickly as possible. However, the act of isolating the computer must be performed correctly by a trained forensic specialist to avoid damage. There are some general steps, most of which we have discussed earlier, that will help you ensure that the evidence on the hard drive stays pristine.

First, remember that there are four general areas of the disk where evidence might hide (besides the active data area, of course):

1. Slack space
2. Unallocated, or free, space
3. Swap files
4. Cache files

All four of these areas are subject to contamination if proper procedures are not followed. As a general rule, there are four specific criteria for forensic analysis:

1. The tools you use to collect the evidence
2. The techniques you use to collect the evidence
3. The tools you use to analyze the evidence
4. The techniques you use to analyze the evidence

Additionally, there are some specific criteria for the selection of your forensic tool kit:

- They must not alter the data as a side effect of the collection process.
- They must collect all of the data we want, and only the data we want.
- We must be able to establish that they worked properly, e.g., as advertised.
- They must be generally accepted by the computer forensic investigative community.
- The results produced must be repeatable.

With this in mind, we have selected the Forensic Tool Kit from New Technologies, Inc., to analyze evidence, and SafeBack, the standard of the law enforcement community, to collect the evidence.

Here, we should make an important distinction. The analyzing of evidence produces *leads,* not more evidence. The evidence resides on the disk image you create with SafeBack. The NTI tools simply allow you to analyze it and pluck out some useful leads to assist you in the investigation. You also can use the information collected with the NTI tools to demonstrate your findings to the finder of fact in a legal action.

At the end of the day, however, the evidence is on your physical image, where it must be protected. You may want to protect the information you gleaned from your analysis as well. It is a good practice to do so. That way, several months after the fact, you will be able to satisfy yourself that the data you collected, in your analysis, is still as pristine as the day you collected it.

Once you have collected evidence in the form of a physical image of the hard disk, you will have to be able to account for its custody until it is needed in court as part of a legal action. This includes both physical and logical protection of your disk images. If you should pass the images on to another custodian, you must ensure that the new custodian takes official control of your data. Evidence must be stored in such a manner that no one except the custodian could have access. Additionally, you (if you are the custodian) must be able to testify that, of your own firsthand knowledge, such is the case. This means you should have a way to secure the evidence physically (bagged, tagged, and placed under lock and key) as well as logically (cryptographically signed).

Part of the problem with computer evidence is that, if it is not still on the computer, you are dealing with a copy. Recall our best evidence rule. The copy must be a full and accurate reproduction; we must be able to so testify of our own firsthand knowledge; and it must be the best example of the original available. When we apply this to a full bitstream copy of a hard drive, we must be able to answer some questions about the copy.

- If we restore the backup to another machine, will it contain all of the files, no more and no less, that were on the original?
- Will the restored version's files be identical, faithful copies of the original?
- Will hidden space be faithfully reproduced?

- Will the restored backup contain all the data, and only the data, on the original?
- How do you know that your answers to these questions are accurate?

How we handle the backup process will determine our answers to these questions. To answer these questions and ensure, months or years in the future, that our data is as pristine as the day it was created on the original disk, we have some tools and techniques. We'll begin by discussing how to mark computer evidence logically using encryption.

"MARKING" EVIDENCE WITH AN MD5 HASH AND ENCRYPTION — CRCMD5 AND PGP

If we have a paper document, a gun, or any other physical object, we can mark it using a physical tag with some unique mark (such as a signature), which we will recognize in the future. That, along with our physical custody measures, helps us to verify collection of the evidence and that it has remained pristine since its collection. This process is not quite so simple with computer data on magnetic media.

Magnetic media is subject to physical stresses such as magnetism, extremes of heat and cold, and, even, physical or electrical shock. Additionally, it is a simple matter to alter logical evidence if you can gain access to it. Knowing and being able to prove that the evidence has been altered can be very difficult because the alteration may leave no indication that it ever occurred.

In order to ensure that the evidence you use in court is the same evidence you collected, you need to be able to mark it logically and seal it in such a manner that it simply is not accessible to anyone, except you. Additionally, so that nobody can create their own, slightly different (presumably, to their benefit) version of the evidence, and present it as identical to your own, you need a method of establishing that all evidence meets the best evidence rule and that it is all identical to the original.

We have three tools to ensure these things. The first allows us to take an inventory of the original disk and document it so thoroughly that even the slightest alteration to any disk file will be revealed.

The second allows us to validate our bitstream backup so completely that if another is made and altered, in even the slightest way, the alteration will be revealed. Finally, we have a method of sealing and signing any file we wish to place in evidence so completely that it cannot be opened without our assistance. However, it can be duplicated as an unprotected file for anyone to examine and analyze without the slightest effect on the original. We begin with the NTI FileList program.

FileList

I should point out that we do not use FileList as the first step in collecting and preserving our evidence. We must first take a bitstream back with SafeBack. We'll discuss the specific use of FileList in the next chapter. For now, I'll just describe what it is and how it works.

FileList is an NTI utility that allows us to take a complete inventory of every file on a disk. It presents the inventory logically — that is, displayed in a standard directory tree format. However, it gives us much more than the typical directory tree. FileList gives us the date of last change and file size, but it also provides an MD5 message digest of the file.

Since MD5 is 128-bit hash algorithm, it is nearly impossible to alter the file, even in the slightest manner, without altering the MD5 value. Thus, a listing from FileList is a nearly perfect and practically unalterable representation of the files present in logical disk space. It does not, of course, make any representations as to hidden space such as slack, unallocated, etc.

CRCMD5

CRCMD5 is an NTI tool that performs two calculations on a file and reports the results in the form of a unique file fingerprint. The first calculation is a 32-bit cyclic redundancy check (CRC). Because it is possible, though difficult, to alter a file, such that the CRC stays the same, CRCMD5 additionally performs an MD5 message digest. Taken together, these two calculations form a fingerprint that is, for all intents and purposes, completely unique to the file. Any attempt to alter the file will be reflected, either in the CRC, the MD5 or, more likely, both.

By running CRCMD5 against the bitstream backup files created by SafeBack, future copies can be compared, ensuring that they are genuine and meet the best evidence rule. The file fingerprint can be saved, both together with the file for which it was taken and separately, thus ensuring that an accurate copy exists and is available if needed.

SEALING EVIDENCE

We can add one additional element to CRCMD5 and make it essentially impossible with today's technology to forge evidence. It also gives us the ability to say, with nearly absolute certainty, that the evidence about which we are testifying is the same evidence we collected months or years earlier.

The process has several parts. First, we must validate (or ensure that we can validate in the future) the evidence, file by file. Second, we must seal and sign the evidence such that only we can retrieve it. For convenience, we also should add a "back door" so that our opposition can access the evidence without affecting our sealed, original copy. The tools we need to do these things are CRCMD5 and PGP (Pretty Good Privacy) public key encryption.

We have described the use of CRCMD5 to create a fingerprint of a file in evidence. Now, a little discussion about public key encryption is in order. Public key encryption differs from secret key encryption in a very important way. Secret key encryption has only one key: the secret key. In order to reveal a file encrypted with secret key encryption you have to reveal the secret key. A secret revealed is no longer a secret. If I tell you my secret key, I cannot testify that you could not have opened the file, altered it, and reencrypted it with the same key. So, if I decide to seal evidence with a secret key, I cannot share it without extracting a copy myself.

Public key encryption, such as PGP, on the other hand, has two keys: a public key and a private key. I can encrypt a file with my private key, which only I know, and give a copy of the encrypted file to you with my public key. The public key can be used only to decrypt the file, not to encrypt it again. So, you can access the file for analysis, but I still have a pristine copy that only I can open and reencrypt because only I know the secret or private key.

In court testimony, then, I could open the real original file, perform a CRCMD5 on it, and determine that it was either the same or different from your version. Because the secret, or private, key is known only to me, if I hadn't shared it (and, why would I, because you can use the public key to access a copy of the file), I can testify that my seal is intact.

SUMMARY

In this chapter, we have had an introduction to a couple of basic techniques for handling and preserving computer file evidence. We have examined the use of CRCMD5 to fingerprint a file, PGP public key encryption to sign and seal it, and FileList to document a hard drive's contents.

In the next chapter, we will take a bitstream image with SafeBack and perform a FileList listing. These are the first two steps in collecting and preserving computer evidence. We will assume a DOS/Win95-98 environment.

17 Collecting Evidence — First Steps

Now we begin the actual step-by-step process of making a bitstream image and collecting our forensic evidence from the disk of a computer. Our examples use MS-DOS/Win95-98 as the operating system, but many of our procedures are the same for other operating systems.

In this chapter, we will take our first two important steps. We will collect a bitstream image using SafeBack and will inventory the hard drive using FileList. This chapter refers, specifically, to SafeBack release 2.0 and FileList release 1.3.

USING SAFEBACK 2.0 TO TAKE AN IMAGE OF A FIXED DISK

We begin by examining, briefly, the SafeBack program and its various screens. SafeBack comprises several programs, including Master, Remote, and Restpart. There are two ways to use SafeBack. You can connect your backup medium (tape drive, Jaz drive, etc.) directly to the computer under examination, or you can connect two computers together, using a special parallel cable connected to one of the LPT ports on the two computers. The controlling computer is the Master, the computer under test is the Slave. This type of connection places the image directly on the controlling computer and is extremely slow due to the parallel port connection.

We will focus on two ways to make a bitstream backup directly, using a single computer: the computer under test. The first way is to use some external form of backup device (tape, Jaz, etc.). Even though SafeBack refers to this as "Local," we will need to use the LTP port on our target computer to connect the backup device. This approach gives us (usually) a bitstream backup from which we can create a mirror image if we wish.

The second way to use the Local connection is to use a second drive, directly, to hold our data. I generally use this approach to create a direct mirror of the computer under test by using the "Copy" capability of SafeBack. Copy is the equivalent of an immediate physical backup and restore. In this section, we will discuss the details, step by step, of these two techniques. Let's begin, however, by taking a brief look at the SafeBack program itself.

When you start SafeBack, you get a nice splash screen. Hit [ENTER] and you will see the audit trail dialog box. SafeBack is always started from a DOS bootable floppy disk containing the portions of the SafeBack program you will need for this backup. Usually, this means the Master program only. You may want to include Restpart.exe because you may need that when you perform the restore function. Restpart restores partition table information when it is destroyed.

The reason you may need that is when you restore a backup to a disk, the physical backup will overwrite all of the original partition information on the target. When you are finished with your analysis, you may wish to restore your working disk to its original partition information. By saving its partition data with Restpart, prior to restoring your bitstream image, you can restore the original partition table (which Restpart saves in a separate file for you) and be back to where you were before analyzing the mirror.

Your first step is to connect your backup device, which must be a SCSI device (for Jaz, use the Traveler option which converts parallel to SCSI), to the computer you wish to test. Next boot the computer with a DOS bootable floppy containing the SafeBack programs you need and all of the drivers required to run your backup device.

After booting, make sure you are seeing the A:> drive prompt, and start SafeBack by typing "master." That will get you the SafeBack splash screen and [ENTER] gets you the audit trail dialog. Hit [ESC]ape and enter the path on the *A: drive* to the audit file, for example: A:\backup-1.txt. Hit [ENTER] and you will be taken to the SafeBack main menu.

There are four modes of operation on SafeBack, called, on the main menu, "functions." They are:

1. Backup
2. Restore
3. Copy
4. Verify

In the Backup mode, SafeBack creates a single (or, if it's necessary to span several backup media, due to available backup space, multiple) DOS file containing your backup. It also contains everything SafeBack needs to recreate partitions and other aspects of the disk geometry. This is the *bitstream image* we have been talking about throughout this book. Because it is a single DOS file, with minimum compression, you can use it to search for keywords using other search tools (which we'll discuss in the next chapter).

In the Restore mode, you can restore the bitstream image created using Backup to another disk. The disk must be at least as big as the one you made the image of. It may be bigger. If the two disks (source and mirror) are not the same size (assuming the disk you will use for the mirror is the larger), SafeBack will adjust (in most cases) the geometry of the two disks to appear the same.

The Copy mode is, essentially, an immediate Backup and Restore without creating an image file.

Verify allows SafeBack to perform all of the tasks associated with a successful Restore without actually restoring anything. The point is that Verify makes sure you have a restorable backup. You should always perform a verify before abandoning a backup procedure.

There are some other choices on the main menu. Remote Connection allows you to select Local or LTP1. The only time you use LTP1 is when you will set up two computers in a master/slave configuration.

The third selection is Try Direct Access. This choice is No or Yes. If you select "No" (the default), SafeBack will use the system BIOS to access the drives on the computer. "Yes" allows SafeBack to bypass the system BIOS and go directly to the drive controller.

The final menu choice is Adjust Partitions. This needs a bit of explanation. When you Store (or Copy) to a drive with different partition data than the drive you backed up, there may be differences in the physical disk geometries of the two drives. SafeBack can try to reconcile those differences such that the two drives appear to be identical. This is the desired approach (and the default).

However, sometimes there is no way to get SafeBack to adjust the two geometries (this can happen during a direct disk-to-disk copy) and you must turn the automatic adjustment off by selecting No. Finally, the Custom choice lets you enter the geometries of the two disks manually and then let SafeBack adjust.

To make our backup, simply select the Backup choice from the main menu, leave everything else alone, and then press [ENTER] to move to the next screen. The next screen will present a table of available drives for you to select the source of the data you want to back up. You will notice that there will be one or more drives labeled using numbers (0,1,2,etc.). There will also be some with familiar letter labels (C,D,E,etc.). The numbered drives are the *physical* drives. The lettered drives are *logical volumes*. We are going to back up physical drives only at this point.

Place the cursor bar on the physical drive you want to back up and press the [SPACE] bar. This will mark the drive. There are several other things that you can do on this screen, but, since they don't relate directly to this process, we'll let them pass. The SafeBack manual is very complete in describing all of the software's functions and I recommend it to the reader prior to using SafeBack in a production environment.

Upon moving from the source drive menu, you will be given the opportunity to tell SafeBack where you want the backup to go and, if appropriate, what you want to name it. I use the Iomega Jaz drive as my backup device. When I install the Jaz drive, using the traveler option, traveler tells me what drive letter it has assigned to the Jaz drive. SafeBack asks me where I want the backup to go and I respond with a standard path/filename, for example, D:\backup-1.

You don't have to give the file an extension because SafeBack will provide that automatically. If your backup is larger than a single copy of your backup media (in the example, Jaz disks), SafeBack will tell you now how many disks (or other media) you will need to hold the entire backup. You can back out at this point if you don't have enough media to continue. Otherwise, continue and the backup will begin.

The Restore process is the opposite of the backup process. Most adjustments required by the differences in disk geometry are handled by SafeBack. If the destination disk is bigger than the original source, SafeBack will backfill the unused space with binary zeros, overwriting any ambient data which may be present on the disk.

The other approach is a direct copy. We have shown an example of this technique when we discussed Unix images. The technique is, essentially, the same for a DOS mirror. Recall that we said a copy creates a mirror image of the source disk on a target disk. The mirroring process is the same as a combination backup and restore without creating a backup image in between.

For our purposes, the terms "mirror" and "copy" are interchangeable. The first step is to establish the target disk. We have several issues to deal with here. First, we need to know how the current source is configured. We must be very cautious here because we are working with a live, original copy of our evidence. Any slip could damage or pollute our original evidence. My strong suggestion is that you *not* perform this process until you have made a bitstream backup of the original evidence in case something goes wrong.

In order to get a picture of how your system is currently set up, you need to boot from your DOS floppy and select the setup option when your PC offers it. Some PCs use [F1], some use the [DEL]ete key, and others use a combination of keys to enter setup during the boot process.

Once you are in the setup program, observe how the hard drive you will be copying is configured. It is possible that you will alter the CMOS and may need the current configuration to recover easily. Most current PCs automatically sense the drive settings, but it never hurts to have the information written down. You want all of the hard drive settings, such as number of cylinders, heads, etc.

You also want the disk type number and want to know how the drive is installed. It usually will be the primary master, but in multi-drive systems it may be a secondary or a slave. Primary master is the desired connection. Verify this by examining the jumper settings on the drive. If you don't know what the settings mean for a particular drive, contact the drive manufacturer, check their Web site, or refer to the best book on the subject, *The Hard Disk Technical Guide*, published by Micro House and written by Douglas T. Anderson and Michael Tribble. Everyone doing computer forensics needs the current copy of this book.

Your next step is to shut down the computer and install your target disk. This disk must be at least the same size as the source. You can mix drive types (IDE, SCSI, etc.) if you have the appropriate controllers installed. I routinely mirror SCSI disks to a 10GB IDE drive by using two different controllers.

If your source drive is the primary master, you'll want your destination drive to be the primary slave. Make sure that the jumpers on the target disk are set properly and connect the same ribbon cable that connects the primary master to the connector on the target drive. There should be two connectors on the cable. Don't forget the power plug. Make sure that the DOS boot disk is in the boot drive (usually A:>) and turn on the PC.

At this point, if the PC uses auto sensing (if it does, you should have made sure that it will select auto sense when you checked the primary/source drive), the PC will now try to detect your second drive. If it doesn't, you'll need to use your references to set up CMOS manually for the primary slave (your destination disk).

Once the two disks are both configured and the PC recognizes them both, the PC will want to reboot. Make sure that the DOS bootable floppy is in the boot drive and reboot. Now, start SafeBack as before, set up the audit file, and proceed to source disk screen. There are a couple of differences now. First, there will be a second, destination, screen after you finish with the source screen. When you were in the main menu, instead of selecting Backup, you should have selected Copy.

Both drives will now appear as physical drives. I am ignoring any other drives that might be in the computer for the moment to keep this simple. For this exercise, we will assume only two drives: the original source and the mirror/destination you are copying to. If you have done everything correctly, the drives should be 0 and 1. But, just to make sure, look at the partitions on drive 0. Does it look as you expect? How about the size? Drive 0 should be smaller than the target drive (drive 1), unless you happen to have an exact duplicate of the source drive to use as the target — not the normal occurrence.

Now using the [SPACE] bar, select drive 0 as the source drive. Press [ENTER] and go to the target screen. Select drive 1 as the destination and press [ENTER] again. The copy will begin and you will see a source box and a destination box displaying the action. The source will be reading and the destination will be writing. When the process is finished, the destination may keep writing. This is because it is backfilling unused space.

TAKING A HARD DISK INVENTORY WITH FILELIST

Once you have your bitstream backup made and placed into evidence, it is safe to run the FileList utility. There is, occasionally, debate about running FileList first. The reason we don't do that is because, if the computer should crash irretrievably, we would not have a bitstream backup of our evidence to fall back on. FileList is very robust, however; it uses a lot of resources when it is calculating MD5, and you never know how an unknown computer might react. In this work, we always take the coward's way out.

FileList is a very simple program to run. I put it on a DOS bootable floppy and keep its results on the same floppy. The syntax of the command to invoke FileList is:

FILELIST [/m] Output-file   drive: [drive:...]

If the "/m" option is specified, an MD5 digest will be performed on each file.

The following is from the text file included with FileList, courtesy of NTI:

FILELIST tests to see if the output file is to reside on a removable disk (e.g., floppy disk or Zip cartridge). If the output file is on a nonremovable hard disk, a file extension of .L00 is suffixed to the basic file name. Otherwise, files are created on removable media with the first disk containing a file with the extension .L01; the second, .L02; and so on. The final disk in a set also contains a zero-length file having an extension of .L99.

Regardless of output media type, each file is prefixed with licensing information, followed by output data.

The output data consists of compressed data and it requires another program to convert it into a dBASE III file. That program is named FILECNVT.EXE and a copy has been provided for your use. The program should be run in a subdirectory with the output file created by FILELIST.

Notes:

1. More than one drive letter can be specified on the command line.
2. File dates and times for creation and last access are implemented in Windows NT and Windows95 only. These fields are not maintained in MS-DOS and have "year" byte values of zero when undefined.
3. Note that the record size is the file name size + 37 bytes (the rest of the fields).[1]

Boot the computer with your DOS bootable floppy containing FileList and Filecnvt and run FileList as above. You can then copy everything to your test PC and review the results if you wish. The reason we keep everything on the same disks (or set of disks) is to ensure that, when we eventually testify, we have the exact version of FileList that we used to take the inventory in the first place.

You can sign and seal the files created by FileList, as we discussed earlier, and bag them as evidence. Our primary evidence for any computer is the SafeBack image and the FileList inventory. Make sure that you create additional copies if you plan to use them later.

SUMMARY

In this chapter, we began the evidence-gathering process. All of the "real" evidence is in the two procedures we performed in this chapter: the bitstream image and the file inventory. Everything from here on is done to generate leads. We use the image we obtained here, both as an image and as the basis for a mirror, but we are only analyzing the evidence, not producing anything new.

In the next chapter we begin that process.

REFERENCE

1. Copyright © 1998, New Technologies, Inc., Excerpt from the text file included with FileList version 1.3.

18 Searching for Hidden Information

In this chapter, we will introduce you to the tools we use to process the data collected, in the previous chapter, for leads. I should caution you here that we cannot cover everything in the depth that a work devoted to forensic computer science could. However, I will introduce the tools, their use, and a bit of the specific hands-on procedure you need for each of them.

There is a small caveat associated with this chapter as well. The tools I will describe are current as of April 1999. However, tools and releases, along with capabilities, change with time. Use this as a starting point.

We'll begin by describing the NTI Intelligent Filter program. Next, we'll look at IP Filter, a wonderful program developed by NTI to help law enforcement investigate child pornography. GetSlack and GetFree are neat little utilities that grab data in slack and unallocated space for you to analyze, while TextSearch Pro is a fast, flexible tool for searching for keywords. We'll end with a brief discussion of the Norton Utilities, although, due to the complexity of the techniques associated with this tool, we won't go into great detail.

Generally, our discussions will apply to DOS file systems. However, you will recall I said in the last chapter that we can perform a bitstream backup of just about any file system as long as we can put the disk into a DOS PC so that we can boot from a DOS floppy and run SafeBack. Thus, although some of these utilities won't do us any good on non-DOS file systems such as Unix, NetWare, and Microsoft NT, some of the others will. I'll point out, in those cases, how to apply the utility to the non-DOS file system.

We owe a debt of thanks to Mike Anderson, Chuck Guzis, and the rest of the folks at New Technologies, Inc., in Gresham, OR, for the tools we'll discuss here, and their significant contributions to computer forensic evidence processing. Unless stated otherwise, the tools in our kit are from NTI. You can contact them for more information at http://www.secure-data.com.

THE INTELLIGENT FILTER — FILTER_I V. 4.1

When we finish a bitstream backup of any file system, we have a DOS file that contains a bit-by-bit backup of everything that was on our source disk. Some of that information is ASCII and some is binary. The binary data, for our purposes in this book, is not of much use. In fact, it takes up a lot of space that causes our other search tools to take much longer to run. On a very large disk, that can have a serious impact.

Further, if we could get rid of the binary data, limiting our bitstream file to ASCII data only, we would still have a large amount of information that contains nothing useful. We need a tool to help us reduce the size of our bitstream files without sacrificing useful information. There is such a tool available from NTI called Filter_I, or the intelligent filter program.

We run Filter_I against any file we wish to filter. Filter_I removes binary data and allows us to filter out any ASCII that is not a pattern likely to be a word. Caution: We will run this first against our entire bitstream backup. Make sure *not* to run it against your original. Make a work copy. Your original bitstream backup must remain pristine and be placed into a chain of custody.

To use Filter_I on the first pass, we run it against the file containing our bitstream backup, as copied from the one made with SafeBack. We'll create a smaller file containing only ASCII data. Filter_I must be on the same disk, in the same directory as the target file. The new file will also be on that disk. Make sure you have enough space to work on both the source file and to write the result file.

Filter_I has a simple DOS menu. The functions are self-explanatory. Once we have created a file with nothing but ASCII characters, we can use one of our text search tools against it for more details. The new file will be, in most cases, between half and two-thirds the size of the original.

The next step is to create a second file that contains only probable words. Here, we have two menu choices: names and English text. Before you run this pass, change the file name of the first result file to something that makes its contents clear. Now run the two text passes: names and words. That creates two new files. Again, rename each before the next run to label them clearly as to their contents. Finally, run the choice that searches probable keyboard entry and rename that result file to something less cryptic than the program creates.

Although we are running this utility against the entire bitstream backup, we could run it against individual slack and unallocated files, as produced by GetSlack and GetFree. We'll discuss those shortly. I recommend that you run in the following order:

- Binary filter — create an ASCII result file
- Name filter — run against the ASCII file for a result file with proper names
- Word filter — run against the ASCII file for a result file with probable English words
- Keyboard filter — run against the ASCII file for a result file with possible keyboard input

You can use the same order against a slack or unallocated file. However, one benefit of running against the entire bitstream backup is that you can get slack, free, swap, and cache in one pass. You can do each of those separately, of course, and it might be worthwhile on a large, well-seasoned (fragmented) disk. Fragmented disks may or may not present hidden information on the bitstream in useful order.

IP FILTER — V. 2.2

IP Filter is probably the most interesting and useful of the Forensic Utilities. It was developed by NTI to help law enforcement track down leads in child pornography cases. It has the same simple DOS user interface as all of the NTI tools have, and is used in pretty much the same way as Filter_I. The difference is that it searches for instances of e-mail addresses, Web URLs, and graphic or Zip file names.

IP Filter must be run the same as Filter_I, from the same directory as the target file. It then, again in the same way as Filter_I, creates a result file. I recommend that you run it against the first ASCII result file from Filter_I.

You have two choices on the simple menu: find probable e-mail addresses or find probable graphics file names. The e-mail addresses include URLs and the graphics files include Zip files. The Zips are suitable in software piracy investigations because a great deal of pirated software is moved and stored using pkZip.

Run the IP Filter program twice — once for addresses and once for file names — renaming the result files, as we did with Filter_I. The result files will be dBASE format files containing every instance of the appropriate information that IP Filter found. Remember that the file names are just the names, not the files, which may or may not still be present in any useful form.

NTI provides a simple DOS utility called DM, which you can use to read the dBASE format result files. You can also use something like Excel. The benefit of DM is that it lets you do an analysis of which addresses or file names most often seen. By selecting "Field Occurrence" in the Reporting pull-down menu, you will see the entries ordered from most to least occurrences, with the number of occurrences shown. To use DM, simply start with the "Use Datafile" choice from the Datafiles pull-down. Select the file you wish to analyze. Only dBASE format files will be shown, limiting your choices to those created by IP Filter. Next, select "Field Occurrence" as above to see the list.

There is one time when IP Filter can give false information. If a large number of the same message appears in a UseNet newsgroup, it is possible for every occurrence to appear, even though the messages were never read. Similarly, if a list of newsgroup message headers is downloaded, all will show when IP Filter checks because the list of headers appeared on the disk, even if the messages did not.

GETSLACK AND GETFREE

GetSlack and GetFree are the simplest of the NTI forensic utilities. One creates a file containing all of the slack space data on the target drive, while the other performs the same task for free or unallocated space. The syntax is the same for both and is very simple. Again, boot from your DOS floppy and run these to create separate slack and free space files. Some analysts create four files: slack, free, swap, and cache. They then run their analysis tools against these files.

The syntax is:

Getslack [filename] [drive:]

where [filename] is the name and path of the file that will hold the slack or free space, and [drive:] is the drive letter (with colon) of the drive to be analyzed. If you leave out the [filename], you will get an estimate of the size of the file, were it to be created. As you can see, unlike Filter_I and IP Filter, there is no menu interface with GetSlack and GetFree. The latter two utilities run straight from the command line.

Also, unlike other NTI utilities, GetSlack and GetFree do not run on the disk they are analyzing. I generally run them from a Jaz drive attached to my test computer. There is a good use for these two utilities that might not be readily obvious. Since they run from an external disk, such as a Jaz disk, you could (after you have a bitstream backup, of course) run them against the actual computer under test.

Once you have taken your bitstream backup for evidence and run your FileList program, you could reboot from a DOS floppy with your Jaz drivers and run GetSlack and GetFree, storing their result files on the Jaz. Then, copy any cache or swap files to the same Jaz and you'll have at hand a collection of all of the hidden space in files on a large enough disk to run other utilities against (such as IP Filter, Filter_I, or, as we'll soon see, TextSearch Plus). That single disk could contain everything you need (except, perhaps, a mirror) to look for leads in hidden space.

TEXTSEARCH PLUS V. 2.04

TextSearch Plus is a utility for searching a disk for text strings. It can search both allocated space and unallocated/slack space. When used to search the physical disk, it can be used against any file system. However, you should be cautious when interpreting text searches on an NT file system because NTFS automatically performs compressions of files of a certain size or greater.

TextSearch Plus does not need to be run from the directory it is searching. Although it has roughly the same menu layout as other NTI tools, TextSearch Plus allows a great deal more flexibility. For the purposes of this book, I'll give you a simple example of its use. However, a bit of practice with the utility will show you a number of tricks that make it a very useful utility.

A side note here: TextSearch Plus makes an excellent tool for parsing very large logs in an Internet backtracing investigation. It uses fuzzy logic and is designed to process a large amount of data in a relatively short time.

The main menu of TextSearch Plus is a bit more comprehensive than other NTI software. This is because it has a number of different functions, whereas other products have, at most, two or three. I'll list the functions available on the main menu, and then we'll examine a typical session.

- Drive/Path — set this for your target file's drive and path. You can look at any drive and path you can see, unlike other NTI programs that see only their local directory.
- Continuous Search — if "on," searches through successes; if "off," pauses at each match; default is off.
- Editor/Lister — allows you to select a default editor.
- File Specs — allows you to specify the file or files on which you want to perform keyword searches; default is *.*.

- DOS Gateway — shell to DOS.
- IntelliSearch — if "on," strips out all control characters and punctuation; default is "off."
- Log File — outputs the results of your search to a file; default is to screen.
- Multiple Matches — doesn't stop after the first match.
- Printer Flag — if "on," output to printer.
- Text Pattern File — search words or text strings listed in this file; if no file is shown, you will have a chance to enter your search strings manually.
- Subdirectory Search — search or ignore subdirectories.
- Exclude File Specs — if "on," the file specs in the choice above will be for files to *exclude* instead of being the files you search.
- WordStar Flag — set it "on" if you are searching WordStar files.
- Physical Drive — allows a physical search of the drives on the target computer. Useful for non-DOS file systems. The drives are listed as physical drives H1: Hn (fixed drives) or F1: Fn (floppy drives).
- Alert — Graphics File — alerts when the search finds a compressed file that may contain useful data, but which must be analyzed manually.

In a typical session with TextSearch Plus, you might be analyzing the slack file created by GetSlack. The file is called slack.txt. We will assume that you have TextSearch Plus and the target file on your PC in c:\txtsrch\. You have created a simple text file, with the text strings for which you want to search — one string per line — in a file called words.txt, and placed it in the same directory. You want to save to a log called valids.log in the same directory. Here is what your Options Menu setting might look like:

- Drive/Path: c:\txtsrch
- Continuous Search: off (let's stop and look at each match)
- Editor/Lister: leave the default (TYPE)
- File Specs: slack.txt
- DOS Gateway: skip this one
- IntelliSearch: on
- Log File: valids.log
- Multiple Matches: on
- Printer Flag: off
- Text Pattern File: words.txt
- Subdirectory Search: off
- Exclude File Specs: off
- WordStar Flag: off
- Physical Drive: ignore this one, too
- Alert — Graphic File: off

Go to the Areas drop-down menu and select Files. Now, go to Proceed in the Search drop-down and your search will begin. If you did not have a pattern file, you would be prompted at this point to enter any strings for which you wanted to search, one string per line.

Your results will be saved in your log file. Each result will be displayed on a single line enclosed in square brackets surrounded by any accompanying data. This helps you to see the context of the match. A typical line might look like:

b atrun 15 Jan 98 22 20 USER root p[id] 3718 cmd usr lib atrun 15 Jan 98 22 2

In this example we were searching for the string "ID." TextSearch Plus is not case sensitive. Note the "[id]" in the center of the line. The surrounding data is present in the file. We could, perhaps, gain leads from the displayed information.

To perform a similar search on an entire disk at the physical level, we would simply select Physical Disk Search from the Areas pull-down menu. We would not, of course, select a file. Instead, we would retain the default *.*. Naturally, this is meaningless, as is any other setting that refers to files or directories, because we will search at the sector level instead of the logical file level.

We must be careful not to have our program, log file, or search string file on the target disk since that would overwrite the hidden areas we want to include in our search.

USING THE NORTON UTILITIES

The Norton Utilities can be a very useful set of programs for our forensic work. In fact, before the NTI tools came along, Norton (now Symantec) was about all that forensic specialists had to work with.

We are concerned with just a few of the utilities, and we will not go into great detail here. The use of Peter Norton's tools is very complex in a forensic environment and is well beyond the scope of this book. The main tools we need are unerase (although we won't usually unerase a file), disk editor, and Norton Commander. All versions should be older DOS versions, which can be difficult to obtain. Sometimes the international versions are still DOS.

Commander is useful for viewing the logical directory structure on a disk and manipulating files. Unerase identifies erased files (which we also can do using Disk Editor) and, in some cases, we may want to recover those files from a mirror. Never recover an erased file on your original disk as this, of course, corrupts the evidence. Always use a mirror image.

The most useful, and difficult to use, tool from Norton is the Disk Editor. Its primary use is rebuilding fragmented files using a technique called "chaining." We briefly discussed chaining in an earlier chapter, but here is a bit more complete discussion.

Disk Editor allows you to view and capture information in all areas of a disk. That includes the master boot record, boot record, file allocation table, root directory, data area, file slack, and unallocated space. By being able to view these areas, you can see file fragments and their contents, files that have been deleted, directory entries that have been manually altered (usually using Disk Editor), so that live files are hidden as "deleted" files.

The point in chaining is to use Disk Editor to identify fragments of a file and copy those fragments to a new location, connecting them together to reassemble the original file. Let's take a brief look at the environment where we would want to do this.

First, even if the file is fragmented, if the entire file exists, unerase will fetch it for us. However, sometimes one or more fragments becomes partially overwritten, and unerase will report it as unrecoverable. Maybe it is, and maybe it isn't. Here's how we'll approach the problem.

First, we should understand why the file is "unrecoverable" in the first place. When a disk becomes badly fragmented ("well-seasoned"), there aren't enough contiguous unallocated clusters to save a large file. Therefore, DOS will break the file up into smaller chunks and save the chunks wherever it can. Each chunk has a sequence number, which the file allocation table keeps track of. As long as the file is in "allocated" space (i.e., not deleted), we have no trouble reading it, because DOS performs the chaining functions automatically. Once we delete the file, the block where it was stored becomes available for saving other, new files. If nothing has overwritten one of our deleted file blocks, unerase can restore it. If one or more blocks (or portions of blocks) has been claimed by DOS ("allocated" to a new file), unerase won't recover the file and it must be done manually, using Disk Editor.

Basically, the chaining process requires that we use Disk Editor to locate the deleted file entry in the directory. We can identify our target, because all of the file name characters are intact except the first, which is a Hex E5 (Greek letter sigma). The file length and starting cluster numbers are there as well.

Using Disk Editor, we go to the starting cluster. To get the number of clusters, we'll need we divide the cluster length into the file size and take the next whole number (since we use entire clusters, leaving the remaining space in the last cluster as slack, we don't ever have fractional clusters). If possible, we want to verify the header information in the first cluster as being the real beginning of the desired file. For word processing files (or other documents), this usually works.

We copy the first cluster to our floppy work disk. We find the rest of the file's clusters, copying each to our work floppy using different filenames (temp1, temp2, etc.), until we find the cluster containing the EOF (end of file) marker, which signifies that we have reached the end of the file. Finally, we copy all off the temp files together into a single file:

Copy /b temp1+temp2+... tempn newfile

This new file may or may not constitute evidence because it has, unarguably, been manipulated. However, it may serve to offer us a lead for further examination, or it may corroborate something we think we already know. If we are lucky and can find an original of the file (perhaps on another computer), we can perform a CRC check on both the original and the recovered file and, if the CRCs match, we can say with some certainty that we have a good copy of the original.

SUMMARY

In this chapter, we have examined a set of forensic tools from NTI that we can use to examine the evidence on a hard disk (or, in some cases, on floppies). In the next, and last, chapter we will cover the one area we have ignored so far: floppy disks themselves. We will look at Anadisk, a program from Sydex that permits us to do a physical examination of a floppy. We'll wrap up by showing you how to copy floppies to a larger work disk.

19 Handling Floppy Disks

Floppy disks present a special case for the investigator. We often find floppies that may contain evidence at the crime scene. We don't want to pollute the data on the disk, but we may need to examine it for hidden files, useful data, or other important information.

In this chapter, we will address the handling of floppy disks. The first step, of course, is to write-protect the floppy so that we cannot alter any data on it. Second, we want to examine the disk to see if there is likely to be anything useful on it. Finally, we may want to copy the full contents to a work disk. We can do that in two ways.

The easy way is to use the DOS Diskcopy command. Diskcopy, unlike Copy, makes a physical duplicate of a floppy onto another, identical, floppy disk. In this regard, Diskcopy is a bit like SafeBack for floppies. However, this process is time-consuming. We have, as you will soon see, another method of creating a work copy of as many floppies as we can fit on a Jaz or Zip disk. We'll begin by examining the original with AnaDisk.

ANADISK V. 2.10LE

AnaDisk is a Sydex product. Basically, AnaDisk lets us do many of the things on a floppy that the Disk Editor allows us to do on a larger disk.

AnaDisk runs on the hard disk of your PC against the floppy drive on the same computer. When you invoke AnaDisk, you will see the Main Menu, which contains several choices.

- Scan: reads the diskette and locates physical problems
- Sectors: allows editing of disk sectors
- Files: manages files at the logical level
- Search: allows searching the disk for strings
- Copy: physical disk to disk copy
- Repair: repairs bad data errors due to diskette damage
- FAT: displays the file allocation table
- Format: custom formatting features
- Dump: allows a physical dump of disk areas, whether or not the diskette is a DOS diskette.

By using AnaDisk, we can examine the entire disk in detail, usually at the physical level, for any hidden information or other useful data or evidence it may contain.

Once we determine we have a diskette that contains evidence, we should copy it to another diskette, or to a larger storage medium, for further analysis. Remember, the diskette itself is the evidence. Write-protect it, tag it so it can be identified, bag it, and put it into chain of custody. Next, we will analyze the contents of the diskette on our work copy.

COPYING FLOPPIES TO A WORK DISK

We have, as I pointed out, two choices for creating a work copy of a diskette that contains evidence. Our first choice, and probably the best, is to use Diskcopy to make a "mirror" diskette. We can then use AnaDisk to examine all areas of the diskette using the copy. We can use the Copy function of AnaDisk, in place of Diskcopy, for convenience.

Another possibility, useful when we have large numbers of diskettes to analyze, is to place them on a larger medium, such as a Jaz or Zip drive. If we use this approach, we need to go back and recall the areas of the hard disk in which we have an interest. Floppies have the same areas. One caveat here, however: we cannot use this technique to move boot or directory areas of the source floppy. If our preliminary AnaDisk analysis tells us that there has been some hanky-panky with the boot sector, we'd be far better off to mirror the evidence floppy to a physical copy, using Diskcopy or AnaDisk.

There are several techniques for hiding data on a floppy. Tools exist for creating disks within disks, for writing data between the tracks of the floppy, and hiding data inside other files, such as graphics files (called "steganography"). While those techniques are beyond the scope of this book, suffice to say that you will need a physical copy of the diskette to analyze them.

If we opt to copy floppies to a larger work disk, we will need to copy three areas: the logical data, the slack, and the unallocated space. Start by preparing a large work disk by creating several directories. Each directory will hold a single floppy's data.

Next, use Copy to copy all logical files on the floppy to its directory on the work disk. Once the logical data is copied, use GetSlack and GetFree to copy slack and unallocated space to the floppy's work directory on the work disk.

Once you have copied data, slack, and unallocated space, you can analyze these files using other NTI tools in the same manner as you would any other files.

SUMMARY

In this chapter, we have discussed the handling of floppy disks that may contain evidence. We used AnaDisk and showed how to create a work copy of a large number of diskettes on a larger medium.

This concludes our effort. I hope we have covered all of the areas of investigation of computer-related crime that you will need to conduct your investigations effectively.

Appendix A

Introduction to Denial of Service Attacks*

FOREWORD

In this paper I have tried to answer the following questions:

- What is a denial of service attack?
- Why would someone crash a system?
- How can someone crash a system?
- How do I protect a system against denial of service attacks?

I have also included a section called "Suggested Reading" where you can find sources for good, free information that can give you a deeper understanding about individual areas.

Note that I have very limited experience with Macintosh, OS/2, and Windows, and most of the materials are therefore for Unix use.

You can always find the latest version at the following address:

http://www.student.tdb.uu.se/~t95hhu/secure/denial/DENIAL.TXT

Feel free to send comments, tips, and so on to address:

t95hhu@student.tdb.uu.se

INTRODUCTION

WHAT IS A DENIAL OF SERVICE ATTACK?

Denial of service is about knocking off services without permission; for example, through crashing the whole system. These kinds of attacks are easy to launch and it is hard to protect a system against them. The basic problem is that Unix assumes that users on the system or on other systems will be well behaved.

---

* Excerpted from "Introduction to Denial of Service" by Hans Husman; edited for publication by CRC ' Press.

WHY WOULD SOMEONE CRASH A SYSTEM?

Introduction

Why would someone crash a system? I can think of several reasons and have presented them more precisely in a section for each reason, but, for short:

1. subcultural status
2. to gain access
3. revenge
4. political reasons
5. economic reasons
6. nastiness

I think that numbers one and six are the more common today, but that numbers four and five will be the more common ones in the future.

Subcultural Status

After all of information about syn flooding had been dispersed, a number of such attacks were launched around Sweden. Most of these attacks were not a part of an IP-spoof attack; it was "only" a denial of service attack. Why?

I think that hackers attack systems as a subcultural pseudo career and believe that many denial of service attacks, for example, syn flooding, were performed for these reasons. I also think that many hackers begin their careers with denial of service attacks.

To Gain Access

Sometimes a denial of service attack could be a part of an attack to gain access to a system. At the moment, I can think of several reasons and specific holes:

- Some older X-lock versions could be crashed with a method from the denial of service family, leaving the system open. Physical access was needed to use the work space afterwards.
- Syn flooding could be a part of an IP-spoof attack method.
- Some program systems could have holes under the start-up, which could be used to gain root, for example, SSH (secure shell).
- Under an attack, it could be possible to crash other machines in the network or to deny certain persons the ability to access the system.
- Also a system being booted could sometimes be subverted, especially rarp-boots. If we know at which port the machine listens (69 could be a good guess), under the boot we can send false packets to that port and almost totally control the boot.

Revenge

A denial of service attack could be a part of a revenge against a user or an administrator.

Political Reasons

Sooner or later both new or old organizations will understand the potential of destroying computer systems and find tools to do it.

For example, imagine Bank A loaning Company B money to build a factory, which may threaten the environment. Organization C crashes A's computer system, maybe with the help of an employee. The attack could cost A a great deal of money if the timing is right.

Economic Reasons

Imagine the small Company A moving into a business totally dominated by Company B. A and B customers order by computer and depend heavily that the order is done in a specific time (A and B could be stock trading companies). If A and B can't process the order, the customers lose money and change companies.

As a part of a business strategy, A pays a computer expert a sum of money to get him to crash B's computer systems a number of times. A year later, A is the dominating company.

Nastiness

I know a person that found a workstation where the user had forgotten to log out. He sat down and wrote a program that made a kill -9 -1 at a random time, at least 30 minutes after the login time, and placed a call to the program from the profile file. That is nastiness.

ARE SOME OPERATING SYSTEMS MORE SECURE?

This is a hard question to answer and I don't think that it will benefit to compare different Unix platforms. You can't say that one Unix is more secure against denial of service; it is all up to the administrator.

A comparison between Windows 95 and NT on one side and Unix on the other could, however, be interesting.

Unix systems are much more complex and have hundreds of built-in programs, services ... . This always opens up many ways to crash the system from the inside.

In the normal Windows NT and 95 network there are few ways to crash the system, although there are methods that will always work.

That gives us the fact that no big difference exists between Microsoft and Unix regarding inside attacks. But, there are a couple of points left:

- Unix has many more tools and programs to discover an attack and to monitor users. To watch what another user is up to under Windows is very difficult.
- The average Unix administrator probably also has more experience than the average Microsoft administrator.

The last two points lead us to believe that Unix is more secure against inside denial of service attacks.

A comparison between Microsoft and Unix regarding outside attacks is much more difficult. However, I would like to say that the average Microsoft system on the Internet is more secure against outside attacks, because they normally have fewer services.

WHAT HAPPENS WHEN A MACHINE CRASHES?

Typically, the following happens:

- X-Windows will be aborted.
- A panic message will be printed on the console.
- A core file, crashdump or something called something else will be written to the disk on the machine or to another machine on the network.
- A reboot attempt will be made.

HOW DO I KNOW IF A HOST IS DEAD?

You can use ping. Ping sends network packets of the ECHO_REQUEST type, which is a part of ICMP, and ICMP is a part of the Internet Protocol. It is possible to block echo_request packets, but it has unlikely been done.

To use ping:

Ex:

$ ping host

USING FLOODING — WHICH PROTOCOL IS MOST EFFECTIVE?

ICMP and UDp are the most effective due to the fact that they don't need to set up a connection like TCP. The synflooding attack is, however, a way to go around that problem with TCP.

ATTACKING FROM THE OUTSIDE

TAKING ADVANTAGE OF FINGER

Most finger installations support redirections to another host.

Ex:

$finger @system.two.com@system.one.com

Finger will, in this example, go through system.one.com and on to system.two.com. As far as system.two.com knows, it is system.one.com who is fingering. So this method can be used for hiding, but also for a very dirty denial of service attack. Look at this:

$ finger @@@@@@@@@@@@@@@@@@@@@@@@@@@@@@host.we.attack

All those @ signs will get finger to finger host.we.attack again and again and again ... . The effect on host.we.attack is powerful and the result is high bandwidth, short free memory, and a hard disk with less free space, due to all child processes.

The solution is to install a finger which doesn't support redirections, for example, GNU finger. You could also turn the finger service off, but I think that is just a bit too much.

UDP AND SUNOS 4.1.3.

SunOS 4.1.3. is known to boot if a packet with incorrect information in the header is sent to it. This is the case if the ip_options indicate a wrong size of the packet. The solution is to install the proper patch.

FREEZING UP X-WINDOWS

If a host accepts a telnet session to the X-Windows port (generally somewhere between 6000 and 6025 — in most cases, 6000), that could be used to freeze up the X-Windows system. This can be done with multiple telnet connections to the port or with a program which sends multiple XOpenDisplay() to the port.

The same thing can happen to Motif or Open Windows. The solution is to deny connections to the X-Windows port.

MALICIOUS USE OF UDP SERVICES

It is simple to get UDP services (echo, time, daytime, chargen) to loop, due to trivial IP-spoofing. The effect can be high bandwidth, which causes the network to become useless. In the example, the header claimed that the packet came from 127.0.0.1 (loopback) and the target is the echo port at system.we.attack. As far as system.we.attack knows, it is 127.0.0.1 system.we.attack and the loop has been established.

Ex:

> from-IP=127.0.0.1
> to-IP=system.we.attack
> Packet type:UDP
> from UDP port 7
> to UDP port 7

Note that the name system.we.attack looks like a DNS-name, but the target should always be represented by the IP-number.

The following is quoted from the proberts@clark.net (Paul D. Robertson) comment on comp.security.firewalls on the matter of "Introduction to Denial of Service."

A great deal of systems don't put loopback on the wire, and simply emulate it. Therefore, this attack will only effect that machine in some cases. It's much better to use the address of a different machine on the same network. Again, the default services should be disabled in inetd.conf. Other than some hacks for mainframe IP stacks that don't support ICMP, the echo service isn't used by many legitimate programs, and TCP echo should be used instead of UDP where it is necessary.

ATTACKING WITH LYNX CLIENTS

A World Wide Web server will fork an httpd process as a response to a request from a client, typically Netscape or Mosaic. The process lasts for less than one second and the load will, therefore, never show up if someone uses ps. In most cases it is therefore very safe to launch a denial of service attack that makes use of multiple W3 clients, typically Lynx clients. But, note that the netstat command could be used to detect the attack (thanks to Paul D. Robertson).

Some httpd:s (for example http-gw) will have problems besides the normal high bandwidth, low memory ... And the attack can in those cases get the server to loop.

MALICIOUS USE OF TELNET

Study this little script:
    Ex:

```
                      while : ; do
                      telnet system.we.attack &
                      done
```

An attack using this script might eat some bandwidth, but it is nothing compared to the finger method, or most other methods. The point is that some pretty common firewalls and httpd:s think that the attack is a loop and turns them down, until the administrator sends kill -HUP.

This is a simple, high risk vulnerability that should be checked and, if present, fixed.

ICMP REDIRECT ATTACKS

Gateways use ICMP redirect to tell the system to override routing tables; that is, telling the system to take a better way. To be able to misuse ICMP redirection we must know an existing connection (we could make one for ourselves, but there is not much use for that). If we have found a connection, we can send a route that loses its connectivity or we could send false messages to the host if the connection we have found doesn't use cryptation.

Ex: (false messages to send)

DESTINATION UNREACHABLE
TIME TO LIVE EXCEEDED
PARAMETER PROBLEM
PACKET TOO BIG

The effect of such messages is a reset of the connection. The solution could be to turn ICMP redirects off, not a very proper use of the service.

E-Mail Bombing and Spamming

In an e-mail bombing attack, the attacker will repeatedly send identical e-mail messages to an address. The effect on the target is high bandwidth, a hard disk with less space, and so on ... . E-mail spamming is about sending mail to all (or rather many) of the users of a system. The point of using spamming instead of bombing is that some users will try to send a reply and, if the address is false, the mail will bounce back. In that case one mail will be transformed to three mails. The effect on the bandwidth is obvious.

There is no way to prevent e-mail bombing or spamming. However, have a look at CERT's paper, "E-mail Bombing and Spamming."

Hostile Applets

A hostile applet is any applet that attempts to use your system in an inappropriate manner. The problems in the Java language could be sorted in two main groups:

1. Problems due to bugs
2. Problems due to features in the language

In group one we have, for example, the Java bytecode verifier bug, which makes it possible for an applet to execute any command that the user can execute. This means that all the attack methods described [in the rest of this appendix] could be executed through an applet. The Java bytecode verifier bug was discovered in late March 1996 and no patch has yet been available (correct me if I am wrong!!!).

Note that two other bugs could be found in group one, but they are both fixed in Netscape 2.01 and JDK 1.0.1.

Group two is more interesting and one large problem found is the fact that Java can connect to the ports. More information and examples could be found at the following address: http://www.math.gatech.edu/~mladue/HostileArticle.html.

If you need a high level of security you should use some sort of firewall for protection against Java. As a user, you could have Java disabled.

Attacking Name Servers

A name server is the program that holds the information about the domain and answers questions. The part of the domain name space that the name server holds is referred to as a zone.

The name server is seldom the only one, it is too important a service. Instead at least two can be found, the primary master and the secondary master. However, too many secondary masters cannot exist. The secondary master provides a backup to the primary.

Every time the name server makes a request, it collects and stores information, and the next time another query is made for the information, it already has it in the cache.

An attack at the name server could have a very big impact. Many servers depend heavily on proper working name servers, for example: rlogin, rsh, rcp, xhost, NFS, smtp, ftp, etc.

To attack the name server we could of course use any method described in this paper, but the machine running the name server seldom does anything except DNS-work. The DNS-server is also very important and has had several well-known security problems. Because of these reasons, the DNS-server will most likely be well protected and other services besides DNS will probably not exist (although ping flooding could be a threat if there is not a firewall that filters ping from the outside). The attack that is left is to attack the service itself at port 53. We could, for example,

1. send random garbage to it
2. send true queries to it
3. use syn flooding

Alternative two should be the most effective, because it will do everything that alternative one does and will also keep the service program itself busy looking up DNS-names. Putting together a long, random list with DNS-name will also mostly contain addresses outside the zone, making the name server try to query other name servers.

ATTACKING FROM THE INSIDE

MALICIOUS USE OF FORK()

If someone executes this C++ program, it will result in a crash on most systems.
Ex:

```
#include
#include
#include

main()
{

        int x;
        while(x=0;x<1000000;x++)
            {
                    system("uptime");
                    fork();
            }
}
```

You can use any command you want, but uptime is nice because it shows the workload.

However, to get a bigger and very ugly attack you should replace uptime (or fork them both) with sync. This is very bad.

If you are really mean, you could also fork a child process for every child process and cause an exponential increase of workload.

There is no good way to stop this and similar attacks. A solution could be to place a limit on the time of execution and size of processes.

CREATING FILES THAT ARE HARD TO REMOVE

All files can be removed, but here are some ideas:
Ex. I:

```
$ cat > -xxx
^C
$ ls
-xxx
$ rm -xxx
rm: illegal option — x
rm: illegal option — x
rm: illegal option — x
usage: rm [-fiRr] file ...
$
```

Ex. II:

```
$ touch xxx!
$ rm xxx!
rm: remove xxx! (yes/no)? y
$ touch xxxxxxxxx!
$ rm xxxxxxxxx!
bash: !": event not found
$
```

(You see, the size does count!)

Another well-known method is files with odd characters or spaces in the name.

These methods could be used in combination with "FILLING UP THE HARD-DISK." If you do want to remove these files, you must use some sort of script or a graphical interface, like OpenWindow's File Manager. You can also try to use: rm ./. It should work for the first example if you have a shell.

DIRECTORY NAME LOOKUPCACHE

Directory name lookupcache (DNLC) is used whenever a file is opened. DNLC associates the name of the file to a vnode. But DNLC can only operate on files with names that have less than N characters (for SunOS 4.x, up to 14 characters; for Solaris 2.x, up to 30 characters). This means that it's very easy to launch a pretty discreet denial of service attack.

Create, let's say, 20 directories (for a start) and put 10 empty files in every directory. Let every name have over 30 characters and execute a script that makes a lot of ls -al on the directories.

If the impact is not big enough, you should create more files or launch more processes.

HOW DO I PROTECT A SYSTEM AGAINST DENIAL OF SERVICE ATTACKS?

BASIC SECURITY PROTECTION

Introduction

You cannot make your system totally secured against denial of service attacks but, for attacks from the outside, you can do a lot. I put this work list together and hope that it can be of some use.

Security Patches

Always install the proper security patches. As for patch numbers, I don't want to put them out, but that doesn't matter because you want anyway to check that you have all security patches installed; so get a list and check! Also note that patches change over time, and that a solution suggested in security bulletins (i.e., CERT) often is somewhat temporary.

Port Scanning

Check which services you have. Don't check with the manual or some configuration file. Instead, scan the ports with a strobe or some other port scanner. Actually, you should do this regularly to see that anyone hasn't installed a service that you don't want on the system (it could, for example, be a service used for a pirate site).

Disable every service that you don't need, for example, it could be rexd, fingerd, systat, netstat, rusersd, sprayd, pop3, uucpd, echo, chargen, tftp, exec, ufs, daytime, time ... . Any combination of echo, time, daytime and chargen is possible to get to loop. There is, however, no need to turn off discard. The discard service will just read a packet and discard it; so if you turn it off, you will become more sensitive to denial of service and not the opposite.

Actual services can be found on many systems that may be used for denial of service and brute force hacking without any logging. For example, Stock rexec never logs anything. Most popds also don't log anything.

Check the Outside Attacks Described in This Paper

Check for attacks described in this paper and look at the solution. Some attacks you should perform to see if they apply to your system, for example:

- freezing up X-Windows
- malicious use of telnet

- how to disable services
- SunOS kernel panic
- attacking with Lynx clients
- crashing systems with ping from Windows 95 machines

That is, stress test your system with several services and look'at the effect. Also have a look in section "Tools That Help You Check."

Note that Solaris 2.4 and later have a limit on the number of ICMP error messages (1 per 500 ms, I think) that can cause problems when you test your system for some of the holes described in this paper. But you can easily solve this problem by executing this line: $ /usr/sbin/ndd -set /dev/ip ip_icmp_err_interval 0.

Check the Inside Attacks Described in This Paper

Check the inside attacks; although it is always possible to crash the system from the inside, you don't want it to be too easy. Also, have several of the attack applications, besides denial of service, for example:

- crashing the X-Server: if stickybit is not set in /tmp, a number of attacks can be performed to gain access
- use resolv_host_conf: could be used to expose confidential data like /etc/shadow
- core dumped under wuftpd: could be used to extract password-strings

Tools That Help You Check

First, we have a very good free packet by Darren Reed (darrenr@cyber.com.au). The text below is quoted from a posting Mr. Reed made to Bugtraq Thu, October 24, 1996 10:50:00 +1000.

I wrote a program called "ipsend" some time ago that I later split up into iptest/ipsend/ipresend. Iptest basically does lots of nasty things, including attempting to send huge packets, etc. It does it using NIT/BPF and DLPI — but I've only tested on Solaris/BSD/Linux. If you want to have a look at it:

ftp://coombs.anu.edu.au/pub/net/misc/ipsend.tar.gz

To give you a brief of the other programs:

• ipresend takes a tcpdump binary dump/snoop binary dump or other input (such as textual descriptions of IP packets) and sends that out through the above
• ipsend is a command line interface for sending a single packet or doing "stealth scanning"

Ideally, ipresend could be used with a known set of inputs which create a set of nasty packets (that aren't covered in iptest) and you could use that to test the rigidity of your IP stack after making any changes. Iptest is a quick and fixed implementation of a fixed number of tests.

Darren

The packet is very good to stress test systems.

We also have ISS, which is not a free tool. According to W3-page: http://www.iss.net/tech/techspec.html.

ISS checks [for many] denial of service attacks. ISS is a very good security checker and checks for many holes, not only denial of service.

Extra Security Systems

Also think about if you should install some extra security systems. The basics that you should always install are a logdaemon and a wrapper. A firewall could also be very good, but expensive. Free tools can be found on the Internet. Note that you should be very careful if building your own firewall with TIS or you might open up new and very bad security holes. But, it is a very good security packer if you have some basic knowledge.

It is also very good to replace services that you need, for example, telnet, rlogin, rsh, or whatever, with a tool like ssh. Ssh is free and can be found at URL: ftp://ftp.cs.hut.fi/pub/ssh.

The addresses I have listed are the central sites for distributing and I don't think that you should use any other except for CERT.

For a long list on free general security tools I recommend: "FAQ: Computer Security Frequently Asked Questions."

Monitoring Security

Also, regularly monitor security, for example through examining system log files, history files, etc. Even in a system without any extra security systems, several tools can be found for monitoring, for example:

- uptime
- showmount
- ps
- netstat
- finger

(see the main text for more information).

Keeping Up to Date

It is very important to keep up to date with security problems. Also understand that when, for example CERT, warns of something, it has often been in the dark-side public for some time, so don't wait. The following resources, which help you keep up to date, can, for example, be found on the Internet:

CERT mailing list
Bugtraq mailing list
WWW-security mailing list
[NT Bugtraq Mailing List]

Read Something Better

Let's start with papers on the Internet. I am sorry to say that there are not many good free papers that can be found, but here is a small collection. I apologize if have overlooked a paper.

1. The Rainbow books is a long series of free books on computer security. U.S. citizens can get them from:
   INFOSEC Awareness Office
   National Computer Security Center
   9800 Savage Road
   Fort George G. Meader, MD 20755-600
   Other papers can be read on the World Wide Web, although every paper cannot be found on the Internet. Following is an address for a large collection of Rainbow books: http://csrc.ncsl.nist.gov/secpubs/rainbow/.
2. *Improving the Security of Your Unix System* by Curry is also a very good source if you need the very basic things. If you don't know anything about computer security, you can't find a better start.
3. *The WWW Security FAQ* by Stein is the very best bet on the Internet about computer security, although it deals with W3-security.
4. CERT has also published several good papers, for example:
   • Anonymous FTP Abuses
   • E-mail Bombing and Spamming
   • Spoofed/Forged E-mail
   • Protecting Yourself from Password File Attacks
   However, I think that the last paper has overlooked several things.
5. For a long list of papers, I can recommend: *FAQ: Computer Security Frequently Asked Questions.*
6. Also see section, SUGGESTED READING.

You should also get some large commercial books, but I prefer not to recommend any.

MONITORING PERFORMANCE

Introduction

There are several commands and services that can be used for monitoring performance. And, at least two good free programs can be found on the Internet.

Commands and Services

For more information, read the main text.

netstat	Shows network status
nfsstat	Shows NFS statistics
sar	System activity reporter

vmstat	Reports virtual memory statistics
timex	Times a command, report process data, and system activity
time	Times a simple command
truss	Traces system calls and signals
uptime	Shows how long the system has been up

Note that if a public netstat server can be found, you might be able to use netstat from the outside. Netstat can also give information like tcp sequence numbers and much more.

Programs

Proctool: Proctool is a freely available tool for Solaris that monitors and controls processes: ftp://opcom.sun.ca/pub/binaries/.

Top: Top might be a simpler program than Proctool, but it is good enough.

Accounting

In order to monitor performance, you have to collect information over a long period of time. All Unix systems have some sort of accounting logs to identify how much CPU time, memory each program uses. You should check your manual to see how to set this up.

You could also invent your own account system by using crontab and a script with the commands you want to run. Let crontab run the script every day and compare the information once a week. You could, for example, let the script run the following commands:

- netstat
- iostat -D
- vmstat

SOME BASIC TARGETS FOR AN ATTACK, EXPLANATIONS OF WORDS, CONCEPTS

Swap Space

Most systems have several hundred Mbytes of swap space to service client requests. The swap space is typically used for forked child processes which have a short lifetime. The swap space will, therefore, almost never, in a normal case, be heavily used. A denial of service could be based on a method that tries to fill up the swap space.

Bandwidth

If the bandwidth is too high, the network will be useless. Most denial of service attacks influence the bandwidth in some way.

KERNEL TABLES

It is trivial to overflow the kernel tables, which will cause serious problems on the system. Systems with write-through caches and small write buffers are especially sensitive.

Kernel memory allocation is also a target that is sensitive. The kernel has a kernelmap limit; if the system reaches this limit, it cannot allocate more kernel memory and must be rebooted. The kernel memory is not only used for RAM, CPUs, screens, and so on, it is also used for ordinary processes. This means that any system can be quickly crashed and with a mean (or in some sense, good) algorithm.

For Solaris 2.X, how much kernel memory the system is using is measured and reported with the sar command, but for SunOS 4.X there is no such command. Under SunOS 4.X you don't even can get a warning. If you do use Solaris you should write sar -k 1 to get the information. Netstat -k can also be used and shows how much memory the kernel has allocated in the subpaging.

RAM

A denial of service attack that allocates a large amount of RAM can make a number of problems. NFS and mail servers are actually extremely sensitive because they do not need much RAM and, therefore, often don't have much RAM. An attack at an NFS server is trivial. The normal NFS client will do a great deal of caching, but an NFS client can be anything, including the program you wrote yourself.

DISKS

A classic attack is to fill up the hard disk, but an attack at the disks can be so much more. For example, an overloaded disk can be misused in many ways.

CACHES

A denial of service attack involving caches can be based on a method to block the cache or to avoid the cache.

These caches are found on Solaris 2.X:

- Directory name lookup cache: associates the name of a file with a vnode
- Inode cache: cache information read from disk in case it is needed again
- Rnode cache: holds information about the NFS filesystem
- Buffer cache: cache inode indirect blocks and cylinders to reeled disk I/O

INETD

Once inetd has crashed, all other services running through inetd no longer will work.

TMPFS

Tmpfs is a filesystem of RAM disk type. As long as RAM is available the files that are written will not be put out to the disk. If the system gets short on RAM, the page however will be stored in the swap space. SunOS 4.x does not use tmpfs as default, but Solaris 2.x does.

LOOPBACK

Loopback is always 127.0.0.1 and is always the same machine making the connection to it.

NFS

NFS is a protocol that makes it possible to work with filesystems coming from a remote host.

SUGGESTED READING — INFORMATION FOR DEEPER KNOWLEDGE

1. Hedrick, C. Routing Information Protocol. RFC 1058, 1988.
2. Mills, D.L. Exterior Gateway Protocol Formal Specification. RFC 904, 1984.
3. Postel, J. Internet Control Message Protocol. RFC 792, 1981.
4. Harrenstien, K. NAME/FINGER Protocol, RFC 742, 1977.
5. Sollins, K.R. The TFTP Protocol, RFC 783, 1981.
6. Croft, W.J. Bootstrap Protocol, RFC 951, 1985.

Many in this category were RFC-papers. An RFC-paper is a paper that describes a protocol. The letters RFC stands for Request For Comment. Hosts on the Internet are expected to understand at least the common ones. If you want to learn more about a protocol, it is always a good idea to read the proper RFC. You can find an RFC index search form at URL: http://pubweb.nexor.co.uk/public/rfc/index/rfc.html.

Appendix B

Technical Report 540-96

Edward W. Felten, Dirk Balfanz, Drew Dean, and Dan S. Wallach
Department of Computer Science, Princeton University

INTRODUCTION

This paper describes an Internet security attack that could endanger the privacy of World Wide Web users and the integrity of their data. The attack can be carried out on today's systems, endangering users of the most common Web browsers, including Netscape Navigator and Microsoft Internet Explorer.

Web spoofing allows an attacker to create a "shadow copy" of the entire World Wide Web. Accesses to the shadow Web are funneled through the attacker's machine, allowing the attacker to monitor all of the victim's activities including any passwords or account numbers the victim enters. The attacker can also cause false or misleading data to be sent to Web servers in the victim's name, or to the victim in the name of any Web server. In short, the attacker observes and controls everything the victim does on the Web.

We have implemented a demonstration version of this attack.

SPOOFING ATTACKS

In a spoofing attack, the attacker creates misleading context in order to trick the victim into making an inappropriate security-relevant decision. A spoofing attack is like a con game: the attacker sets up a false but convincing world around the victim. The victim does something that would be appropriate if the false world were real. Unfortunately, activities that seem reasonable in the false world may have disastrous effects in the real world.

Spoofing attacks are possible in the physical world as well as the electronic one. For example, there have been several incidents in which criminals set up bogus automated-teller machines, typically in the public areas of shopping malls.[1] The machines would accept ATM cards and ask the person to enter their PIN code. Once the machine had the victim's PIN, it could either eat the card or "malfunction" and return the card. In either case, the criminals had enough information to copy the victim's card and use the duplicate. In these attacks, people were fooled by the context they saw: the location of the machines, their size and weight, the way they were decorated, and the appearance of their electronic displays.

People using computer systems often make security-relevant decisions based on contextual cues they see. For example, you might decide to type in your bank account number because you believe you are visiting your bank's Web page. This belief might arise because the page has a familiar look, because the bank's URL appears in the browser's location line, or for some other reason.

To appreciate the range and severity of possible spoofing attacks, we must look more deeply into two parts of the definition of spoofing: security-relevant decisions and context.

SECURITY-RELEVANT DECISIONS

By "security-relevant decision," we mean any decision a person makes that might lead to undesirable results such as a breach of privacy or unauthorized tampering with data. Deciding to divulge sensitive information, for example by typing in a password or account number, is one example of a security-relevant decision. Choosing to accept a downloaded document is a security-relevant decision, since in many cases a downloaded document is capable of containing malicious elements that harm the person receiving the document.[2]

Even the decision to accept the accuracy of information displayed by your computer can be security-relevant. For example, if you decide to buy a stock based on information you get from an online stock ticker, you are trusting that the information provided by the ticker is correct. If somebody could present you with incorrect stock prices, they might cause you to engage in a transaction that you would not have otherwise made, and this could cost you money.

CONTEXT

A browser presents many types of context that users might rely on to make decisions. The text and pictures on a Web page might give some impression about where the page came from; for example, the presence of a corporate logo implies that the page originated at a certain corporation.

The appearance of an object might convey a certain impression; for example, neon green text on a purple background probably came from Wired magazine. You might think you're dealing with a popup window when what you are seeing is really just a rectangle with a border and a color different from the surrounding parts of the screen. Particular graphical items like file-open dialog boxes are immediately recognized as having a certain purpose. Experienced Web users react to such cues in the same way that experienced drivers react to stop signs without reading them.

The names of objects can convey context. People often deduce what is in a file by its name. Is manual.doc the text of a user manual? (It might be another kind of document, or it might not be a document at all.) URLs are another example. Is MICR0S0FT.COM the address of a large software company? (For a while that address pointed to someone else entirely. By the way, the round symbols in MICR0S0FT here are the number zero, not the letter O.) Was dole96.org Bob Dole's 1996 presidential campaign? (It was not; it pointed to a parody site.)

People often get context from the timing of events. If two things happen at the same time, you naturally think they are related. If you click over to your bank's page and a username/password dialog box appears, you naturally assume that you should type the name and password that you use for the bank. If you click on a link and a document immediately starts downloading, you assume that the document came from the site whose link you clicked on. Either assumption could be wrong.

If you only see one browser window when an event occurs, you might not realize that the event was caused by another window hiding behind the visible one.

Modern user-interface designers spend their time trying to devise contextual cues that will guide people to behave appropriately, even if they do not explicitly notice the cues. While this is usually beneficial, it can become dangerous when people are accustomed to relying on context that is not always correct.

TCP AND DNS SPOOFING

Another class of spoofing attack, which we will not discuss here, tricks the user's software into an inappropriate action by presenting misleading information to that software.[3] Examples of such attacks include TCP spoofing,[4] in which Internet packets are sent with forged return addresses, and DNS spoofing,[5] in which the attacker forges information about which machine names correspond to which network addresses. These other spoofing attacks are well known, so we will not discuss them further.

WEB SPOOFING

Web spoofing is a kind of electronic con game in which the attacker creates a convincing but false copy of the entire World Wide Web. The false Web looks just like the real one: it has all the same pages and links. However, the attacker controls the false Web, so that all network traffic between the victim's browser and the Web goes through the attacker.

CONSEQUENCES

Since the attacker can observe or modify any data going from the victim to Web servers, as well as controlling all return traffic from Web servers to the victim, the attacker has many possibilities. These include surveillance and tampering.

SURVEILLANCE

The attacker can passively watch the traffic, recording which pages the victim visits and the contents of those pages. When the victim fills out a form, the entered data is transmitted to a Web server, so the attacker can record that too, along with the response sent back by the server. Since most on-line commerce is done via forms, this means the attacker can observe any account numbers or passwords the victim enters.

As we will see below, the attacker can carry out surveillance even if the victim has a "secure" connection (usually via Secure Sockets Layer) to the server, that is, even if the victim's browser shows the secure-connection icon (usually an image of a lock or a key).

TAMPERING

The attacker is also free to modify any of the data traveling in either direction between the victim and the Web. The attacker can modify form data submitted by the victim. For example, if the victim is ordering a product on-line, the attacker can change the product number, the quantity, or the ship-to address.

The attacker can also modify the data returned by a Web server, for example by inserting misleading or offensive material in order to trick the victim or to cause antagonism between the victim and the server.

SPOOFING THE WHOLE WEB

You may think it is difficult for the attacker to spoof the entire World Wide Web, but it is not. The attacker need not store the entire contents of the Web. The whole Web is available on-line; the attacker's server can just fetch a page from the real Web when it needs to provide a copy of the page on the false Web.

How the Attack Works

The key to this attack is for the attacker's Web server to sit between the victim and the rest of the Web. This kind of arrangement is called a "man in the middle attack" in the security literature.

URL Rewriting

The attacker's first trick is to rewrite all of the URLs on some Web page so that they point to the attacker's server rather than to some real server. Assuming the attacker's server is on the machine www.attacker.org, the attacker rewrites a URL by adding http://www.attacker.org to the front of the URL. For example, http://home.netscape.com becomes http://www.attacker.org/http://home.netscape.com.

(The URL rewriting technique has been used for other reasons by two other Web sites, the Anonymizer and the Zippy filter.)

Once the attacker's server has fetched the real document needed to satisfy the request, the attacker rewrites all of the URLs in the document into the same special form by splicing http://www.attacker.org/ onto the front. Then the attacker's server provides the rewritten page to the victim's browser.

Since all of the URLs in the rewritten page now point to www.attacker.org, if the victim follows a link on the new page, the page will again be fetched through the attacker's server. The victim remains trapped in the attacker's false Web, and can follow links forever without leaving it.

Forms

If the victim fills out a form on a page in a false Web, the result appears to be handled properly. Spoofing of forms works naturally because forms are integrated closely into the basic Web protocols: form submissions are encoded in URLs and the replies are ordinary HTML Since any URL can be spoofed, forms can also be spoofed.

When the victim submits a form, the submitted data goes to the attacker's server. The attacker's server can observe and even modify the submitted data, doing whatever malicious editing desired, before passing it on to the real server. The attacker's server can also modify the data returned in response to the form submission. "Secure" connections don't help.

One distressing property of this attack is that it works even when the victim requests a page via a "secure" connection. If the victim does a "secure" Web access (a Web access using the Secure Sockets Layer) in a false Web, everything will appear normal: the page will be delivered, and the secure connection indicator (usually an image of a lock or key) will be turned on.

The victim's browser says it has a secure connection because it does have one. Unfortunately the secure connection is to www.attacker.org and not to the place the victim thinks it is. The victim's browser thinks everything is fine: it was told to access a URL at www.attacker.org so it made a secure connection to www.attacker.org. The secure-connection indicator only gives the victim a false sense of security.

STARTING THE ATTACK

To start an attack, the attacker must somehow lure the victim into the attacker's false Web. There are several ways to do this. An attacker could put a link to a false Web onto a popular Web page. If the victim is using Web-enabled email, the attacker could email the victim a pointer to a false Web, or even the contents of a page in a false Web. Finally, the attacker could trick a Web search engine into indexing part of a false Web.

COMPLETING THE ILLUSION

The attack as described thus far is fairly effective, but it is not perfect. There is still some remaining context that can give the victim clues that the attack is going on. However, it is possible for the attacker to eliminate virtually all of the remaining clues of the attack's existence.

Such evidence is not too hard to eliminate because browsers are very customizable. The ability of a Web page to control browser behavior is often desirable, but when the page is hostile it can be dangerous.

THE STATUS LINE

The status line is a single line of text at the bottom of the browser window that displays various messages, typically about the status of pending Web transfers.

The attack as described so far leaves two kinds of evidence on the status line. First, when the mouse is held over a Web link, the status line displays the URL the link points to. Thus, the victim might notice that a URL has been rewritten. Second, when a page is being fetched, the status line briefly displays the name of the server being contacted. Thus, the victim might notice that www.attacker.org is displayed when some other name was expected.

The attacker can cover up both of these cues by adding a JavaScript program to every rewritten page. Since JavaScript programs can write to the status line, and since it is possible to bind JavaScript actions to the relevant events, the attacker can arrange things so that the status line participates in the con game, always showing the victim what would have been on the status line in the real Web. Thus the spoofed context becomes even more convincing.

THE LOCATION LINE

The browser's location line displays the URL of the page currently being shown. The victim can also type a URL into the location line, sending the browser to that URL. The attack as described so far causes a rewritten URL to appear in the location line, giving the victim a possible indication that an attack is in progress.

This clue can be hidden using JavaScript. A JavaScript program can hide the real location line and replace it by a fake location line which looks right and is in the expected place. The fake location line can show the URL the victim expects to see. The fake location line can also accept keyboard input, allowing the victim to type in URLs normally. Typed-in URLs can be rewritten by the JavaScript program before being accessed.

VIEWING THE DOCUMENT SOURCE

There is one clue that the attacker cannot eliminate, but it is very unlikely to be noticed.

By using the browser's "view source" feature, the victim can look at the HTML source for the currently displayed page. By looking for rewritten URLs in the HTML source, the victim can spot the attack. Unfortunately, HTML source is hard for novice users to read, and very few Web surfers bother to look at the HTML source for documents they are visiting, so this provides very little protection.

A related clue is available if the victim chooses the browser's "view document information" menu item. This will display information including the document's real URL, possibly allowing the victim to notice the attack. As above, this option is almost never used so it is very unlikely that it will provide much protection.

BOOKMARKS

There are several ways the victim might accidentally leave the attacker's false Web during the attack. Accessing a bookmark or jumping to a URL by using the browser's "Open location" menu item might lead the victim back into the real Web. The victim might then reenter the false Web by clicking the "Back" button. We can imagine that the victim might wander in and out of one or more false Webs. Of course, bookmarks can also work against the victim, since it is possible to bookmark a page in a false Web. Jumping to such a bookmark would lead the victim into a false Web again.

TRACING THE ATTACKER

Some people have suggested that this attack can be deterred by finding and punishing the attacker. It is true that the attacker's server must reveal its location in order to carry out the attack, and that evidence of that location will almost certainly be available after an attack is detected.

Unfortunately, this will not help much in practice because attackers will break into the machine of some innocent person and launch the attack there. Stolen machines will be used in these attacks for the same reason most bank robbers make their getaways in stolen cars.

REMEDIES

Web spoofing is a dangerous and nearly undetectable security attack that can be carried out on today's Internet. Fortunately there are some protective measures you can take.

SHORT-TERM SOLUTION

In the short run, the best defense is to follow a three-part strategy:

1. disable JavaScript in your browser so the attacker will be unable to hide the evidence of the attack;
2. make sure your browser's location line is always visible;
3. pay attention to the URLs displayed on your browser's location line, making sure they always point to the server you think you're connected to.

This strategy will significantly lower the risk of attack, though you could still be victimized if you are not conscientious about watching the location line.

At present, JavaScript, ActiveX, and Java all tend to facilitate spoofing and other security attacks, so we recommend that you disable them. Doing so will cause you to lose some useful functionality, but you can recoup much of this loss by selectively turning on these features when you visit a trusted site that requires them.

LONG-TERM SOLUTION

We do not know of a fully satisfactory long-term solution to this problem. Changing browsers so they always display the location line would help, although users would still have to be vigilant and know how to recognize rewritten URLs.

For pages that are not fetched via a secure connection, there is not much more that can be done.

For pages fetched via a secure connection, an improved secure-connection indicator could help. Rather than simply indicating a secure connection, browsers should clearly say who is at the other end of the connection. This information should be displayed in plain language, in a manner intelligible to novice users; it should say something like "Microsoft Inc." rather than "www.microsoft.com."

Every approach to this problem seems to rely on the vigilance of Web users. Whether we can realistically expect everyone to be vigilant all of the time is debatable.

RELATED WORK

We did not invent the URL rewriting technique. Previously, URL rewriting has been used as a technique for providing useful services to people who have asked for them.

We know of two existing services that use URL rewriting. The Anonymizer, written by Justin Boyan at Carnegie Mellon University, is a service that allows users to surf the Web without revealing their identities to the sites they visit. The Zippy filter, written by Henry Minsky, presents an amusing vision of the Web with Zippy-the-Pinhead sayings inserted at random.

Though we did not invent URL rewriting, we believe we are the first to realize its full potential as one component of a security attack.

ACKNOWLEDGMENTS

The URL-rewriting part of our demonstration program is based on Henry Minsky's code for the Zippy filter. We are grateful to David Hopwood for useful discussions about spoofing attacks, and to Gary McGraw and Laura Felten for comments on drafts of this paper.

FOR MORE INFORMATION

More information is available from our Web page at http://www.cs.princeton.edu/sip, or from Prof. Edward Felten at felten@cs.princeton.edu or (609) 258-5906.

REFERENCES

1. Peter G. Neumann. *Computer-Related Risks.* ACM Press, New York, 1995.
2. Gary McGraw and Edward W. Felten. *Java Security: Hostile Applets, Holes and Antidotes.* John Wiley & Sons, New York, 1996.
3. Robert T. Morris. "A Weakness in the 4.2BSD UNIX TCP/IP Software." *Computing Science Technical Report 117,* AT&T Bell Laboratories, February 1985.
4. Steven M. Bellovin. "Security Problems in the TCP/IP Protocol Suite." *Computer Communications Review* 19(2):32–48, April 1989.
5. Steven M. Bellovin. "Using the Domain Name System for System Break-ins." *Proceedings of Fifth Usenix UNIX Security Symposium,* June 1995.
6. Web site at http://www.anonymizer.com
7. Web site at http://www.metahtml.com/apps/zippy/welcome.html

Index

Index